One Baptism

*Ecumenical Dimensions of the
Doctrine of Baptism*

Susan K. Wood

A Michael Glazier Book

LITURGICAL PRESS
Collegeville, Minnesota

www.litpress.org

Ferm Amaz 7/09 29.95

A Michael Glazier Book published by Liturgical Press

Cover design by David Manahan, OSB. Photo courtesy of Maria Laughlin and the St. James Cathedral in Seattle, Washington.

1	2	3	4	5	6	7	8	9

Library of Congress Cataloging-in-Publication Data

Wood, Susan K.
    One baptism : ecumenical dimensions of the doctrine of baptism / Susan K. Wood.
        p. cm.
    "A Michael Glazier book."
    Includes bibliographical references and index.
    ISBN 978-0-8146-5306-7 (pbk.)
    1. Baptism.   I. Title.
BV811.3.W66 2009
234'.161—dc22

2008048344

There is one body and one Spirit,

just as you were called to be the one hope of your calling,

one Lord, one faith, one baptism,

one God and Father of all,

who is above all and through all and in all.

Ephesians 4:4-6

Contents

Abbreviations

DS	Denzinger-Schönmetzer
DV	*Dei Verbum*
JDDJ	*Joint Declaration on the Doctrine of Justification*
JSNTSup	*Journal for the Study of the New Testament*, Supplement Series
LBW	*The Lutheran Book of Worship*
LC	*The Book of Concord: The Confessions of the Evangelical Lutheran Church*
LC-MS	Lutheran Church-Missouri Synod
LG	*Lumen Gentium*
MPL	Migne's *Patrologia Latina*
NPNF	*Nicene and Post-Nicene Fathers*
PL	*Patrologia Latina*
RCIA	Rite of Christian Initiation of Adults
SC	*Sacrosanctum Concilium*
ST	St. Thomas Aquinas, *Summa Theologiae*
TI	Karl Rahner, *Theological Investigations*
UR	*Unitatis Redintegratio*
WELS	Lutheran Church-Wisconsin Synod
Werke	*D. Martin Luthers Werke* (Weimar: Hermann Böhlau, 1912–21)

Introduction

The question "What does baptism do?" has haunted me for much of my theological career. At one level any catechized Christian can answer this question, yet from the perspective of systematic theology, the answer remains elusive and complex. The reason is that baptism, the sacrament that makes Christians, lies at the intersection of all the great themes of theology: Christology, pneumatology, salvation, faith, church, justification, and Christian discipleship. Yet the medieval concern to determine the minimum elements necessary for sacramental validity and efficacy barely touches many of these themes. Conversely, the systematic and dogmatic treatment of such themes often does not allude to baptism. This is partially due to the fragmentation of theology today. Even though today sacramental theology is more in tune with liturgical theology, both need stronger bonds with systematic theology. This study attempts to forge those bonds by integrating sacramental, liturgical, historical, and systematic theology in an examination of baptism.

Christian churches claim baptism as the foundation of their unity, citing Ephesians 4:4: "There is one body and one Spirit, just as you were called to the one hope of your calling, one Lord, one faith, one baptism, one God and Father of all, who is above all and through all and in all." It is rather commonplace to assert that baptism constitutes the source of ecumenical unity of the Christian churches, but all too often this assumption remains unexamined. When our practice of baptism is different and what we say baptism does is different, can we really claim that there is one baptism? This is a study that relies on a number of theological disciplines to determine how common our doctrine and practices of baptism are.

This project examines baptism through an ecumenical lens. The discerning reader will discover that perhaps more attention is given to Lutheran sources than to some other ecclesial traditions. That is due to the fact that I have been engaged in ecumenical dialogue with Lutherans since 1994 and am simply more familiar with this tradition. At times, to manage the complexity of the ecumenical variety I group ecclesial traditions into "families" that share certain common characteristics. While this generalization is helpful, I acknowledge that at times it obscures details of difference with respect to individual ecclesial groups. Even within these groups ecumenical documents and even confessional statements do not necessarily represent all the members. Nevertheless, I believe this synthetic approach helpfully sketches the large contours of the ecumenical landscape. Although I try to accurately describe all the traditions represented in this study, it is written from a Roman Catholic perspective. This fact simply represents the hermeneutical truth that we ask questions and see the world from our own front yard.

These are some of the questions that drive this project:

Chapter 1: Baptism, Eschatology, and Salvation

- How can we reconcile the two dominant paradigms for the sacrament of baptism: Christ's baptism in the Jordan, with its trinitarian theophany, and the theme of death and resurrection in Romans 6? The first paradigm is dominant in Eastern traditions while the second is a major theme in Western traditions.

- Baptism seems to be about beginnings, yet it is oriented to the eschaton. How does eschatology illuminate the initiation achieved in baptism? The Scriptures affirm the necessity of baptism for salvation, yet Roman Catholics have a long history of affirming the possibility of salvation for non-Christians, the nonbaptized. How can these two affirmations, the necessity of baptism and the salvation of non-Christians, be reconciled? Is baptism really necessary for salvation? What is at stake? How is Christian baptism related to the salvation of non-Christians?

Chapters 2 and 3: The Doctrine of Baptism

- When Christians cite Ephesians 4:4-6, saying there is one baptism, what is common in our doctrine of baptism and where do we differ? How do different traditions answer the question "What does baptism do?"

- What have been some of the misrepresentations of sacramental teaching contributing to ecumenical disagreements?

- Does eschatology or forensic justification shape Luther's theology of baptism?

Chapters 4 and 5: Baptism and Patterns of Initiation

- The World Council of Churches has suggested that ecumenical agreement on baptism may be reached through common patterns of initiation. How fruitful is this approach, and what is the relationship between patterns of initiation and the doctrine of baptism? Do the baptismal liturgical texts of various traditions reflect their doctrine?

- What are the theologies of baptism imbedded in the ancient catechumenate?

- What really constitutes the difference between traditions reflecting the ancient catechumenate and those that restrict the practice of baptism to the ordinance given in Matthew 28:19?

Chapter 6: Baptism, Faith, and Justification

- Baptism is a sacrament of faith, both requiring faith for a fruitful reception of the sacrament and imparting the infused theological virtue of faith. The requirement of faith is what leads some churches to limit baptism to believers. Yet all churches, including the paedo-baptists, require faith for baptism. This raises the question of the role of the community of faith in the baptismal event and how that relates to personal confessions of faith. Are we initiated into a faith community or do we come to faith individually and then seek out persons who also believe to form a faith community?

- How is baptism as a sacrament of justification related to justification by faith? Why were Roman Catholics out of communion with Reformation churches for 480 years on the issue of justification, while differences in the doctrine and practice of baptism were not considered to be church dividing in many instances? Where these differences were church dividing, this was more from the perspective of other traditions than from the side of the Roman Catholic Church.

Chapter 7: Baptism and the Church

- How is a tradition's understanding of baptism profoundly linked to its view of the church? How do different traditions come to different conclusions on baptism because of their different understanding of the nature and boundaries of the Christian community and how that community is constituted? What is the relationship between baptism and church membership?

I hope that this study contributes to a clearer understanding of what we mean when we say that baptism is the foundation of unity among Christian churches. May it also lead to a deeper integration of doctrine and sacramental practice in the church, or at least a better awareness of how they are interrelated. Finally, may its modest proposals contribute to Christian unity.

*   *   *

I am grateful to Marquette University for granting me the sabbatical and two summer fellowships that made this project possible. My religious community, the Sisters of Charity of Leavenworth, enabled me to extend my sabbatical to the entire year, but they sustain me in so many other more important ways. I also owe a debt of thanks to Mickey Mattox, Jakob Rinderknecht, and Katy Leamy, who read parts of the manuscript and commented on them, and to Lisa Cullison who prepared the indexes. Linda Maloney was indefatigable in her copy editing. I deeply value the support and assistance of Peter Dwyer and Hans Christoffersen at the Liturgical Press. Finally, but not least, I have been blessed in the many conversations with my ecumenical dialogue partners. May we one day be gathered in unity around the Lord's table.

Chapter One

Baptism, Eschatology, and Salvation

Baptism seems to be about beginnings: beginning of a new life as a Christian, inauguration into the Christian community, beginning of life in the Spirit. Yet to understand baptism and the beginnings of Christian life we must begin at the end, with eschatology. Baptism is more than initiation into the Christian life, more than the path to entrance into the church. It is oriented toward the end time and is the sacramental realization of that end time proleptically breaking into the life of the baptized individual and the church. In other words, baptism is inaugurated eschatology, the end time present now.[1]

Baptism receives its eschatological identity from Jesus Christ, who from eternity entered human history in the incarnation, uniting the earthly material of the cosmos to divinity, bringing eternal time into the midst of historical time, when he became human. His resurrection, into which we are baptized, represents the intersection of historical time and the fulfilled time of eschatology. Neville Clark observes that this happens not at the end of history but in the midst of history, and comments: "Resurrection, which belonged to the Last Day, had taken place on the Third Day.

[1] Neville Clark, "Initiation and Eschatology," in *Baptism, the New Testament and the Church: Historical and Contemporary Studies in Honour of R.E.O. White*, ed. Stanley E. Porter and Anthony R. Cross, JSNTSup 171 (Sheffield: Sheffield Academic Press, 1999), 339.

Tomorrow had become Now. The future Eschaton was the Present Eschatos. Yet historical time went on. And the End was not yet."[2]

We express the same idea sacramentally. Sacraments memorialize the past and anticipate the future within present symbolic events and symbolic time, concentrating past and future within a present event. Within the ritual time of the liturgy, past and future are gathered into the present moment through memorial (anamnesis), presence, and anticipation. A past historical event is transposed into the present life of the community in its remembrance and becomes a promise of future fulfillment and completion. Thus in baptism, when we participate in the death and resurrection of Christ, these past events are brought into the present. When we rise sacramentally to new life with Christ and participate in the new creation, the fullness of that new life and new creation still await us in the eschaton. For example, even though we sacramentally celebrate union with Christ and one another in the Eucharist, as we leave church we are often painfully aware of the broken relationships and global enmity that point to reconciliation still to be achieved. Although we die and rise in Christ in baptism, we must still die in the flesh and await our final bodily resurrection. The sacramental event anticipates the final historical and transhistorical event.

This sacramental view is consistent with the Pauline eschatological view of baptism in Romans 6, 2 Corinthians 5:17, and Galatians 6:15, which consider the present experience of Christians as a participation in eschatological reality.[3] The inaugurated aspect of Pauline eschatology consists both in what God has done in the death and resurrection of Jesus and in what happens to a Christian in baptism and how that person lives out the meaning of baptism in daily life. However, there is also a future dimension, the full working out of the power of the resurrection, which remains to be fully accomplished. Thus there is the past event of what Christ did, the present application of that to the life of the Christian, and the future anticipation of fulfillment. Eschatology imparts meaning and value to historical, temporal realities in the light of their ultimate purpose and goal. The dynamism of the Christian life can be summarized as a dying and rising with Christ—not just sacramentally in baptism and the Eucharist or at the end of earthly life, but also in the daily choice to turn from a self-centered, self-affirming preoccupation to an openness of being

---

[2] Ibid., 342.

[3] Zachary Hayes, *Visions of a Future: A Study of Christian Eschatology*, New Theology Series 8 (Wilmington, DE: Michael Glazier, 1989), 58.

for others and for God. This dynamism answers the question: what do Christians hope for? And it becomes the grammar of how they structure their lives.

This relationship between past, present, and future is possible on account of the risen Christ, for as Thomas J. Talley explains:

> By virtue of the resurrection, Christ is now transhistorical and is available to every moment. We may never speak of the Risen Christ in the historical past. The event of his passion is historical, but the Christ who is risen does not exist back there, but here, and as we live on this moving division line between memory and hope, between the memory of his passion and the hope of his coming again, we stand always in the presence of Christ, who is always present to everyone. This is where the real substance of our anamnesis lies.[4]

At the beginning of the Easter Vigil liturgy the celebrant cuts a cross in the wax of the Easter candle, saying: "Christ yesterday and today, the beginning and the end, Alpha and Omega. All time belongs to him and all the ages; to him be glory and power through every age for ever. Amen." The key to eschatology is Christology. Jesus Christ is the one who has come and entered our history, who comes in the present through word and sacrament, and who will come again. He does not replace or annihilate history, but enters history, just as he becomes flesh rather than merely appearing in the flesh in a docetic fashion. Incarnation and redemption are not two separate events, the bookends of his life, but represent an unbroken continuum. Becoming flesh leads to the grave. Yet, because he has taken to himself the earthly matter of creation, that stuff of the earth is transformed through Christ's resurrection. Creation becomes the new creation.

Christians experience the inauguration of this new creation in the baptismal waters administered in the Triune name. Just as Christ did not bypass the matter of creation in uniting himself to humanity, so too Christians use the waters of baptism to unite themselves to divinity and begin to live the eschatologically transformed life through sacramental mediation. In being baptized, Christians imitate the actions of Christ who announced the coming reign in his own baptism. Christ not only

---

[4] Cited by Robert Taft in "What Does Liturgy Do? Toward a Soteriology of Liturgical Celebration: Some Theses," *Worship* 66, no. 3 (May 1992): 200.

assumed earthly elements in his incarnation, but submitted himself to John's baptism as a prophetic sign of his messianic identity and mission.

Jesus' Baptism by John: An Eschatological Action

One of the earlier ecumenical documents, "One Lord, One Baptism," situates the eschatological meaning of Christian baptism against the background of John the Baptist's activity.[5] John's baptism, more than a call to repentance or a symbol of purification from sin, is best understood as the proclamation of an eschatological reality: namely, the drawing near of the messianic kingdom. John's baptism had as its purpose the gathering of a messianic people who would be prepared for the coming Messiah. His baptism pointed forward to that event as he cried, "Prepare the way of the Lord, make his paths straight" (Matt 3:3). The difference between John's baptism and Christian baptism is that John pointed forward toward the messianic time, while for Christian baptism the messianic kingdom has already come. Baptism admits a person to the kingdom of the Messiah, Christ. The baptism of John is solely a baptism of water; the baptism of the church confers the Holy Spirit, who belongs to the new age and the last days, the messianic time (Isa 11:2; Acts 2:17).

The accounts of Jesus' baptism by John mark the transition from the preparation for the messianic age to its arrival, the seal of Jesus' messianic vocation, and the inauguration of his messianic mission. The puzzle for John was why Jesus should present himself for a baptism of repentance. He had foretold a different baptism:

> I baptize you with water for repentance, but one who is more powerful than I is coming after me; I am not worthy to carry his sandals. He will baptize you with the Holy Spirit and fire. His winnowing fork is in his hand, and he will clear his threshing floor and will gather his wheat into the granary; the chaff he will burn with unquenchable fire. (Matt 3:11-12)

[5] Commission on Faith and Order, World Council of Churches, *One Lord, One Baptism* (Minneapolis: Augsburg, 1960), 50. I am indebted to this document for the connection between Jesus' messianic vocation and identity and the eschatology presented here. This document was written without Roman Catholic participation because it predated Vatican II and Catholic membership on the Faith and Order Commission.

Here we have reference to the Holy Spirit, associated with the messianic age, and the reference to the final, eschatological judgment. The separation of wheat and chaff symbolizes the eschatological judgment of Matthew 25:31-46, where the Son of Man comes in glory and separates people one from another as a shepherd separates the sheep from the goats. The blessed inherit the kingdom of the Father and are received into eternal life, while the others are sent into eternal punishment.

When Jesus presented himself to John to be baptized, John's response was "I need to be baptized by you, and do you come to me?" (Matt 3:14). Jesus replied, "Let it be so now; for it is proper for us in this way to fulfill all righteousness" (Matt 3:15). When Jesus came up from the water, the heavens were opened to him. Jesus saw the Spirit of God descend like a dove and alight on him. A voice from heaven said, "This is my Son, the Beloved, with whom I am well pleased" (Matt 3:17). The appearance of the Spirit and the voice from heaven confirm his being baptized. Jesus' baptism by John is immediately followed by his being led by the Spirit into the wilderness to be tempted, the arrest of John the Baptist, Jesus' proclamation, "Repent, for the kingdom of heaven has come near" (Matt 4:17), and his gathering of a messianic community through the call of Simon (now called Peter), Andrew, James, son of Zebedee, and his brother John. In the Gospel of Matthew this is followed by the Sermon on the Mount, which gives the characteristics of the new age that Jesus introduces.

In the Gospel of Luke, Jesus' public ministry begins with his teaching in the synagogues, including the one in Nazareth where he reads the prophecy of Isaiah:

> The Spirit of the Lord is upon me, because he has anointed me to bring good news to the poor. He has sent me to proclaim release to the captives and recovery of sight to the blind, to let the oppressed go free, to proclaim the year of the Lord's favor. (Luke 4:18-19)

He ends with the announcement: "Today this scripture has been fulfilled in your hearing" (Luke 4:21). The prophecy announces the characteristics of the messianic era. Jesus proclaims that this time has arrived, and, in citing the text from Isaiah, gives a clear indication of how his self-interpretation is influenced by the Isaian text.

The theological question raised by Jesus' baptism is why Jesus, the sinless one, must necessarily receive John's baptism of repentance along with all the other sinners. The Commission on Faith and Order locates the answer in the connection between the voice from heaven proclaiming "This is my Son, the Beloved, with whom I am well pleased" and the first line of the first servant song in Isaiah, which says, "Here is my servant, whom I uphold, my chosen, in whom my soul delights; I have put my spirit upon him; he will bring forth justice to the nations" (Isa 42:1). Both the servant and Jesus receive the pleasure and delight of the Father. Both are recipients of the Spirit in these passages. Both share the mission of restoring justice to the nations. Jesus himself reads Isaiah 61:1-11 in the synagogue in Nazareth, a poem that recalls the Servant Songs of chapters 42–53 in Isaiah, where the mission of the prophet is to bring encouragement to the exiled and oppressed.

The echo of Isaiah in the baptism event invites the reader to interpret the inauguration of the messianic age in Jesus through the lens of the suffering servant in such a way that what is said of the suffering servant applies to Jesus Christ. Thus the Commission concludes that Jesus' baptism with John's baptism of repentance for the remission of sins means that Jesus, the Servant of the Lord, as the only righteous One, enters vicariously into "the sin of the many" (Isa 53:12), to bear it as his own sin so that the many may participate in his righteousness.[6] This is also Paul's interpretation in 2 Corinthians 5:21: "For our sake he made him to be sin who knew no sin, so that in him we might become the righteousness of God." The Commission summarizes the meaning of the event:

> It is baptism into solidarity with sinners and the initiation of redemptive action, baptism into obedience to the Father and love for the lost, a stepping into the unknown. It was a baptism that brought an opened heaven, revelation from the Father, and the presence of the Spirit. It was also his consecration to suffering and to death. Only so was "all righteousness" fulfilled (Matt. 3.15). The messianic kingdom was established only through the fact that he, "the righteous one, my servant," makes many righteous by bearing their iniquities (Isa. 53.11).[7]

The fourth servant song depicts a man of suffering acquainted with infirmity, wounded for our transgressions and crushed for our iniquities, upon whom was the punishment that made us whole and by whose bruises we are healed (Isa 53:3, 5). This is the Christian interpretation of Jesus' death. Jesus also interprets his baptism in terms of his death. His

---

[6] Ibid., 53.
[7] Ibid.

baptism led directly to the cross. When Jesus spoke of baptism on the occasion when James and John, the sons of Zebedee, asked for seats immediately to his right and to his left, he interpreted it in terms of his death: "The cup that I drink you will drink; and with the baptism with which I am baptized, you will be baptized" (Mark 10:39). Here both the cup and the baptism are his death.[8] In Luke 12:50 Jesus exclaims, "I have a baptism with which to be baptized, and what stress I am under until it is completed!"

Just as Jesus' baptism in the Jordan foreshadows his death, Christian baptism is interpreted as a baptism into the death of Jesus. Paul asks, "Do you not know that all of us who have been baptized into Christ Jesus were baptized into his death?" (Rom 6:3). Baptism is a dying in Christ, a dying that leads to new life. The baptismal font and water symbolize tomb as well as womb, water that drowns as well as water that sustains life.

Death, however, does not have the last word, but is the gateway to resurrection and everlasting life. The text from Romans continues, "Therefore we have been buried with him by baptism unto death, so that, just as Christ was raised from the dead by the glory of the Father, so we too might walk in newness of life. For if we have been united with him in a death like his, we will certainly be united with him in a resurrection like his" (Rom 6:4-5). Jesus' resurrection constitutes the ground of hope and faith in the resurrection of Christians. The new life inaugurated by baptism is not only a different quality of life in this world, but the foretaste of life everlasting.

In the Gospel of John the promise attached to faith-filled sacramental action is eschatological life. Jesus tells Nicodemus, "no one can enter the kingdom of God without being born of water and the Spirit" (John 3:5). In the conversation with Nicodemus faith is associated with eternal life (John 3:16-17). In this same conversation Jesus says that the Son of Man must be lifted up, a reference to the cross, in order that whoever believes in him may have eternal life (John 3:15, 36). In chapter 6, the discourse on the bread of life, the work of God is believing the one whom God sent (John 6:29). Those who believe are promised eternal life and resurrection on the last day (John 6:40), and those who eat the living bread, the flesh of Christ given for the life of the world, receive the same promise (John 6:51, 54). Although not all traditions interpret these texts sacramentally, the sacramental realism of these eucharistic texts is underscored by the

---

[8] See the reference to death as cup in Mark 14:36.

anti-docetic emphasis on the realism of the Greek verb used for "eating," which carries the connotation of masticating, and the use of "flesh" rather than "body." Faith and sacrament are not a dichotomy in these texts, since the sacramental birth in water and the Spirit and sharing in the bread of life are actions performed in faith.

At times there may be a tendency to read the account of Jesus' baptism in the Jordan, the dominant baptismal text in Orthodox Christianity, separately from the Romans text, the dominant Western text, as two different theologies of baptism. However, the resonances of the Servant Songs in the baptismal event in the Jordan and the Isaiah text inaugurating Jesus' public mission link the two theologies. In the Jordan event and the beginning of his public mission that follows it Jesus proclaims the arrival of the messianic era and appropriates to himself the identity of the servant who inaugurates the messianic time. He then acts on this identity in such activities as reinterpreting the laws of the Sabbath, healing the sick, and forgiving sinners. Jesus' baptismal identity directly leads to his mission, which results in his death.

The end of the journey, however, is not the cross, but rather Jesus' resurrection and exaltation. The theme of exaltation is yet another link to the suffering servant song in Isaiah 52:13: "See, my servant shall prosper, he shall be exalted and lifted up, and shall be very high." Likewise, the same themes occur in connection with Jesus' death in Philippians 2:7-11, where Christ took the form of a slave, became obedient to the point of death on a cross, and was consequently exalted and confessed as Lord.

The Christian's participation in Jesus' death in baptism is also a participation in his resurrection (Rom 6:5). In Paul's theology the ethical dimension of baptism, that is, death to sin, correlates with the eschatological dimensions of baptism, namely the destruction of death itself and the possibility of life everlasting. The newness of life of the baptized is a foretaste of the resurrected life. Having died with Christ, we hope to rise with him. Baptism orients us to a future that does not end in death even while it initiates us into a cruciform pattern of life. This was Christ's path to the resurrection, and thus it is also ours.

Baptism into the Ecclesial Body of Christ

Baptism into Christ is also baptism into his ecclesial body. We do not simply become members of a church as an organization, but are engrafted into Christ. This reality is expressed according to the various biblical images such as that of the body in 1 Corinthians 12:13 or the relationship of branches grafted into the vine in John 15. These images express not only the relationship of the baptized to Christ, but also that of the baptized to one another. We are members of the same body, vines of the same plant. Thus baptism is incorporation or engrafting into a spiritual community identified by its relationship to Christ.

Just as death is no longer the boundary of individual human existence, neither is it the boundary of this spiritual community. Baptism, like the Eucharist, has an eschatological end and a goal inseparable from the eschatological meaning of the church, which is the eschatological destiny of all believers. The unity forged at the baptismal font and around the eucharistic table extends beyond the frontiers of death. Eschatology is not a break from the previous order, but its completion. The community initiated in baptism is the form of salvation in the end time. Even though each person is saved personally, we are not saved individually, but as members of the people of God.

We call this community the communion of saints and profess belief in it in the third article of the Apostles' Creed, which summarizes the eschatological work and hope of baptism:

> I believe in the Holy Spirit,
> the holy Catholic Church
> the communion of saints,
> the forgiveness of sins,
> the resurrection of the body,
> and the life everlasting.

Here the church, the communion of saints, the forgiveness of sin, the resurrection of the body, and life everlasting are all the work of the Spirit. Within sacramental theology these are also the work of the Spirit as received in baptism and the work of the Spirit as operative in the Eucharist. In the invocation of the Spirit in the Eucharist, the epiclesis, the Spirit is not only invoked to transform the gifts of bread and wine into the body and blood of Christ; in a second epiclesis the Spirit is invoked to transform the community of believers into the ecclesial body of Christ. Through baptism we are incorporated into Christ and the church. Through the Eucharist, by partaking of one bread, we become one body (1 Cor 10:17) through the power of the Spirit. Thus these two foundational sacraments are properly sacraments of the church in the strong sense of constituting the church as the body of Christ and temple of the Spirit.

Baptism and Salvation

Salvation is a theme appropriately considered within eschatology, since it is eternal life in communion with God who is Father, Son, and Spirit. Many Christian churches teach the necessity of baptism for salvation.[9] A number of interconnected theological terms refer to the core Christian conviction that because of Christ human beings experience a transition from one state to another, which designates a changed status before God. The first state is characterized as one of sinfulness, bondage, and alienation from God. The second is described as graced union with God that endures after death in eternal life. Thus redemption, based on an economic metaphor, literally means that Jesus buys us back. Atonement literally means at-one-ment, the uniting of parties formerly estranged. Reconciliation has much the same meaning. Justification, a term at home in the forensic world of law, means that we are made and declared righteous before God. Salvation, derived from the Latin word for health, refers to healing and the fact that human woundedness is made whole. All these concepts refer to an initiative taken by Christ on our behalf.

Baptism is necessary for salvation because of the relationship it establishes with the trinitarian life through the work of Christ in the power of the Spirit. In baptism we are incorporated into Christ and thus share in his life of grace and in his saving death and resurrection. We are also anointed by the Spirit, and in Christ we receive the status of adopted sons and daughters of God and brothers and sisters of Christ. Incorporation into Christ is inseparable from incorporation into the church, Christ's ecclesial body. The church is the community of salvation that mediates the saving effects of Christ's redemptive actions through its confession of faith, proclamation of the word of Scripture, and the sacraments.

The Scriptures use various phrases to express the baptized person's relationship to Christ. The baptized is assigned to Christ by being baptized in the name of Jesus (1 Cor 1:13; 3:23; 6:19; 2 Cor 10:17). The baptized puts on Christ like a garment (Gal 3:27; Eph 4:22-24; 6:11-14; Col 2:12;

---

[9] The differences among various Christian traditions will be discussed in chapters 2 and 3.

3:9-10; Rom 13:13-14). More than an external likeness to Christ, the image of putting on Christ signifies that the baptized person becomes the image and likeness of Christ and thus manifests Christ. Through baptism there is a mutual indwelling of the baptized in Christ and Christ in the baptized (Rom 8:9-11; 2 Cor 4:5-14; 13:2-5; Eph 3:16-17; Gal 2:19-20; 4:19-20; Col 1:17; Phil 1:21). Christ lives through his Spirit in the baptized, enabling them to live a justified life modeled on Christ and exhibiting the gifts and fruits of the Spirit. This life freed from the power of sin is characterized by faith, hope, and charity. The baptized person shares in salvation because, in being united with Christ, the baptized lives Christ's justified life.

Before baptism is something an individual does or even what the church does to an individual, it is ultimately the work of Christ ministered through the agency of the church. When the church baptizes, Christ baptizes. What God has already done in Jesus, his being anointed with the Spirit and being proclaimed "beloved," is accomplished in the individual through the Spirit:

> But when the goodness and loving kindness of God our Savior appeared, he saved us, not because of any works of righteousness that we had done, but according to his mercy, through the water of rebirth and renewal by the Holy Spirit. This Spirit he poured out on us richly through Jesus Christ our Savior so that, having been justified by his grace, we might become heirs according to the hope of eternal life. (Titus 3:4-7)

However, the Christian is baptized not only in the name of Jesus, but also in the name of the Father and of the Spirit (Matt 28:19), indicating that baptismal identity, as Christ's identity, is constituted by the trinitarian relationships. The baptized person begins a journey to the Father with whom he or she is reconciled by participating in the salvific work of the Son in the power of the Spirit.

The baptismal life is a foretaste of eternal life, a participation in the trinitarian life that is the goal and fulfillment of the Christian life. This is literally a new life, a rebirth. The supernatural is the proper goal of the natural, even while lying beyond its capabilities. The history of salvation reveals the true meaning of human history. Thus baptism is oriented to the future. As Michael Schmaus expresses it: "Like the whole Church, baptism exists only for the sake of this future. It is the future that gives it its ultimate meaning. All the effects of baptism, accordingly, are to be seen as a liberation from the obstacles on the way and as the granting of freedom of movement toward the future."[10]

The eschatological meaning of baptism, like that of the Eucharist, points to salvation as a social reality. The second sentence in chapter 2 of *Lumen Gentium* makes the remarkable claim: "He (God) has, however, willed to make women and men holy and to save them, not as individuals without any bond between them, but rather to make them into a people who might acknowledge him and serve him in holiness."[11] According to chapter 2 this people is comprised of those elected by Christ's covenant. This new people of God, called together from Jews and Gentiles, is reborn of water and the Spirit, a reference to baptism (John 3:5-6). Its destiny is the kingdom of God, which will be brought to perfection at the end of time. This messianic people, even though it does not include everyone at the present time, is "a most certain seed of unity, hope and salvation for the whole human race" (LG 9). The people, compared to a "seed" because of its limited yet promising scope, is "the instrument for the salvation of all." This people of God is also called the church of Christ, identified as "the visible sacrament of this saving unity." Finally, this people is also a "kingdom of priests" that offers spiritual sacrifices, another reference to baptism since this priesthood of believers is constituted in baptism. These sacrifices include the sacrifice of a holy life, the offering of the Eucharist, prayer, and the reception of the sacraments (LG 10).

Although baptism is oriented to salvation and many churches teach that it is necessary for salvation, salvation is not to be presumed. Although Christ promises eternal life to those who believe in him (John 6:41) and eat his flesh (John 6:51), and entrance into the kingdom of God is associated with birth of water and the Spirit (John 3:5), human beings possess the freedom to reject God's offer of salvation. The Council of Trent taught that the justified baptized person can sin and lose grace.[12] Salvation is not automatic with baptism, but presupposes perseverance in faith, hope, and charity with the help of God. Thus we are only assured of our salvation at the moment of death. A Reformed statement expresses this condition aptly:

[10] Michael Schmaus, *Dogma 5: The Church as Sacrament* (Kansas City, MO: Sheed and Ward, 1975), 160.

[11] LG 9. In *Vatican Council II: The Basic Sixteen Documents*, trans. Austin Flannery (Northport, NY: Costello, 1996).

[12] Council of Trent, Session VI, 13 January 1547, canon 23; Session VII, 3 March 1547, canon 6.

While the promises of Christ in Baptism are such that none need ever fall into despair, the obligations involved in Baptism are such that none dare become complacent regarding his state of salvation. He may quench the Holy Spirit: he may become hardened in sin: he may reject the gift of life. Therefore what is given may become a judgment: what is grafted may wither: what is generated may never grow.[13]

The Salvation of Non-Christians

The Roman Catholic tradition affirms the necessity of baptism for salvation; at the same time it teaches the possibility of salvation for non-Christians. The theological challenge is to show how the salvation of non-Christians is related to baptism. In the second chapter of *Lumen Gentium*, even though covenant and election are the identifiers of the community, salvation is not limited to the people of the covenant but extends potentially to the whole human race.[14] The messianic people, described as a tiny flock, although it does not include everybody, nevertheless has a role of constituting "for the whole human race a most certain seed of unity, hope, and salvation" (LG 9). In fact, not only the whole human race but all creation is destined for eschatological renewal and will participate in the final freedom of the glory of the sons and daughters of God (Rom 8:21). The larger question is not the salvation of the few, those included in the covenant, or even those who profess explicit faith and are baptized. The issue is how non-Christians and even all of creation are related to the seed community that represents explicit, visible profession of faith, conversion of life, and participation in baptism.

The church, then, as a visible sacrament of this saving unity, has a role in the saving unity that potentially can encompass all. As a sort of sacrament, it signifies intimate union with God and the unity of all humanity (LG 1).[15] It is also an instrument facilitating this unity. *Lumen Gentium* suggests several ways in which the church may effect this unity, including

---

[13] Church of Scotland, Special Commission on Baptism, *The Doctrine of Baptism: An Interpretation of the Biblical and Reformed Doctrine of Baptism* (Edinburgh: Saint Andrews Press, 1962), 15.

[14] See LG 16 for how those who have not accepted the Gospel are yet related to the people of God in various ways.

[15] Note that the church is "a sort of" (*veluti*) sacrament. Thus it is a sacrament analogously, not the same way Christ or baptism and the Eucharist are sacraments.

baptism, the law of love, the fact that the church has a single head, a single status of dignity and freedom, a single law, and a single end or purpose (LG 9). This is clear enough insofar as the unity of the church itself is concerned, or insofar as the church itself becomes more extensive through evangelization and the addition of new members. Nevertheless, it remains somewhat unsatisfactory as an explanation of how those peoples who explicitly do not want to be Christians can possibly be considered to be associated with the church in some way.

Various attempts to account for the salvation of non-Christians include the traditional teaching about three kinds of baptism: baptism of water, martyrdom (which is baptism by blood), and baptism by desire. Theologians have interpreted decisions of conscience, a form of the traditional baptism of desire, as representing an implicit faith sufficient for salvation. Karl Rahner built on this in formulating his well-known theory of the anonymous Christian.[16] Admittedly, all these accounts of the salvation of non-Christians only make sense from an intramural perspective, that is, from the Christian perspective of Christians looking outward and trying to account for an inclusive and universalist eschatology and soteriology. They can become quite offensive to the Muslim or Hindu who has no desire to be a Christian, anonymous or otherwise. Yet *Lumen Gentium* clearly taught the possibility of salvation for non-Christians: "Those who, through no fault of their own, do not know the Gospel of Christ or his church, but who nevertheless seek God with a sincere heart, and moved by grace, try in their actions to do his will as they know it through the dictates of their conscience—these too may attain eternal salvation" (LG 16).

Nevertheless, eschatological reconciliation has a universal dimension, not in the sense that all will necessarily be saved, but that all receive the offer of salvation that must be accepted in freedom. Although Christians have the firstfruits of the Spirit, the whole creation, presumably including those who do not know Christ, is groaning to be set free from its bondage to decay—in other words, from the sentence of death—in order to obtain the glory of the children of God: in other words, life eternal (Rom 8:21). If this salvation is to occur beyond the frontiers of the bap-

---

[16] Karl Rahner, "Anonymous Christians," in his *Theological Investigations*, vol. 6 (Baltimore: Helicon Press, 1969), 390–98; "Observations on the Problem of the 'Anonymous Christian,'" *Theological Investigations*, vol. 14 (New York: Seabury Press, 1976), 280–94; "Anonymous and Explicit Faith," *Theological Investigations*, vol. 16 (London: Darton, Longman & Todd, 1979), 52–59.

tized, it will be through the power of the Spirit (Rom 8:14), and because they, too, are called, predestined, and justified and members in some way in the family of Christ (Rom 8:29-30).

The document issued by the Congregation for the Doctrine of the Faith, "Dominus Iesus: On the Unicity and Salvific Universality of Jesus Christ and the Church," interprets this possibility of salvation for non-Christians in relation to Christ and the church:

> For those who are not formally and visibly members of the Church, "salvation in Christ is accessible by virtue of a grace which, while having a mysterious relationship to the Church, does not make them formally part of the church, but enlightens them in a way which is accommodated to their spiritual and material situation. This grace comes from Christ; it is the result of his sacrifice and is communicated by the Holy Spirit; it has a relationship with the Church, which "according to the plan of the Father, has her origin in the mission of the Son and the Holy Spirit."[17]

The precise manner in which the non-Christian is related to Christ and the church remains mysterious. However, any position that would consider the church as one way of salvation alongside those constituted by the other religions, seen as complementary or substantially equivalent to the church, even if converging with the church toward the eschatological kingdom of God, is expressly rejected in the document.[18] At the same time it acknowledges that "the various religious traditions contain and offer religious elements which come from God, and which are part of what the Spirit brings about in human hearts and in the history of peoples, in cultures, and religions."[19]

Even though theologians have not been able to explain the manner of salvation of non-Christians in a completely satisfactory way, either to Christians or especially to non-Christians, the fact of this possibility of salvation; the relationship of this salvation to the God whom Christians confess as Father, Son, and Spirit; and the necessary relationship to the church as the body of Christ and the sacrament of the unity of God and humankind is profoundly related to the idea of unicity and universality.

[17] Congregation for the Doctrine of the Faith, "Dominus Iesus: On the Unicity and Salvific Universality of Jesus Christ and the Church," August 6, 2000, §20. Text available in *Origins* 30, no. 14 (September 14, 2000), 209, 211–19.

[18] "Dominus Iesus," §21.

[19] Ibid.

Salvation reflects our unity as members of the one human race; the recapitulation of that race in Christ, the new Adam; and our interconnectedness with one another and with Christ through the bonds established by the Spirit expressed in various images of the church such as the mystical body of Christ, people of God, or temple of the Spirit. The very fact that even though each is saved personally (but not individually) but as a people implies that the salvation of non-Christians is because of a relationship to the church, even though there appears to be no connection institutionally and non-Christians are not a formal part of the church. The "elements that come from God" and the work of the Spirit in human hearts, history, and cultures, which motivate to seek and desire God through their decisions of conscience and search for the divine, result in what has been traditionally termed "a desire for baptism" even though it is not a conscious desire for the sacramental water bath in the Triune name. Christians have identified that longing as a desire for baptism, but when this is not an explicit desire, this "desire for baptism" becomes a shorthand way of saying that the object of our longing is that holy, good, ultimate personal presence that gives meaning to our living and dying, our loving and failed relationships, our struggles, hopes, joys even in the face of immense personal and global tragedies. Christians know this to be the paschal mystery of Christ's death and rising, the Christ who was sent to reconcile all with the Father in the power of the Spirit. Baptism is insertion into this Triune life and mystery; into the relationship of Father, Son, and Spirit; and into the process of dying and rising in the company of all so initiated. Nevertheless, the church has never required that non-Christians be able to identify the object of that holy longing explicitly in order to name it a "desire for baptism."

Baptismal Life

Eschatology, which articulates the goal of baptism, establishes the pattern of Christian living for the initiated who is "on the way." Once we know where we are going, the contours of the road leading to that destination become clear. Baptism is the beginning of a spiritual growth to maturity and a journey to final consummation.

The baptismal life reflects analogically the inner life of the Triune God and thus is characterized by communion and relationships of interdependence. In baptism we enter into communion with God, who is communion of Father, Son, and Spirit. Moreover, a Christian does not go to

God individualistically, but in the company of the community of the baptized, whose bond is the communion of the Spirit by which this community becomes the body of Christ. Baptism not only takes place within the fellowship of the church or grants membership to the church as to an organization; baptism places a person within the corporate union of the faithful in Christ in the communion of the Spirit. This community, variously described as the body of Christ and the temple of the Spirit, is a primary agent in the Christian formation of the baptized, the place where Christian life is nourished so that it may grow to maturity. Within this communion, the baptized is invited to abandon illusions of self-sufficiency and isolation and live a life poured out for others in the spirit of self-emptying that characterizes the Triune relationships. The baptismal life, however, is not only characterized by generosity; it is also profound receptivity and so is never empty, but is filled to overflowing with the love of the Triune God, the gifts of the Spirit, and the shared life of Christians.

Baptismal life is cruciform in the pattern of Christ's redemption, lived at the intersection of a "vertical" relationship with God and a "horizontal" communion with one another. The "vertical" life of contemplation and "horizontal" service complement one another. Baptismal life is also cruciform in the taking up of one's cross and the laying down of one's life in small as well as larger ways in imitation of Christ's death. Our baptism is completed by going the way of the cross.[20] As the cross is not the end of the road, neither is death, but resurrection to new life, new creation, and new birth.

Monika Hellwig describes the countercultural implications of Jesus' death and resurrection: a radical sharing of material resources (Acts 2:42-47; 4:32-37); a style of leadership characterized by service rather than domination (John 13:6-17); trust in divine providence (Matt 6:25-34); forgiveness and nonviolence (Rom 12:1-21); simplicity, total truthfulness, and a deep level of fellowship (1 Cor 12:4-31); and a style of life permeated by prayer.[21] This reordering of relationships characterizes the commitment to a baptismal life and represents the advent of the reign of God. While ultimate salvation transcends whatever we can achieve, even

---

[20] The Report of the Anglican-Reformed International Commission 1981–1984, *God's Reign and Our Unity* (London: SPCK; Edinburgh: Saint Andrews Press, 1984), 34.

[21] Monika K. Hellwig, "Eschatology," in *Systematic Theology: Roman Catholic Perspectives*, vol. 2, ed. Francis Schüssler Fiorenza and John P. Galvin (Minneapolis: Fortress Press, 1991), 361.

by grace, in this world, the sacramental life and the manner of living it requires proleptically realize in a partial way the reign of God, which will be complete eschatologically. In this respect there is continuity between the political, economic, and social structures that result from baptismal living and ultimate salvation, despite the radical discontinuity between this world and the next.

Baptismal life is fundamentally communal. The general judgment as described in Matthew 25:31-46 demonstrates the essential interrelatedness and community of destiny of humankind. The reward of the kingdom is based on how members of the human family treat one another. The fact that there is a general judgment in addition to an individual judgment means that redemption is not offered to each individual person in isolation. A communal destiny awaits each of us, a destiny to which each has contributed for good or for ill.

The themes of baptism, *parousia*, and mutual life come together in the first epistle of Peter. Some scholars interpret 1 Peter 1:3–4:ll as a baptismal homily or liturgy. This letter describes the Christian community as "a chosen race, a royal priesthood, a holy nation, God's own people (1 Pet 2:9). First Peter 4:7-11 combines the themes of the *parousia* and the Christian life. "The end of all things is near (v. 7)," and Christians are urged to maintain constant love for one another (v. 8) and to serve one another with whatever gift each has received (v. 10). The baptismal life is a life of mutual service oriented to the end time.

Lumen Gentium develops the themes of 1 Peter in its second chapter on the people of God. As *Lumen Gentium* 9 says, "[God] has, however, willed to make women and men holy and to save them, not as individuals without any bond between them, but rather to make them into a people who might acknowledge him and serve him in holiness." Christians are forged into this people of God by baptism, born anew through the word of God (1 Pet 1:23) and through water and the Holy Spirit (John 3:5-6). This people is "one and unique," spread throughout the world, but destined to be "finally gathered together as one (see John 11:52)" (LG 13). The unity of the people of God entails ethical implications for mutual service and also prefigures the unity of final consummation.

One final characteristic of baptismal life in the pattern of the Trinity is that it is oriented to mission. The missionary character of baptism flows out of Word and Spirit, the two missions of the Trinity. The Father sent the Son to give the Spirit. Jesus' baptism inaugurated his mission. Anointed with the Spirit at his baptism, Jesus was tried in the wilderness and then returned to Galilee proclaiming the advent of the kingdom of

God (Mark 1:9-15; Luke 3:21–4:14). The characteristics of this kingdom, the transformation of the world achieved in the person of Jesus, Son of the Father and empowered by the Spirit, were foretold by Isaiah 61:1-2 and announced by Jesus (Luke 4:18-19): good news brought to the poor, captives released, the blind given sight, and the oppressed freed. Similarly, the Christian conformed to Christ in baptism and anointed by the Spirit is sent to build the kingdom of God, to continue Christ's mission while manifesting the love of Father, Son, and Spirit and thus to transform the world.

Chapter Two

The Doctrine of Baptism: Sacramental Concepts and Developments on the Eve of the Reformation

In a very real sense the whole ecumenical movement rests on a mutual recognition of baptism among Christian churches, as is the conviction of Ephesians 4:4-6: "There is one body and one Spirit, just as you were called to the one hope of your calling, one Lord, one faith, one baptism, one God and Father of all, who is above all and through all and in all." If there is any unity among Christians, any hope of mending the divisions that rend the ecclesial body of Christ, that unity and that hope must be grounded in the one baptism in Christ and his Spirit. The convergence document of the World Council of Churches, *Baptism, Eucharist and Ministry*, asserts: "Through baptism, Christians are brought into union with Christ, with each other and with the Church of every time and place. Our common baptism, which unites us to Christ in faith, is thus a basic bond of unity."[1] The Vatican II Decree on Ecumenism states that baptism

---

[1] World Council of Churches, *Baptism, Eucharist and Ministry*, Faith and Order Paper No. 111 (Geneva: World Council of Churches, 1982), No. 6.

in Christ gives us the right to be called Christians and is the basis for accepting as brothers and sisters all who have been justified by faith in baptism.[2]

This raises the question: Just what is "common" in this common baptism? By and large, the churches assume a unity because most Christian churches have a rite they call baptism and they believe this practice to be in response to Jesus' command in Matthew 28:19: "Go therefore and make disciples of all nations, baptizing them in the name of the Father and of the Son and of the Holy Spirit, and teaching them to obey everything that I have commanded you." Mutual recognition of baptism seems to rest on a common confession of Jesus Christ within a trinitarian relationship.

Multiple reasons exist for the nonrecognition of baptism. Sometimes nonrecognition is based on faulty Christology or trinitarian doctrine, the reason for the nonrecognition of Mormon baptism by some Christian groups. Sometimes it is based on the recipient of baptism, the reason for the nonrecognition of infant baptism by proponents of believer baptism. Some nonrecognition of baptism is based on ecclesiological principles by groups who believe that only the true church can validly administer the sacrament. This has been the reason for some Orthodox rebaptism of Christians entering into full communion with some Orthodox churches.

Nevertheless, even with those traditions with which we affirm a mutual recognition of baptism, significant differences lurk beneath assumptions of commonality. We do not believe the same things about baptism. We have different notions of what constitutes a sacrament. We disagree on the relationship between the sign of baptism and the reality it signifies. We disagree about the effect of baptism. We engage in sometimes heated arguments about who can be baptized, some churches baptizing infants while others reserving baptism to adults. We do not necessarily baptize in the same way, some churches using immersion while others sprinkle or pour water over the person being baptized. The very formula of baptism has become contested, with some feminists objecting to the naming of God as "Father." We have different practices of admitting the baptized to the eucharistic table, thereby raising the

---

[2] UR 2. In *Vatican Council II: The Basic Sixteen Documents*, trans. Austin Flannery (Northport, NY: Costello, 1996).

question about the interrelationship of the three sacraments of initiation and the relationship between baptism and church membership.

An examination of what is common in the one baptism professed by Christians must address the doctrine of baptism. That doctrine essentially answers these questions: What does baptism do? How does it do it? What does it mean? This chapter examines the fundamental sacramental concepts such as the character of sacrament as sign, the relationship between word and sacrament, sacramental causality (the relationship between the sign of the sacrament and the reality signified), asking what the sacrament effects and how it achieves its effect. Baptism is really much larger than these questions, which arise out of a medieval theology interested in the minimum action and words required for the existence of a sacrament. For example, medieval concerns did not adequately address the relationship between baptism and the church, baptism and justification, baptism and salvation, and baptism and discipleship. However, in order to understand the responses of the Reformers to the medieval heritage of Catholic theology, it is important to begin with an overview of these categories.

The medieval sources of sacramental theology were much more varied than is sometimes assumed. Until Vatican II, Catholic sacramental theology largely reflected the thought of Thomas Aquinas. However, the Reformers of the sixteenth century were much closer to a more diverse sacramental heritage. A case study of what constitutes an obstacle to baptism will illustrate how problematic histories of interpretation can develop, and how these impede ecumenical agreement.

In addition to the sacramental doctrine inherited from the scholastics, the Reformers inherited rites of initiation that were no longer unified. Baptism had been separated from postbaptismal anointing invoking the Spirit, a rite that had become known as confirmation, and from the Eucharist. This loss of an integrated rite of initiation arguably contributes to divisions among Christians that extend well beyond baptism to the theologies of justification and church, as will be examined later in this study.

Sacraments as Signs

Sacramental theology is heavily indebted to St. Augustine (354–430), who defined a sacrament as a visible sign of invisible grace. In the heat of his struggle with the Donatists, Augustine developed a number of sacramental principles that would remain constant in the Christian tradition. He articulated the principle that Christ is the principal minister of the sacrament and that the personal worthiness of the minister does not affect a sacrament's validity. He also distinguished between the existence of the sacrament and its spiritual fruit, a distinction later identified as the difference between sacramental validity and efficacy. Thus baptism could be received validly outside the Catholic Church in heretical sects, although Augustine, believing heresy to be sinful, thought that sins were not forgiven or grace conferred until the baptized repented and was received into the Catholic Church. Augustine also developed a theology of the permanent effect of certain sacraments, which later developed into the doctrine of the sacramental character that marked a person as a member of Christ and the church. He considered baptism to be essential for salvation and stressed the need to baptize infants, teaching that the church acted as proxy by professing faith on behalf of the infant. A baptism of desire and baptism of blood in martyrdom were alternatives for baptism with water.

Later definitions of a sacrament are variations on Augustine's concept of sacraments as visible signs of invisible grace, as these representative examples show:

Thomas Aquinas	A sacrament is a sign of a sacred reality by which we are sanctified. (ST IIIa, q. 60, a. 1)
The *Baltimore Catechism*, formational for American Catholics prior to the Second Vatican Council	A sacrament is an outward sign instituted by Christ to give grace.
Code of Canon Law (1983)	The sacraments of the New Testament, instituted by Christ the Lord and entrusted to the Church, as they are the actions of Christ and the Church, stand out as signs and means by which the faith is expressed and strengthened, worship is rendered to God and the sanctification of humanity is effected, and they thus contribute in the highest degree to the establishment, strengthening and manifestation of ecclesial communion (c. 840).

Catechism of the Catholic Church (1994)	The sacraments are efficacious signs of grace, instituted by Christ and entrusted to the Church, by which divine life is dispensed to us. The visible rites by which the sacraments are celebrated signify and make present the graces proper to each sacrament. They bear fruit in those who receive them with the required dispositions.[3]
John Calvin, *Geneva Catechism* (1541)	An outward attestation of the grace of God, which, by a visible sign, represents spiritual things to imprint the promises of God more firmly in our hearts, and to make us more sure of them.
Episcopal Church, USA, *The Book of Common Prayer* (1979)	The sacraments are outward and visible signs of inward and spiritual grace, given by Christ as sure and certain means by which we receive that grace.

Figure 1

The more recent definitions stress sacraments as actions of Christ and the church and the role of sacraments as expressing and strengthening faith.

Word in Sacrament

Augustine is also famous for developing the role of the word in a sacrament:

> Why does He [Christ] not say: you are clean because of the baptism with which you were washed, but says: "because of the word that I have spoken to you" [John 15:3], unless the reason is that even in water it is the word that cleanses? Take away the word and what is water but water? The word is joined to the element and the result is a sacrament, itself becoming, in a sense, a visible word as well. . . . Whence this power of water so exalted as to bathe the body and

---

[3] *Catechism of the Catholic Church* 1131, hereafter *Catechism*.

cleanse the soul, if it is not through the action of the word; not because it is spoken, but because it is believed? . . . This word of faith
is of such efficacy in the Church of God that it washes clean not only
the one who believes in the word, the one who presents [the child
for baptism], the one who sprinkles [the child], but the child itself,
be it ever so tiny, even though it is as yet incapable of believing unto
justice with the heart or of making profession unto salvation with
the lips. All this takes place through the word, concerning which the
Lord says: "you are already clean because of the word that I have
spoken to you."[4]

The word conveys the meaning of the sign.[5] When Catholics think of
sacraments, they think first of material signs and what they signify.
Although the sign of the sacrament may include a material element and
an action, it also includes a ritual word. For example, the words "I baptize
you . . ." accompany immersion in the font. The Second Vatican Council
urged that the administration of every sacrament include Scripture readings and a word of explanation and pastoral application by the sacramental minister. The word itself is sacramental because through the word
of Scripture we encounter the Word of God. Conversely, the ritual actions
of sacraments are like words that have taken on a visible form, signs of
grace added to the promises of grace. As we have seen, Augustine defined sacraments as "visible words." Luther defined sacraments as
"promises with signs attached to them." The word is an essential element
in all sacramental activity. The Protestant Reformers built on the role of
word within a sacrament, but this remained largely underdeveloped in
Roman Catholic theology until Karl Rahner would describe sacraments
as "word events"[6] and the *Catechism of the Catholic Church* would call
baptism "a bath of water in which the 'imperishable seed' of the Word
of God produces its life-giving effect." In the same paragraph it cites

[4] *Super Joann.* LXXX, on 15, 2. PL 35, 1840. Eng. trans. in James E. White, *Documents of Christian Worship: Descriptive and Interpretive Sources* (Louisville: Westminster John Knox, 1992), 119–20.
[5] See also Thomas Aquinas, *Summa Theologiae*. Latin text, Eng. trans., Introductions, Notes, Appendices, and Glossary by James J. Cunningham (New York: Blackfriars, in conjunction with McGraw-Hill Book Co., 1975) III, q. 60, a. 6.
[6] Karl Rahner, "What is a Sacrament?" in his *Theological Investigations* (hereafter TI), vol. 14 (New York: Seabury Press, 1976), 135–48, at 137. See also his "The Word and the Eucharist," TI 4 (Baltimore: Helicon Press, 1966), 253–86.

Augustine's famous line, "The word is brought to the material element, and it becomes a sacrament."[7]

Sacramental Theology in the Middle Ages

Roman Catholic sacramental theology in the Middle Ages largely followed that of Augustine, but used the philosophical categories of Aristotle to try to understand and explain the sacraments. According to Aristotle all things are composed of matter and form. Everything has two basic aspects: (a) something sensible or able to be experienced in some way, seen or heard; and (b) intelligibility, the capacity to be understood. We have an idea or concept of what something is. As applied to the sacraments, the matter of a sacrament was the sensible gestures and the objects used. The form, given in the words applied, was the meaning of the rituals. In baptism, water is the matter and the baptismal formula, "I baptize you in the name of the Father, and the Son, and the Holy Spirit" is the form.

The minister brings the matter and form together to confect the sacrament. For Roman Catholics, priests and deacons are the "ordinary" ministers of baptism, which means that it is part of the special office of priests and deacons to baptize. However, in cases of emergency, because of the teaching of the necessity of baptism for salvation, baptism can be conferred by anyone who uses the water rightly and speaks the required formula with the intent to do what the church does when it baptizes. These "extraordinary" ministers of baptism may be laywomen or men, even the nonbaptized, provided they have the intention to do what the church intends when it baptizes. However, since the minister takes the place of the one Christ, there should be only one minister. In other words, baptism may not be conferred by several persons taking various roles (one applying the water, another saying the words, for example). Later, Reformed theology would restrict baptism to an authorized minister. Calvin expressly prohibited women from baptizing, largely from a desire to avoid the emergency baptisms of infants by midwives, since he did not hold baptism to be indispensable for salvation.

In the Middle Ages the scholastics distinguished between the sacramental sign consisting of matter and form (*sacramentum tantum*), the

---

[7] *Catechism* 1228.

sacramental reality (*res et sacramentum*), and the spiritual effect or grace of the sacrament, the reality without the sign (*res tantum*). In baptism, for example, immersion or aspersion with water using the trinitarian formula is the *sacramentum tantum*, the sacramental character that identifies an individual as a member of the common priesthood of Christ and incorporates that person into the church is *res et sacramentum*, and sanctifying grace is the *res tantum*.

Sacramental Causality

Sacramental causality, that is, how a sacrament achieves a spiritual effect, was described in various ways in medieval scholasticism. Efficaciousness means that the sacrament actually occurs, that is, is effected and valid. The principal cause of the effects of baptism is God alone, who works actively to produce the interior effect of the sacrament.[8] The reason for this, according to Thomas, is that God alone enters into the soul in which the sacramental effect takes place and because grace, the interior effect of the sacrament, is from God alone.[9] The sacramental rite is efficacious as an instrumental cause, that is, the instrument through which God works. Thomas Aquinas and the Dominicans advocated an instrumental, efficient causality.[10] Within instrumental efficient causality God alone is the primary efficient agent, while the sacramental rite is only an instrumental, secondary agent. The instrumental agent must do something under the influence of the primary agent, must contribute something proper to itself, and in the effect there must be something that can be attributed to the instrument as cause. Thus, according to Thomas, a saw (instrumental cause) depends on the artisan (primary cause) using it, but has its own effect as a saw cutting through a board. The instrumental cause is a sign of a hidden effect in virtue of the fact that it is not only a cause but in some sense also an effect of the primary cause. Thomas says this is why the sacraments of the New Law are causes and signs at the same time and effect what they signify. The water of baptism, "by

[8] ST III, q. 64, a. 1.

[9] See ST I–II, q. 112, a. 1.

[10] Kenan Osborne notes that Thomas himself is inconclusive with regard to causality, treating it variously in his *Commentary on the Sentences* (IVd. 2, q. 1, a. 4), in *De Veritate* (q. 27, a. 4), in *De Potentia* (q. 3, a. 4), and in the *Summa Theologiae* (III, q. 62, a. 1). Kenan Osborne, *Sacramental Theology: A General Introduction* (New York: Paulist Press, 1988), 51.

the very fact of washing the body of its own connatural power, washes the soul too in virtue of being a unity."[11] The sign of washing the body signifies and effects a washing of the soul. The water is the instrumental cause, and God is the primary cause.

A second account of sacramental causality is moral causality. In moral causality the sacraments are seen as pleading with God to grant grace.[12] Here the sacramental rite is essentially a prayer to God to give grace. God is the real efficient agent who alone causes grace.

What is called "occasional causality" represents the third approach to sacramental efficacy, advocated by Alexander of Hales, Bonaventure, and Duns Scotus. Sacraments are the occasions for God to give grace because God has bound himself to them by a certain pact. According to Scotus a prior ordination by God has determined that he will give grace when someone receives a sacrament. Thus sacraments do not give grace in an absolute or necessary way, but because of God's prior ordination, thus preserving the gratuity of grace. Gabriel Biel's sacramental theology comes out of this tradition.

Contemporary sacramental theology has advanced the discussion of sacramental causality beyond all of these scholastic positions by integrating sacraments as causes with sacraments as signs, these two aspects having been considered separately by the scholastics. For example, Karl Rahner criticizes traditional sacramental theology for juxtaposing the function of sacraments as signs and their function as causes without connecting the two concepts, as if the fact that the sacraments are signs plays no part in explaining their causality. He notes:

> The axiom everywhere quoted, *sacramenta significando efficiunt gratiam* (sacraments effect grace by signifying), is not in fact taken seriously. Nor do these theories take into account the fundamentally human element in the sacraments as sacred rites which have a past and a background in the whole history of man's religious activity. Always and everywhere men have had the conviction that in gestures and rites and figurative representation, what is signified and pointed to is in fact present, precisely because it is "represented," and this conviction should not be rejected off-hand as "analogy magic."[13]

---

[11] ST III, q. 62, a. 1.

[12] Advocates of this position include de Ledesma, Vasquez, Lessius, Lugo, Tournely, Franzelin, Pesch, Sasse, Oten, and Puig (Osborne, *Sacramental Theology*, 54).

[13] Karl Rahner, *The Church and the Sacraments* (New York: Herder and Herder, 1963), 36.

The intrinsic relationship between sacramental sign and sacramental efficacy means that if the sign of the sacrament is not present, the sacrament is not present. Thus water is necessary for baptism, and eucharistic crumbs must be identifiable as bread.

These various approaches to sacramental causality illustrate that medieval scholastic sacramental theology was varied, with a number of competing schools of thought. Among the scholastics, contemporary Roman Catholic sacramental theology is most heavily indebted to Thomas Aquinas. The *Decree for the Armenians* issued by the Council of Florence (1439), the most comprehensive ecclesiastical pronouncement on the sacraments until the Council of Trent's sixth session, included a section on the sacraments taken almost verbatim from St. Thomas. This trajectory was not as neat or evident to the Reformers, who were at times responding to currents of sacramental thought that did not become mainstream within Roman Catholicism. Trent, which did not develop a comprehensive sacramental theology but merely responded to perceived errors in the theology of various Reformers, likewise relied heavily on Thomas, although it did not decide among conflicting schools of thought in its sacramental decrees.[14]

Sacramental Character

The sacramental character is a permanent effect of the sacrament that cannot be lost through sin. The character is also called an indelible seal that is both a sign and a reality. Because of the irrevocability of this character, baptism, confirmation, and holy orders, the three sacraments that confer a character, can be received only once by an individual. The character causes a permanent change in the individual who receives the sacrament. This change is best understood as situating an individual in a particular relationship to Christ and to the church that specifies that person's role within the total act of the Church's worship.[15] Thomas notes that this is "nothing else than a certain kind of participation in the priesthood of Christ deriving from Christ himself."[16] Thus through the baptismal character Christians are deputed for the public worship of the

---

[14] Hubert Jedin, *A History of the Council of Trent*, vol. 2, trans. Ernest Graf (St. Louis: Herder and Herder, 1961), 373.

[15] ST III, q. 63, a. 1 and 2.

[16] ST III, q. 63.

church in its liturgy as members of the baptismal priesthood. Catechumens who are preparing for baptism are dismissed from the liturgy of the Eucharist at the end of the reading of the gospel to indicate that they have not yet received this deputation. Baptism gives us both the right and the responsibility to participate in the eucharistic liturgy.

The sacramental character allows baptism to have the effect of the sacraments of the New Law, namely the forgiveness of sin and the worship of God.[17] The teaching of the Roman Catholic Church is that the sacraments of the Old Law did not cause grace, but were only a figure of the passion of Christ. Because baptism is worship, it is not just about what happens to an individual—the forgiveness of an individual's sin, of an individual's membership in the church—but is fundamentally and foremost an act of worship of God, a participation in Christ's worship of his Father, which was most intense in his death and resurrection in obedience to his Father. Forgiveness of sin and newness of life are secondary effects that flow from participation in Christ. The sacrifice of the Son makes baptism a priestly act because his baptism is his sacrifice.

Reformation Responses to Medieval Sacramental Theology

The Reformers were not directly responding to the scholastic theologians of the twelfth and thirteenth centuries, but to Roman Catholic sacramental theology as it had evolved from then up to the beginning of the sixteenth century. If the Reformers had been responding directly to the theology of Thomas Aquinas many of the disputes between them and Catholic sacramental theology might have been eliminated. However, at Erfurt Martin Luther had learned his scholastic theology as mediated by Gabriel Biel, a nominalist who moderated and interpreted William of Occam. Biel, as will be seen below, did not credit Thomas Aquinas for sufficiently associating sacramental efficacy *ex opere operato* with the active role of the recipient *ex opere operantis*. Biel does grant that sacraments have a sacramental effect, but not by virtue of anything naturally intrinsic to them.[18] John Farthing notes two other areas where Biel

---

[17] ST III, q. 63, a. 6; see also q. 62, a. 1 and 5.

[18] Gabriel Biel, IV *Sent.* d. 1 q. 1 a. 2 c. 1. Cited by John L. Farthing, *Thomas Aquinas and Gabriel Biel: Interpretations of St. Thomas Aquinas in German Nominalism on the Eve of the Reformation*, Duke Monographs in Medieval and Renaissance Studies 9 (Durham, NC: Duke University Press, 1988), 107.

departs from Thomas: (1) by denying that the sacraments effect a prior disposition for the infusion of grace, arguing that the character may exist in one who lacks justifying grace, and (2) by denying "Thomas' thesis concerning the supernatural potency (*virtus*) by which sacraments are able to function causally with respect to the impression of a character (instrumentally) and then with respect to the infusion of grace (dispositively)."[19] Biel points to the contrast between Thomas and doctrine he ascribes to Bonaventure, Scotus, and Occam, who place "such emphasis upon God's will, ordinance, and covenant that little is left of sacramental causality as something inherent in the sacrament itself."[20] To the extent that these writers influence the Reformers, differences regarding the sacramental efficacy of baptism will arise between them and the later Catholic tradition, which largely followed the teaching of Thomas. The seeds of difference regarding sacramental doctrine were sown before the Reformers arrived on the scene.

Furthermore, sacramental theology of the late Middle Ages came under the influence of canon law and corresponding concerns about questions of validity—what was required to cause the sacramental reality. Unfortunately, the effort to arrive at precision in the juridical sphere led to sacramental minimalism in the pastoral sphere: The sacramental signs were minimal—little water, wafers for bread, dabs of oil—and the repeatable sacraments such as the Eucharist were received only rarely. In the popular imagination, all too frequently, sacramental practice assumed a magical quality. The principle of *ex opere operato* was interpreted to mean that the sacraments produced their effect automatically. The connection between the sacrament and an individual's faith and the faith of the community was weakened. The original interpretation, meant to assure that sacraments are acts of Christ and do not depend on the worthiness of the minister or the recipient for their validity, lost its association with its correlative principle, *ex opere operantis*, the insistence that the recipient of the sacrament must be actively engaged in the sacramental act through faith and the proper disposition in order to receive the grace of the sacrament. Within a magical worldview validity and fruitfulness collapse into one another and a valid sacrament becomes automatically a fruitful one. Although this was never official church teaching, such attitudes helped to set the stage for the Protestant Reformation that followed.

[19] Ibid.
[20] Ibid., citing Biel, IV *Sent.* d. 1 q. 1 a. 1 n. 2 op. 2 (D).

History of Interpretation:
Obstacles to Baptism as a Case Study

Another problem that poses a challenge to ecumenical understanding today is that a history of interpretation can develop that is not faithful to the original sources and therefore misrepresents the theological position of another tradition. The issue of an obstacle to baptismal efficacy illustrates these problems of interpretation.

Thomas Aquinas identifies the obstacle to baptismal efficacy as deceit, which he understands as the situation in which a person's will stands in contradiction to baptism itself or to its effect.[21] Thomas cites Augustine when he gives four ways in which a person can be considered deceitful: "first, if he does not believe, whereas baptism is *the sacrament of faith*; secondly, if he has contempt for the sacrament itself; thirdly, if he celebrates the sacrament in a way other than according to the rite of the Church; fourthly, if he approaches the sacrament without devotion. Thus it is obvious that deceit blocks the effect of baptism."[22] Thus serious sin in itself does not block the effect of baptism, through which all sins are forgiven,[23] but only the will to remain unrepentant, the desire to remain in serious sin, for this contradicts the action of presenting oneself for baptism, a sign of repentance. This contradiction is deceitful. Deceit blocks the ultimate effect of the sacrament, what the scholastics called the "reality" (*res*) of the sacrament, which is grace. However it does not block the "reality and sign" (*res et sacramentum*), which is the baptismal character.[24]

John Calvin, as well as some contemporary Protestant theologians, identifies mortal sin as an obstacle to the sacraments inclusive of baptism, although this is not one of the meanings Thomas attributes to deceit. In Roman Catholic theology, by baptism *all sins* are forgiven, original sin and all personal sins as well as all punishments for sins.[25] Thus mortal sin cannot be an impediment to baptism. Sometimes a writer simply identifies mortal sin as an obstacle to all sacraments, not distinguishing baptism and penance from the other sacraments. Calvin expresses this

---

[21] ST III, q. 69, a. 9.

[22] Ibid., resp.

[23] See Eugenius IV, *Decree for the Armenians* from the Bull *"Exultate Deo"* (Nov. 22, 1439). DS 696. For contemporary Roman Catholic teaching see *Catechism* 1263.

[24] ST III, q. 68, a. 8, and n. 5b by James J. Cunningham, the editor.

[25] *Catechism* 1263; Council of Trent, Session VI, Canons on the Sacraments in General, c. 6.

view in his statement, "and we justly repudiate the fiction of Sorbonne, that the sacraments of the new law are available to all who do not interpose the obstacle of mortal sin."[26] However, others specifically mention baptism, for example, William B. Evans:

> Among those who wish to ascribe a more than merely cognitive efficacy to the sacraments, two major options have emerged in the history of Western Christianity. There is, first of all, the tradition of *ex opere operato* efficacy that emerged from the ecclesiology of Augustine and was later developed, clarified, and codified during the twelfth and thirteenth centuries by Peter Lombard, Alexander of Hales, Thomas Aquinas, and others. Here baptism is said to be an instrument whereby the grace of baptism is conveyed to the recipient in a more or less mechanical fashion (the Latin phrase *ex opere operato* means "in the performance of the act"). Grace is conveyed unless an obstacle or impediment (e.g., mortal sin) prevents it.[27]

Mark Tranvik is yet another theologian who identifies mortal sin as an impediment to baptism: "When baptism is received with an impediment of mortal sin, the indelible mark on the soul is received but not the saving graces. When however, that impediment is removed, the saving graces of baptism become effectual."[28]

Such statements usually occur in a polemic against the principle that sacraments are efficacious *ex opere operato*, that is, by virtue of the sacramental rite being performed with the intention of the church. They are responses to two particular canons from the Council of Trent: canon 6, which says: "If anyone says that the sacraments of the New Law do not contain the grace which they signify, or that they do not confer that grace on those who place no obstacles in its way, as though they are only outward signs of grace or justice received through faith and certain marks of Christian profession, whereby among men believers are distinguished from unbelievers, let him be anathema," and canon 8: "If anyone says that by the sacraments of the New Law grace is not conferred *ex opere*

---

[26] John Calvin, "Exposition of the Heads of Agreement," in *Selected Works of John Calvin: Tracts and Letters*, vol. 2, Tracts, Part 2, ed. Henry Beveridge and Jules Bonnet (Grand Rapids: Baker Book House; Edinburgh: Calvin Translation Society, 1846, repr. 1983), 232.

[27] William B. Evans, "'Really Exhibited and Conferred . . . In His Appointed Time': Baptism and the New Reformed Sacramentalism," *Presbyterion* 31, no. 2 (Fall 2005): 72–88, at 77.

[28] Mark D. Tranvik, "Luther on Baptism," *Lutheran Quarterly* 13 (1999): 76.

operato, but that faith alone in the divine promise is sufficient to obtain grace, let him be anathema."[29]

The writers just cited do not give a source for their claim that mortal sin is an obstacle, but mention it in passing as if it were general knowledge. Thus it may be an idea that is in a general culture, "in the air," as it were. Nevertheless, it is interesting to track down what may be one of the sources of this misconception, even though this cannot be proved beyond any doubts. At any rate, it is imperative to clarify the confusion and correct the error.

Martin Chemnitz (1522–86) contributed significantly to the establishment of the Lutheran Reformation and to the development of Lutheran doctrinal theology in the late sixteenth century and is well known to Protestant dogmatic theologians. Chemnitz cites Gabriel Biel's (ca. 1414–95) interpretation of the scholastics: "'A sacrament is said to confer grace *ex opere operato*, so that by the very fact that it (understand sacrament) is performed, grace is conferred on the users, unless the obstacle of mortal sin prevents it,' so that beyond the exhibition of the sign, outwardly exhibited, there is not required a good inner impulse in the recipient."[30] Again, indirectly citing Biel, Chemnitz adds that the sacrament outwardly administered does not suffice for the conferring of grace, but that sacraments confer grace *ex opere operante* through the measure of merit, since there is required a good impulse in the recipient according to whether grace is merited either worthily or suitably (*condigni vel congrui*).[31]

This passage does not specifically mention baptism. What Biel says regarding an obstacle is true of the sacraments of the living but does not apply to the sacraments of the dead. The first require that the recipient of a sacrament be in a state of grace to receive the effects of the sacrament. Within Catholic theology this would include the Eucharist, confirmation, marriage, holy orders, and anointing of the sick. These sacraments impart grace to those who are already spiritually alive through sanctifying grace.

---

[29] Council of Trent, Decree Concerning the Sacraments, Session VII, 3 March 1547.

[30] Martin Chemnitz, *Examination of the Council of Trent*, Part II (St. Louis: Concordia Publishing House, 1978), 83, citing Gabriel Biel, IV *Sent.* d. 1, q. 3, n. 2: *Uno modo ex ipso signo seu sacramento vel, ut* alii *dicunt, ex opere operato; ita quod eo ipso quod opus illud, puta signum aut sacramentum, exhibetur, nisi impediat obex peccati mortalis, gratia confertur, sic quod praeter exhibitionem signi foris exhibiti non requiritur bonus motus interior in suscipiente, quo de condigno vel de congruo gratiam mereatur, sed sufficit quod suscipiens non ponat obicem.*

[31] Translation from Chemnitz, *Examination*, Part II, 83.

The "sacraments of the dead," baptism and penance, are those sacraments which mediate the forgiveness of sin to those who are spiritually dead through the lack of sanctifying grace. For them, repented mortal sin is not an impediment.

A later passage in Biel's commentary, not cited by Chemnitz, accurately explains the nature of the obstacle to baptism; here he says that the general opinion of the scholastics was that baptism removes all sins and punishment due to sin except the deceit of remaining unrepentant of a sin and the sin for which there is no repentance, which must then be presented to the sacrament of penance. Biel clarifies this position with the following example:

> Before baptism someone committed seven mortal sins and coming to baptism he is sorry about six; the seventh actually pleases him and he is in no way sorry for it. That seventh sin alone is the cause of his pretense in baptism. It is necessary therefore that he truly repent over that seventh sin in itself and insofar as it was the cause of his pretense in baptism. I say this inasmuch as someone perhaps sinned, causing irreverence to the sacrament by one other mortal sin by receiving baptism in such a pretense. But when that pretense is withdrawn, which was the impediment to the effect of baptism, by true penitence and contrition (because otherwise that pretense and this sin is not forgiven), God confers baptismal grace as a remedy for those other six sins, which would have been forgiven in baptism if the pretense had not been present.[32]

The obstacle to baptism here is not that the seventh sin was a mortal sin, but that the penitent received baptism insincerely because he repented of six mortal sins but not the seventh. The obstacle is insincerity, not mortal sin as such. According to Biel one who receives baptism insincerely receives the sacramental character, but the insincerity is an obstacle to receiving the full effect of the sacrament, namely the forgiveness of sins. A disputed question during the medieval period was whether, after the insincerity was removed, all guilt and punishment for sins prior to baptism would be remitted by virtue of the baptism (the

---

[32] Gabriel Biel, *Collectorum cira quattuor libros Sententiarum, Libri quarti pars prima* (d. 1–14), ed. Wilfridus Werbeck and Udo Hofmann (Tübingen: J. C. B. Mohr [Paul Siebeck], 1975), IV *Sent.* d. 4 q. 1 a. 3 dub. 3 op. 2, trans. Roland Teske. See Thomas Aquinas, IV *Sent.* d. 4 q. 3 a. 2 qla. 3 sol., and ST III, q. 69, a. 10 corp.

position of Thomas), or whether penance would be required for the sin of insincerity.[33]

In his *Commentary on the Sentences*, Thomas presents the question whether, once the feigning has been withdrawn, baptism should obtain its effect. The argument is that a dead work is never brought back to life, but that is called a dead work which has taken place in mortal sin. Therefore when a feigning person approaches baptism, should that person be in mortal sin, baptism will never be able to bring back life in order to confer grace.[34] However, here again the issue is not that mortal sin is an impediment; the original impediment was the fiction, which is now withdrawn. However, a mortal sin submitted to baptism under the pretense of repentance cannot be brought back to life by baptism, but must be submitted to penance. This is because Thomas teaches that there are two effects of baptism. The first, the *res et sacramentum*, is the sacrament itself, that is, the sacramental character. The second effect is the *res*, but not the *sacramentum*, that is, the grace of the sacrament. A person who receives baptism feigning repentance receives the first, the *res et sacramentum*, the sacramental character, but does not receive the *res*, that is, the grace of the sacrament. Unrepented mortal sin is an impediment to the grace of the sacrament but not to the sacrament itself. The characteristic that makes it an impediment is the fact that it is unrepented. This distinction is not observed in those theologians who say that mortal sin is an impediment to baptism.

There is the further question whether Biel accurately represents Thomas's teaching on the relationship between the concepts *ex opere operato* and *ex opere operantis* when he states "beyond the exhibition of the sign, outwardly conveyed, there is not required a good inner impulse in the recipient." He continues: "however, the sacraments are said to confer grace *ex opere operante* through the measure of merit, namely, because the sacrament outwardly administered does not suffice for the conferring of grace, but that beyond this there is required a good impulse or an inner devotion in the recipient, according to the intention of which grace is conferred as of a worthy or suitable merit (*meritum condigni vel congrui*), exactly and not greater, on account of the giving of the sacrament."[35]

Biel seems to claim that Thomas says that sacraments confer grace without any subjective movement of the soul toward God. As John

[33] See Farthing, *Thomas Aquinas and Gabriel Biel* (n. 18, p. 30 above), 138.
[34] Aquinas, IV *Sent.*, *De Sacramentis*, d. 4, q. 2, a. 2, qla. 3.
[35] Cited by Chemnitz, *Examination*, Part II, 83.

Farthing notes, Biel "obscures Thomas on the actual sacramental bond between the *opus operatum* (considered objectively) and the *opus operantis* (considered subjectively)—or between outer work and inner faith. Thomas does not suggest that the mere absence of obstacles is sufficient for the bestowal of sacramental grace *ex opere operato*."[36] The original purpose of the concept *ex opere operato*, which dates from the Donatist controversy in the fourth century, was not to suggest that faith or some inner movement toward God is required on the part of the sacramental recipient, but to assert that the efficacy of the sacrament derives from the action of Christ and is not therefore affected by the moral state of the minister. Farthing suggests that the source of Biel's misrepresentation of Thomas is that he is reading Thomas through the eyes of Scotus's dictum that "a sacrament . . . confers grace by virtue of the work performed (*ex virtute operis operati*), so that no good interior motion is required, which would merit grace: but it is enough if the one who receives it places no obstacle in the way," even though Scotus does not claim to be interpreting Thomas on this point.[37] John Farthing's study of Biel's interpretation of Thomas shows that Biel, in interpreting Thomas through the eyes of Scotus, misrepresents Thomas's opinion on sacramental efficacy *ex opere operato*.[38] Thomas actually held to a closer bond between the *opus operatum* and the *opus operantis*, that is, between the objective and subjective character of sacramental efficacy, namely, work of the sacrament and the inner faith of the recipient.

Since ecumenical agreement is based on confessional documents where they exist, it is important to check whether the source of claims that mortal sin is an obstacle to baptism lies in confessional texts. Three texts in the Lutheran *Book of Concord* make mention of obstacles with respect to the sacrament, although none of them identifies mortal sin as an obstacle to baptism. In each case these are presented in a polemic against the concept of *ex opere operato*:

1. *Apology of the Augsburg Confession*, Article XIII, 18: "It is much more needful to understand how the sacraments are to be used. Here we condemn the entire crowd of scholastic doctors who teach that the sacraments confer grace *ex opere operato* without a good disposition in those receiving them, as long as the recipients do not place an obstacle in the way."

---

[36] Farthing, *Thomas Aquinas and Gabriel Biel*, 109.
[37] Ibid., 110.
[38] Ibid.

2. *Apology of the Augsburg Confession*, Article XXIV, 63: Here the reference to mortal sin is correct since the context refers to a "sacrament of the living," the Mass.

3. *Apology of the Augsburg Confession*, Article XXVI, 96: Here the nature of the obstacle is not named, but the reference is to the effects of the Mass, not baptism.

The erroneous notion that mortal sin is an obstacle to baptism does not come from Lutheran confessional writings. Whatever its source, the error is significant, for if mortal sin is erroneously considered to be an obstacle to baptism, this jeopardizes baptism's role as a sacrament of justification. It also contributes to the polemic against a theology of sacramental efficacy *ex opere operato* by emphasizing a mechanistic and automatic conferral of grace by the sacrament if this obstacle is absent.

This case study in a history of interpretation demonstrates how theologians from the heritage of the Reformation, which was influenced by nominalism, differed from the Thomistic heritage of Catholicism. In addition to these mistaken references to the nature of an obstacle to baptism, these two streams of thought led to different conclusions regarding sacramental efficacy. Moreover, these were not the only two schools of thought offering theological opinions on the matter.

Changes in Baptismal Practice: The Disintegration of an Integrated Rite

A number of shifts in the practice of Christian initiation in the West in the late medieval period also had an impact on baptismal theology. For the early Christians the implications of baptism were enormous, demanding a total conversion that immediately placed them in a countercultural position at odds with the dominant faith systems, whether Jewish, Roman, or Greek. This conversion was a process that proceeded in stages over what was frequently a three-year period of probation known as the catechumenate. Initiation was not easy, and halfhearted Christians were discouraged from undertaking the process. Since the early sixth century, however, the candidates for baptism have been primarily infants, implying that they are baptized into a Christian culture rather than making an adult commitment to personal conversion.

Eventually the disintegration of the integral unity of the initiation rites consisting of baptism, postbaptismal anointing, and Eucharist also contributed to the diminishment of awareness of the radical change wrought by baptism and affected baptismal theology, particularly as it relates to the other sacraments of initiation. The first step in this disintegration was the dissociation of baptism from communion in the West. Mark Searle describes the breakup of Christian initiation in the sixth century and attributes it largely to the fact that the candidates for baptism were almost exclusively infants. Because of high infant mortality and the widely accepted doctrine of Augustine on original sin, the preoccupation shifted from forming Christians for life to saving children from dying unbaptized.[39] This resulted in the gradual abandonment of Easter and Pentecost as the annual festivals of initiation, although the unified rite of initiation survived in Rome, with the exception of emergencies involving the danger of death, until the twelfth century.[40]

Before the twelfth century infants were given communion of the wine at the time of their baptism. J. D. C. Fisher reports that "in all the Churches of the West those who were granted Paschal initiation, whether or not they then received confirmation, were all, irrespective of age, communicated at the Mass which formed the climax of the rite."[41] Once the Eucharist had been received, another reception of the sacrament could be deferred for a long time, but there was great emphasis that the Eucharist should be received before death. In this context it is not a question of receiving the Eucharist when death was imminent; the emphasis is on a person having received the Eucharist at all, including infants. The

[39] Mark Searle, *Christening: The Making of Christians* (Collegeville, MN: Liturgical Press, 1980), 14.

[40] Maxwell Johnson drew my attention to recent scholarship questioning the assumed normativity of Easter as the occasion for baptism as well as a Romans 6 paschal theology for interpreting Christian initiation in the early church. See Gabriele Winkler, *Das armenische Initiationsrituale*, Orientalia Christiana Analecta 217 (Rome: Pontifical Oriental Institute, 1982); and eadem, "Die Licht-Erscheinung bei der Taufe Jesu und der Ursprung des Epiphaniefestes," *Oriens Christianus* 78 (1994): 177–229. Thomas Talley, *The Origins of the Liturgical Year*, 2nd ed. (Collegeville, MN: Liturgical Press, 1986); Paul Bradshaw, "'*Diem baptismo sollemniorem*': Initiation and Easter in Christian Antiquity," in *Living Water, Sealing Spirit: Readings on Christian Initiation*, ed. Maxwell Johnson, 137–47 (Collegeville, MN: Liturgical Press, 1995); Maxwell Johnson, "From Three Weeks to Forty Days: Baptismal Preparation and the Origins of Lent," 118–36 in the same volume; idem, "Preparation for Pascha? The Origins of Lent in Christian Antiquity," in *Passover and Easter*, Two Liturgical Traditions Series, vol. 5, ed. Paul Bradshaw and Lawrence Hoffman, 36–54 (Notre Dame: University of Notre Dame Press, 1999).

[41] J. D. C. Fisher, *Christian Initiation: Baptism in the Medieval West* (London: SPCK, 1965), 101.

Scripture text of John 6:53, "Very truly, I tell you, unless you eat the flesh of the Son of Man and drink his blood, you have no life in you," seemed to mandate the reception of communion by all.[42]

This changed in the twelfth century, following eucharistic controversies and an emphasis on sacramental realism that raised doubts about whether infants should be communed with eucharistic bread since they would be unable to swallow the host. Even though communing them with eucharistic wine remained a possibility, the chalice was soon withdrawn from the laity, with the effect of excommunicating children. The general rule was then that they could not be admitted until they reached "years of discretion."[43] The Fourth Lateran Council (1215) imposed the discipline of going to confession and receiving the Eucharist at Easter on those faithful who had reached the age of discretion.[44] In 1562 the Council of Trent decreed that children under the age of discernment are not bound by any obligation to sacramental holy communion.[45] When Pope Pius X lowered the age for the reception of communion, but not for confirmation, in 1910, the sequence for the rites of initiation became baptism-penance-Eucharist-confirmation. Within this sequence Eucharist is not experienced as the culmination of initiation, regardless of whatever theologies might be in place.

The second step was the separation of confirmation from baptism. In the sixteenth century the Council of Trent decreed that a child should not be confirmed until the age of reason, generally reckoned to be about seven years of age. The Anglican communion inaugurated the same restriction with the first *Book of Common Prayer* of 1549.

Effects of the Loss of an Integrated Rite

In the baptismal rites of the third century recounted for us in the *Apostolic Tradition*, generally attributed to Hippolytus (d. 215), baptism clearly culminates in the Eucharist. After their baptism the neophytes join the faithful in their prayers and exchange the kiss of peace with

---

[42] Ibid., 103.

[43] This history of infant communion in the West is described by Paul Bradshaw in "Christian Initiation," in *The New Dictionary of Sacramental Worship* (Collegeville, MN: Liturgical Press, 1990), 606.

[44] Fourth Lateran Council, c. 21.

[45] Session XXI, 16 July 1562, chap. 4, canon 4.

them. Then the Eucharist begins, and the newly baptized celebrate their incorporation into the body of Christ by sharing in eucharistic communion. The Eucharist is the climax of their process of conversion and they are only admitted to it after perhaps as much as three years of association with the church.

The disintegration of the unity of the rites of initiation produced numerous effects. Christian initiation ceased to be a process and became a series of three separate rites. Not only have these rites been separated, but the order of their reception has been changed. Today children are usually admitted to communion before they are confirmed, and Roman Catholic sacramental legislation prescribes that they receive first reconciliation before their first communion. The separation and reordering destroy the direct trajectory from baptism to Eucharist, although a eucharistic doctrine that loses its connection with the mystical body of Christ, that is, its ecclesial meaning, and becomes solely associated with an individual's reception of the sacramental body of Christ is also to blame.[46] Within our faith traditions we are very clear that we receive the body of Christ when we receive the Eucharist, but generally we are not as conscious that we also sacramentalize our communion with one another within the church, which is the mystical body of Christ. The ecclesial meaning of the Eucharist has largely been lost. Some who try to restore it may be accused of a certain horizontalism in their eucharistic piety, implying a neglect of the transcendent nature of the Eucharist. Such criticisms, however, fail to acknowledge that the ecclesial meaning of the Eucharist is rooted in the identity of the ecclesial community as the body of Christ within the Pauline theology of 1 Corinthians 10:16-17.

Initiation also became privatized and isolated from the faith community. Most often baptisms were celebrated on Sunday afternoon with only a remnant of the community, predominantly the family, even present to receive and welcome the new member. The communal meaning of baptism was replaced by a more individualistic focus.

The emphasis on the removal of original sin eclipsed baptism's formational function of "making a Christian" and incorporating that person into the Christian community. The emphasis became the salvation of an individual through the removal of sin and the bestowal of grace rather than incorporation into an eschatological community identified as the body of Christ. Eventually, too, the concept of grace became reified,

---

[46] Henri de Lubac traces this separation in *Corpus Mysticum: L'Eucharistie et l'Église au Moyen Age*, Coll. Théologie 3 (Paris: Aubier-Montaigne, 1944).

imagined as a quantifiable substance rather than a relationship of communion.

Aidan Kavanagh eloquently describes the relationship between baptism and the Eucharist when he articulates the principle on which the Rite's norm of baptism rests:

> that baptism is inadequately perceptible apart from the eucharist; that the eucharist is not wholly knowable without reference to conversion in faith; that conversion is abortive if it does not issue in sacramental illumination by incorporation into the Church; that the Church is only an inept corporation without steady access to Sunday, Lent, and the Easter Vigil; that evangelization is mere noise and catechesis only a syllabus apart from conversion and initiation into a robust ecclesial environment of faith shared. In baptism the eucharist begins, and in the eucharist baptism is sustained. From this premier sacramental union flows all the Church's life.[47]

The ecclesial dimension of baptism is associated with the conviction that all who are baptized into Christ have become one in Christ Jesus (Gal 3:27-28). This unity in Christ is expressed by Paul in the image of the body: "For just as the body is one and has many members, and all the members of the body, though many, are one body, so it is with Christ. For in the one Spirit we were all baptized into one body—Jews or Greeks, slaves or free—and we were all made to drink of one Spirit" (1 Cor 12:12-13). By being baptized into the death and resurrection of Christ we become his body, not individually, although there is a transformation in grace whereby we are formed into the likeness of Christ, but corporately.

Here the trajectory between baptism and Eucharist, the sacrament of Christ's body and blood, is evident. They are both sacraments of the same body and we participate in the body through different sacramental modalities. Just as Christ is sacramentalized on the altar, so is the church. The communion into which we are baptized, both Christic and ecclesial, is represented by the sacrament of the altar. In terms of sacramental symbolism, the water bath symbolizes our immersion in the death and resurrection of Christ and the Eucharist represents our communion in Christ. The Eucharist is the repeatable communal form of the incorporation into Christ achieved under different sacramental signs in baptism.

---

[47] Aidan Kavanagh, *The Shape of Baptism: The Rite of Christian Initiation* (New York: Pueblo, 1978), 122.

In the following chapters, as we examine the theology of the Reformers, the legacy of this disintegrated rite of initiation will be evident in an individualistic notion of justification considered apart from membership in a community of salvation, in a theology of baptism considered apart from its fulfillment in the Eucharist, and in a divorce of sacramental theology from a theology of the church. In short, this disintegration no doubt contributed to divisions among Christians at the time of the Reformation.

Chapter Three

The Doctrine of Baptism: The Reformers and Catholic Responses

This chapter tests the assumption of a common baptism by illustrating the major differences and similarities embedded in the historical origins of several major Protestant traditions: Lutheran, Anabaptist, Reformed, and Baptist. By inquiring into the definition of sacrament, examining the relationship between the sign of the sacrament and the reality signified, and asking what the sacrament effects and how it achieves its effect, this chapter addresses the questions: What does baptism do? How does it do it? What does it mean?

Baptism is really much larger than these questions, which arise out of a medieval theology interested in the minimum action and words required for the existence of a sacrament. This narrow and rather juridical consideration of baptism developed at the same time that its administration occurred in a private and individualistic ceremony that took place apart from the communal liturgical experience of a faith community. Nevertheless, these questions, which dominated medieval sacramental theology, continued to influence the baptismal theology of the Reformers, whose theology was largely a reaction to the medieval theology outlined in the preceding chapter. Eventually we will have to move beyond these questions, but a comparison of various ecclesial traditions must begin by addressing them.

The Lutheran Tradition

Baptism is a recurring theme in Martin Luther's writing.[1] His early works on the topic were comparatively free from polemics, for Luther did not have any major disagreements with Catholic baptismal doctrine or practice, but when the Anabaptists came on the scene in the early 1520s, this changed dramatically. Luther directed his polemical energies toward refuting the Anabaptists, who disapproved of the baptism of children and asserted that children are saved without baptism.

The Lutheran confessions include Luther's baptismal theology in his *Small* and *Large Catechisms*, both written in 1529, and the *Smalcald Articles* of 1537. In answer to the question "what is baptism?" the *Small Catechism* replies: "Baptism is not simply plain water. Instead it is water enclosed in God's command and connected with God's Word."[2] Baptism "brings about forgiveness of sins, redeems from death and the devil, and gives eternal salvation to all who believe it."[3] It accomplishes this through the "Word of God, which is with and alongside the water, and faith, which trusts this Word of God in the water."[4] With the Word of God, water is a baptism, which is a "new birth in the Holy Spirit" (Titus 3:5-8). Major themes in Luther's baptismal theology include the role of the word of God in the sacrament, the reception of the sacrament in faith, and the new birth and forgiveness of sin effected by the sacrament.

Luther's Disagreement with Thomas Aquinas

Even though Luther had no major disagreements with the baptismal theology he inherited from medieval theology, the one point in Thomas Aquinas's theology of baptism that did concern Luther was whether there is a "heavenly power" in the water that imprints a character in the

---

[1] Luther's teaching on baptism is set out in two treatises, "The Holy and Blessed Sacrament of Baptism" (1519) and "The Babylonian Captivity of the Church" (1520), in his *Small* and *Large Catechisms* (1529), and in at least twenty-three sermons on baptism: four in 1528, three in 1532, seven in 1534, six in 1538, and three in 1539. A number of his other writings also contain frequent references to baptism.

[2] Luther, *The Small Catechism*, "The Sacrament of Holy Baptism," first article. *The Book of Concord: The Confessions of the Evangelical Lutheran Church* (= LC), ed. Robert Kolb and Timothy J. Wengert (Minneapolis: Fortress Press, 2000).

[3] Ibid., second article.

[4] Ibid., third article.

soul.[5] This question recurred several times: in the *Smalcald Articles* (1537),[6] in a sermon on baptism (10 February 1538),[7] in his lectures on Genesis (1535–45),[8] and in a sermon in which is found his last recorded reference to Thomas Aquinas (10 January 1546).[9] The issue was whether there was a spiritual power joined to the water that, through the water, washes away sin. Luther objected to separating the "word" from the element of the sacrament and attributing the power of the sacrament to the water itself. Nevertheless, in his sermon he does recognize that only the power of the Holy Spirit, not the water itself, washes away sin. Luther rejects an attribution of justification to the baptismal water, insisting that the water is no better than the water that cows drink.[10]

The *Smalcald Articles* incorporate Augustine's definition of a sacrament as the Word added to the element.[11] However, on the basis of this Luther says: "Therefore we do not agree with Thomas[12] and the Dominicans who forget the Word (God's institution) and say that God has placed a spiritual power in the water which through the water, washes away sin. We also disagree with Scotus and the Franciscans,[13] who teach that baptism washes away sin through the assistance of the divine will, that is, that this washing takes place only through God's will and not at all through the Word and the water." Luther makes a similar point in "The Babylonian Captivity of the Church," where he comments: "There is a dispute, some saying there is a hidden spiritual power in the word and water, which works the grace of God in the soul of the recipient."[14] In this text Luther is referring to a medieval dispute regarding how sacraments cause grace.

---

[5] This discussion is indebted to Denis R. Janz, *Luther on Thomas Aquinas: The Angelic Doctor in the Thought of the Reformer* (Stuttgart: Steiner Verlag, 1989), 66–68, citing *D. Martin Luthers Werke: Tischreden* (Weimar: Böhlau, 1912–21), 2, 202, 21ff. (18 Aug. 1532).

[6] *D. Martin Luthers Werke. Kritische Gesamtausgabe* (Weimar: Böhlau, 1883), 50, 241, 12ff.

[7] Ibid., 46, 168, 18ff.

[8] Ibid., 42, 170, 8ff.

[9] Ibid., 51, 122, 25ff.

[10] Ibid.

[11] *Smalcald Articles*, III, 5.

[12] Thomas Aquinas, ST III, q. 62, a. 4.

[13] John Duns Scotus, *Commentary on the Sentences* IV, d. 1, q. 2. He was followed by Franciscans like William of Occam, *Sent.* IV, q. 1.

[14] Martin Luther, "The Babylonian Captivity of the Church," in *Three Treatises*, 2nd rev. ed. (Minneapolis: Fortress Press, 1970), 186.

Although attributing the spiritual power of baptism to the water may strike a contemporary reader as strange, this was actually a disputed point among the scholastics of the Middle Ages. Hugh of St. Victor held that the grace of the sacrament was contained in the sacramental sign and directly imparted through it. Others, such as Bonaventure and Duns Scotus, contended that the sign was merely a symbol, but that God, according to an agreement, imparted the grace of the sacrament when the sign was used.[15] Luther disagreed with what he thought was Thomas's position, namely that a spiritual power exists in the baptismal water. He also disagreed with the voluntarist position that the washing is an occasion for the will of God, which actually effects the washing of sin apart from the Word and the water.

Since in the *Smalcald Articles* Luther explicitly refers to Aquinas, Thomas's position must be examined more carefully in its context. In *Summa Theologiae* III, 62 it is especially important to study the replies to the objections in article 4. There Thomas is actually referring to the water as an instrumental cause of grace, not as a container for grace. Furthermore, he says that when a spiritual entity exists fully in something, it contains that thing and is not contained by it. He actually says that grace is not in the sacrament as in a subject or a vessel inasmuch as a vessel is a certain kind of place, but rather in the way that an instrument is a tool by means of which some work is performed. Furthermore, Thomas cites the authority of Augustine throughout his treatment of the nature of a sacrament, including the very citation Luther is using to object to him. In ST III, 60, 4, Thomas states: "On the other hand, Augustine says, *The word is conjoined to the material element and the sacrament is constituted.* Here he is speaking of the kind of element which is perceptible by the senses, namely, water. Therefore sensible realities are needed for the sacraments."[16] Thus even though Luther may be referring to a question disputed among the scholastics, in the *Smalcald Articles* he does not accurately reflect the teaching of Thomas Aquinas.

As Denis Janz observes, such an assertion actually distorts Thomas's view when it fails to take into account his qualifications, namely, that God himself is the principal cause of grace while the sacraments are instrumental causes.[17] Although a spiritual power can be in the water "insofar as a body can be moved by a particular spiritual substance so

---

[15] "The Babylonian Captivity of the Church," n. 123, p. 187.
[16] ST III, q. 60, a. 4, ad 1.
[17] ST III, q. 62, a. 4.

as to produce a particular spiritual effect,"[18] and there can be a spiritual power in the water in the same way that a voice perceived by the senses can bear within it a spiritual power,[19] spiritual power, properly speaking, is in both words and things as they combine to form one sacrament.[20] Thus the spiritual power is not just in the water as such, but is in the sacrament as comprised by both matter and form, external matter and the words of the sacrament.[21] Because for Thomas, the words and the water are inseparable and because the sacrament derives its power from Christ as received in faith, Luther's position is much closer to that of Thomas than he supposes.[22]

The Lutheran Tradition: Baptism and the Word

Luther's major contribution to baptismal theology is to connect it to God's word of promise. As we have seen, he adopts Augustine's understanding of a sacrament: "When the Word of God is added to the element or the natural substance, it becomes a sacrament, that is, a holy, divine thing and sign."[23] For Luther, sacraments are external things in which God's Word is enclosed.

The *Smalcald Articles* describe baptism as "nothing other than God's Word in the water, commanded by God's institution, or, as Paul says, 'washing by the Word.'"[24] The connection between word and water is made in Augustine's definition of a sacrament: "Let the Word be added

---

[18] Ibid. III, q. 62, a. 4, ad. 1.

[19] Ibid.

[20] Ibid. III, q. 62, a. 4, ad. 4. See also ST III, q. 66, aa. 4 and 5, and ST III, q. 66, a. 6.

[21] Ibid. III, q. 62, a. 5, ad. 2.

[22] Janz (*Luther on Thomas Aquinas*, 68) suggests that Luther's misunderstanding of Thomas on this point might be attributable to a one-sided and distorted presentation of Thomas's teaching among Thomists.

[23] *The Large Catechism*, Fourth Part: Concerning Baptism, l. 19–21, citing Augustine, *Tractate 80*, on John 15:3: "Accedat verbum ad elementum et fit sacramentum" (MPL 35:1840; NPNF, ser. 1, 7:344, which reads *accedit*). The note from *The Book of Concord* reads: "Luther cites from memory the Latin of Augustine's *Tractates on the Gospel of St. John* 80, 3 on John 15:3 (MPL 35:1840; NPNF, ser. 1, 7:344). Augustine's actual words were, 'The Word is added to the element, and a sacrament results.' (*Accedat verbum ad elementum et fit sacramentum*)." Luther referred to this statement in other contexts: LC (see n. 2 above), "Baptism," 18, and LC, "Lord's Supper," 10, p. 320.

[24] *Smalcald Articles*, III, 5.

to the element, and a sacrament results."[25] Sacraments are enacted forms of the word of God, word being understood as "gospel." Thus "baptism is a demonstration of what God has done and still does for our salvation in and through Christ, and God's application to the individual in the church of the objective reconciliation and atonement that he has accomplished in Christ."[26] There is a reciprocal relationship between word and sacrament in that the word is an audible sacrament and sacraments are visible words.

The Lutheran concern is to keep the water and the word of command and promise inseparably together, for the Lutheran confessions define sacraments as "rites which have the command of God and to which the promise of grace has been added."[27] The connection between sacrament and promise is especially important in Lutheran theology because of the correspondence between the promise, the faith by which it is received, and the sacrament. Thus the connection between word and sacrament is essential for the doctrine of justification by faith to be linked to a theology of baptism as a justifying sacrament.

Whether Baptism is Regenerative

Luther says that in baptism we should pay attention to three things: "the sign, the significance of it, and the faith."[28] The sign of the sacrament is being thrust into the water in the name of the Father, Son, and Spirit, and being drawn out again. This signifies a dying to sin and a resurrection in the grace of God. Luther's language in "The Holy and Blessed Sacrament of Baptism" is strongly regenerative. He speaks of a new

---

[25] Ibid.

[26] Arthur Carl Piepkorn, "The Lutheran Understanding of Baptism—A Systematic Summary," in *Lutherans and Catholics in Dialogue II: One Baptism for the Remission of Sins*, ed. Paul C. Empie and William W. Baum, published jointly by Representatives of the U.S.A. National Committee of the Lutheran World Federation and the Bishops' Commission for Ecumenical Affairs (Washington, DC: Publication Office, National Catholic Welfare Conference, 1966), 31.

[27] *Apology of the Augsburg Confession*, XIII, 3.

[28] Martin Luther, "The Holy and Blessed Sacrament of Baptism," in *Luther's Works*, vol. 35, *Word and Sacrament*, ed. E. Theodore Bachmann (Philadelphia: Muhlenberg Press, 1955), §2. In his sermon of 1540 at the baptism of Bernard von Anhalt, Luther says that baptism has three parts: natural water, God's word beside and with the water, and the institution or the Word that institutes and ordains baptism. See *Luther's Works*, vol. 51, *Sermons I* (Philadelphia: Muhlenberg Press, 1959), 320–21.

person, "born in grace," who "comes forth and rises." He cites Paul in Titus 3:5, who calls baptism a "washing of regeneration" since "in this washing a person is born again and made new." In this spiritual birth of baptism a person "is a child of grace and a justified person."[29]

In the essay "The Babylonian Captivity of the Church," Luther insists that the new creation, regeneration, and spiritual birth should not be understood only allegorically as the death of sin and the life of grace, but as actual death and resurrection, since baptism is not a false sign.[30] Luther considered washing to be too weak a concept to express what happens in baptism, which is more powerfully a symbol of death and resurrection: "The sinner does not so much need to be washed as he needs to die, in order to be wholly renewed and made another creature, and to be conformed to the death and resurrection of Christ, with whom he dies and rises again through baptism."[31] This same emphasis on innocence, regeneration, and the removal of "the inherited disease of our impure and condemned birth from Adam" also occurs in his 1540 sermon delivered at the baptism of Bernard von Anhalt.[32] In this essay Luther says that baptism makes a person holy in body and soul and altogether new.[33] Baptism is efficacious because in baptism we put on Christ, who sanctified and instituted baptism through his own baptism in the Jordan. This relationship in Christ is what renews and regenerates.

The relationship between baptism and justification is much more nuanced in "The Babylonian Captivity of the Church."[34] There Luther states that "it is not baptism that justifies or benefits anyone, but it is faith in that word of promise to which baptism is added. This faith justifies and fulfills that which baptism signifies."[35] This essay also qualifies the efficaciousness of baptism:

> It cannot be true, therefore, that there is contained in the sacraments a power efficacious for justification, or that they are "effective signs" of grace. All such things are said to the detriment of faith, and out

---

[29] "The Holy and Blessed Sacrament of Baptism," §3.

[30] "The Babylonian Captivity of the Church," 191.

[31] Ibid.

[32] "Sermon at the Baptism of Bernard von Anhalt" (1540), in *Luther's Works*, vol. 51, *Sermons I*, 323–24.

[33] Ibid., 324.

[34] The relationship between faith and justification will receive a more extended discussion in chap. 5.

[35] "The Babylonian Captivity of the Church," 188.

of ignorance of the divine promise. Unless you should call them "effective" in the sense that they certainly and effectively impart grace where faith is unmistakably present. But it is not in this sense that efficacy is now ascribed to them; as witness the fact that they are said to benefit all men, even the wicked and unbelieving, provided they do not set an obstacle in the way—as if such unbelief were not in itself the most obstinate and hostile of all obstacles to grace.[36]

In both instances Luther is arguing against an automatic or mechanical notion of sacramental efficacy that is divorced from faith. Baptism justifies when it is received in faith. Grace is only received in faith. Faith is, therefore, an integral part of baptism.

Luther's insistence on the efficacy of baptism is also related to his criticism of the sacrament of penance. He does not wish to support any theology of penance that may suggest that baptism has lost its efficacy: "We must therefore beware of those who have reduced the power of baptism to such small and slender dimensions that, while they say grace is indeed inpoured by it, they maintain that afterwards it is poured out again through sin, and that then one must reach heaven by another way, as if baptism had now become entirely useless."[37] To preserve the efficacy of baptism, Luther taught that once received, it is always present to be returned to in faith. When the promise of baptism is received again in faith, a person is continually baptized by faith, continually dies, and continually lives.[38]

Through the grace of this bath of rebirth and renewal in the Holy Spirit we are "righteous and heirs in hope of eternal life."[39] Baptism "signifies that the old creature in us with all sins and evil desires is to be drowned and die through daily contrition and repentance, and on the other hand that daily a new person is to come forth and rise up to live before God in righteousness and purity forever."[40] The scriptural basis for this theology is Romans 6:4, where Paul says: "We were buried with Christ through baptism into death, so that, just as Christ was raised from the dead through the glory of the Father, we, too, are to walk in a new life."

---

[36] Ibid., 189.
[37] Ibid., 192.
[38] Ibid.
[39] *The Small Catechism*, "The Sacrament of Holy Baptism," third article.
[40] Ibid., fourth article.

Eschatology as the Key to Understanding Luther's Theology of Baptism

At times Luther's theology of baptism appears to be in tension with the theme of *simul justus et peccator*, especially when he states that "therefore sins are drowned in baptism, and *in place of sin*, righteousness comes forth" (emphasis added).[41] Yet the very next section of the 1519 essay hastens to assert that "sin never ceases entirely while the body lives, which is so wholly conceived in sin that sin is its very nature."[42] This same tension is expressed in paragraph seven:

> . . . when someone comes forth out of baptism, he is truly pure, without sin, and wholly guiltless. Still there are many who do not properly understand this. They think that sin is no longer present . . . it should be properly understood and known that our flesh, so long as it lives here, is by nature wicked and sinful.

The eschatological explanation for this tension appears in paragraph eight:

> A baptized person is therefore sacramentally altogether pure and guiltless. This means nothing else than that he has the sign of God; that is to say, he has the baptism by which it is shown that his sins are all to be dead, and that he too is to die in grace and at the Last Day is to rise again to everlasting life, pure, sinless, and guiltless. With respect to the sacrament, then, it is true that he is without sin and guilt. Yet because all is not yet completed and he still lives in sinful flesh, he is not without sin. But although not pure in all things, he has begun to grow into purity and innocence.[43]

The source of this tension is to be found in the eschatological character of baptism in Luther's thought. For Luther, baptism is an event that has very real effects in the life of the recipient. The sacrament really causes what it signifies. However, this same significance and effect is not fulfilled completely in this life.[44] He distinguishes between sacramental baptism and spiritual baptism, a drowning of sin, which lasts throughout

---

[41] "The Holy and Blessed Sacrament of Baptism," §3, p. 30.

[42] Ibid., §4, p. 31.

[43] This same eschatological point is made in "The Babylonian Captivity of the Church, " p. 19, where he says: "Neither does sin completely die, nor grace completely rise, until the sinful body that we carry about in this life is destroyed, as the Apostle says in the same passage (Rom. 6:6-7)."

[44] Ibid.

life and is only completed in death. This seems to amount to a distinction between (1) sacramental sign: baptism in water; (2) sacramental reality: regeneration, innocence, new life, on the one hand, and spiritual baptism: the daily dying to sin; and (3) the spiritual reality that is only achieved fully at death. Thus "a baptized person is therefore *sacramentally* altogether pure and guiltless," which means that a person is pure by way of sign that is future-directed, but not in terms of historical, existential, daily reality. Thus baptism, for Luther, is not simply a past event accomplished once and for all, but is a continuing event in the life of the Christian. We are not completely born until we are born into eternal life. He explains: "The sacrament has taken place. But the work of the sacrament has not yet been fully done, which is to say that death and the resurrection at the Last Day are still before us." In other words, the sign of the sacrament has occurred and the promise directed to future fulfillment has been received, but the reality it signifies, namely, death to sin and resurrection in grace, is a reality worked out in the process of daily living and only completed in our personal death. The sacramental sign points to a historical reality, shows us the end result of that historical reality, and assures us with God's promise that that reality will be achieved because the sign of the sacrament is truly efficacious.

This is not how Catholics, who emphasize an ontological change effected by the sacrament, think about baptism. However, there are some similarities between this model and a Catholic understanding of the unity signified in the sacrament of the Eucharist. Although Luther rejected scholastic theories, categories, and language for thinking about sacramental realities, his thought here seems to exhibit remnants of the scholastic system. According to the scholastic analysis of the sacraments the sign of the sacrament is the *sacramentum tantum*, the reality of the sacrament is the *res et sacramentum*, and that which is signified by the sacrament is the *res tantum* or the *res sacramenti*. In the case of the Eucharist, the bread and wine are the *sacramentum tantum*, the sacramental real presence of Christ is the *res et sacramentum*, and the unity of the church is the *res tantum*. This unity, the ultimate purpose of the sacrament, is none other than the communion of saints in the mystical body of Christ.[45] Most importantly, this is a unity that is inaugurated in the sacrament, that exists in fullness under the sacramental sign, but that is completed in its existential fullness only eschatologically. We truly experience the fullness of unity sacramentally, but when we leave the Eucharist to return

[45] Ibid., 24.

to our daily lives we become painfully aware of unreconciled relationships, war, social disorder, and all manner of ways our lives still await unity. Likewise, even though we are sacramentally united with Christ, that union and our sanctification remain capable of growth and intensification. In the present we experience this unity in fullness under the sacramental sign, but at the end time there will be no more sacramental sign, but only reality. The grace of the *res tantum*, insofar as it characterizes Christian life, is always incomplete in the present time and oriented to future fullness. The parallel with Luther's thought, but not his expression, would seem to be that the sign of baptism is the water bath in the trinitarian name; the enduring reality of baptism is the word added to the element, that is, the promise of Christ, and the grace of the sacrament is regeneration and forgiveness of sin.

The eschatological meaning of the *res tantum* is reinforced by the parallelism between the scholastic sacramental schema *sacramentum tantum / res et sacramentum / res tantum* and the threefold meaning of Scripture interpreted through spiritual exegesis: the literal meaning / the allegorical meaning / the anagogical meaning. The literal meaning corresponds to the sacramental sign. The allegorical meaning, referring to the christological or ecclesial meaning of the text, corresponds to the *res et sacramentum*. The anagogical or eschatological meaning of the text corresponds to the *res tantum*.

Sacrament		Spiritual Exegesis	
sacramentum tantum (sign)	bread and wine	literal sense	exodus
res et sacramentum (reality)	real presence of Christ	allegorical sense	Christ's passion, death, resurrection
res tantum (spiritual effect achieved in fullness eschatologically)	unity of the church in Christ	anagogical sense	Christ in glory, united with the members of his body

Figure 2

Within this relationship the preceding term functions as the figure of the reality represented by the succeeding term. Only the last term is reality, but not figure. Thus the bread and wine are the figure of the real presence of Christ. But the sacramental presence of Christ is itself a figure of the church as the *totus Christus*. Similarly, in spiritual exegesis the Old Testament is a figure of the New Testament; the exodus is a figure of Christ's passion. Both Christ and the Eucharist are figures of the church viewed as the "whole Christ," the members of the church in union with their head, Christ.[46]

This seems to be the structure behind Luther's text. He is not speaking here of *simul justus et peccator* in the language of a forensic justification wherein my sin is no longer imputed to me because Christ's grace or justice stands in for me. The context here is rather the tension between sacramentally signified reality and eschatological realization. *Sacramentally* a person is sinless and therefore will be sinless eschatologically. Under sign or figure, which inherently contains the notion of promise, a person is sinless. At the end time there will be no more sign, but only the reality of sinlessness. In the meantime the Christian lives in sinful flesh and is not without sin. The present time is a time of inaugurated eschatology. Thus the person is both justified and sinner. In this schema eschatology, not forensic justification, is the controlling paradigm. This eschatological tension and paradigm therefore also differ from the usual discussion as to whether baptism effects an ontological change in the baptized or whether grace is imputed to the person without effecting a real interior change.

Baptism and the Christian Life

A final theme in the *Large Catechism* concerning baptism is its relationship to the Christian life. For Luther, baptism is not a past event, but a continuing presence that endures and remains until we enter into eternal glory. Access to baptism in faith gives a Christian "the grace, Spirit and strength to suppress the old creature." Repentance is "a return and approach to baptism, to resume and practice what has earlier been begun but abandoned."[47] This is a return to the promise that was abandoned in the sin of the Christian.[48] The promise cannot be changed by sins, but receives us back when we turn to it. This continuing efficacy of the promise of baptism is what constitutes this sacrament as the first and the foundation of all the others, without which none of the other sacraments

---

[46] See Susan K. Wood, *Spiritual Exegesis and the Church in the Theology of Henri de Lubac* (Grand Rapids: Eerdmans, 1998), chap. 3.

[47] *The Large Catechism*, IV: 79.

[48] "The Babylonian Captivity of the Church," 180–81.

can be received. Baptism takes away sin daily and daily strengthens the new person, when turned to in faith.

Comparison of Lutheran and Catholic Doctrines of Baptism

The following chart summarizes the points of agreement and difference between Lutherans and Catholics on the doctrine of baptism:

Lutherans	Catholics
Baptism brings about forgiveness of sins (*Small Catechism*, Sacrament of Holy Baptism, III, 5–6).	By baptism we receive full and complete remission of all sins (Council of Trent, Session XIV, Sacrament of Penance, chap. 2; *Catechism* 1263, 1279).
Baptism is a "bath of the new birth in the Holy Spirit" (*Small Catechism*, Sacrament of Holy Baptism, III, 9–10; *Large Catechism*, Washing of Regeneration, IV, 27).	By baptism we put on Christ and are made in him an entirely new creature (Council of Trent, Session XIV, Sacrament of Penance, chap. 2). Baptism makes the neophyte "a new creature" (*Catechism* 1265). The two principal effects are purification from sins and new birth in the Holy Spirit (*Catechism* 1262).
Baptism is necessary for salvation (*Large Catechism*, Concerning Baptism, 6, 24).	Baptism is necessary for salvation (Council of Trent, Session VII, Canons on Baptism, 5; *Catechism* 1257, 1277).
Infant baptism remains valid even if he or she did not have true faith (*Large Catechism*, 60; *Apology of the Augsburg Confession*, Article IX).	If anyone says that children, because they have not the act of believing, are not after having received baptism to be numbered among the faithful, and that for this reason are to be rebaptized when they have reached the years of discretion; or that it is better that the baptism of such be omitted than that, while not believing by their own act, they should be baptized in the faith of the Church alone, let him be anathema (Council of Trent, Session VII, Canons on Baptism, 13; *Catechism* 1282).
Baptism signifies the slaying of the old Adam and the resurrection of the new creature (*Large Catechism*, IV, 65).	The believer enters through baptism into communion with Christ's death, is buried with him, and rises with him (*Catechism* 1227).
Christian life is a daily baptism (*Large Catechism*, IV, 65).	By the sacraments of rebirth, Christians have become "children of God," "partakers of the divine nature." Coming to see in the faith their new dignity, Christians are called to lead henceforth a life "worthy of the gospel of Christ" (*Catechism* 1692).

Lutherans	Catholics
Where faith is present with its fruits, there baptism is no empty symbol, but the effect accompanies it; but where faith is lacking, it remains a mere unfruitful sign (*Large Catechism*, IV, 73).	The fruitful reception of the sacraments depends on the disposition of the recipient (Pius X, Decree *Sacra Tridentina* [1905] 1204/4; Leo X, Bull *Exsurge Domine* [1520]; Council of Trent, Session VII, Decree on the Sacraments, canon 6; Pius XII, *Mediator Dei* [1947]; Vatican II, *Sacrosanctum Concilium* [1963] 59).
Penance is really nothing else than baptism. If you live in repentance, you are walking in baptism. Repentance is nothing else than a return and approach to baptism (*Large Catechism*, IV, 74–75, 79).[49]	Christ instituted the sacrament of penance for all sinful members of his church: above all for those who, since baptism, have fallen into grave sin, and have thus lost their baptismal grace and wounded ecclesial communion. It is to them that the sacrament of penance offers a new possibility to convert and to recover the grace of justification. The fathers of the church present this sacrament as "the second plank [of salvation] after the shipwreck which is the loss of grace" (*Catechism* 1446).
The baptized are truly reborn; they now have *arbitrium liberatum* [a freed will or freed choice] (*Solid Declaration*, Article II, 67).	Entry into Christian life gives access to true freedom (*Catechism* 1282). If anyone says that, after the sin of Adam, human free will was lost and blotted out, or that its existence is purely nominal . . . let him be anathema (Council of Trent, Session VI, Canons Concerning Justification, 5).
Baptism is God's own act (*Large Catechism*, IV, 6, 10, 35).	They [sacraments] are actions of the Holy Spirit at work in his Body, the Church. They are "the masterworks of God" in the new and everlasting covenant (*Catechism* 1116).
The Word and the water must by no means be separated from each other (*Large Catechism*, IV, 22).	Word, faith, and sacrament are linked together (Paul VI, Apostolic Exhortation, *Evangelii Nuntiandi* [1975] 47). The preaching of the Word is required for the sacramental ministry itself, since the sacraments are sacraments of faith, drawing their origin and nourishment from the Word (Vatican II, *Presbyterorum Ordinis* 4).

[49] In the Kolb and Wengert edition of *The Book of Concord* (see n. 2 above), 465, the editors note that when Luther occasionally referred to penance as a sacrament he regarded it as part of baptism, emphasizing the declaration of forgiveness, or absolution, pronounced by the administrator.

Lutherans	Catholics
They are able to assent to and accept the Word, although in great weakness (*Solid Declaration*, Article II, 67).	Yet certain temporal consequences of sin remain in the baptized, such as suffering, illness, death, and such frailties inherent in life as weaknesses of character, and so on, as well as an inclination to sin that Tradition calls *concupiscence . . . (Catechism* 1264).
But those who are righteous have it as a gift, because after the washing [of baptism] they were justified (*Apology of the Augsburg Confession*, Article IV, 103).	The Most Holy Trinity gives the baptized sanctifying grace, the grace of justification, enabling them to believe in God, to hope in him, and to love him through the theological virtues; giving them the power to live and act under the prompting of the Holy Spirit through the gifts of the Holy Spirit; and allowing them to grow in goodness through the moral virtues (*Catechism* 1266; see also 1992).
It means that the old Adam in us should be drowned by daily sorrow and repentance, and die with all sins and evil lusts, and, in turn, a new person daily come forth and rise from death again. He will live forever before God in righteousness and purity (*Small Catechism*, IV).	For God hates nothing in the reborn, because there is no condemnation for those who are truly buried with Christ by baptism into death, who do not walk according to the flesh but, putting off the old person and putting on the new person created according to God, become innocent, stainless, pure, blameless and beloved children of God, heirs of God and fellow heirs with Christ, so that nothing at all impedes their entrance into heaven (Council of Trent, Session V, Decree on Original Sin, canon 5). Justification is a translation from that state in which man is born a child of the first Adam, to the state of grace and of the adoption of the sons of God through the second Adam, Jesus Christ (Council of Trent, Session VI, chap. 4).
Baptism removes original sin even if the "material element" of sin remains, namely, concupiscence (*Apology of the Augsburg Confession*, 35; Luther's marginal notes on Lombard's *Sentences* [1509/10], *Werke* 9:74–75).	In the baptized, concupiscence or a tendency to sin remains (Council of Trent, Session V, Decree on Original Sin, canon 5).

Figure 3

The Anabaptists

The Anabaptists were the radical arm of the Reformation, a movement that originated in Zürich, Switzerland in 1525 under the leadership of Conrad Grebel and Felix Manz. Even though they separated from

Zwingli, the Anabaptists can only be understood in terms of his theology since many of their members had been Zwingli's closest followers. They inherited major theological themes from him, such as discipleship as the formal principle of ethics, a theology of the local congregation where valid church action is located, and a rejection of infant baptism.[50] Since they rejected infant baptism, many of them chose to be baptized as believing adults. Thus their enemies called them ana-baptists, that is, "re-baptizers," although they themselves reject the name "Anabaptist," not considering this to be a rebaptism since they do not consider infant baptism to be a baptism at all. Descendants of the original Anabaptist movement include the Mennonites, the Amish, the Hutterites, and the Church of the Brethren.

The beliefs held by the Anabaptists include adherence to the Bible alone as the rule of life, the complete separation of church and state, baptism only upon confession of faith, nonresistance to violence, nonconformity to the world, an emphasis on individual conscience, and a commitment to a holy life. They oppose the baptismal teaching of both the Roman Catholics and the magisterial Reformers, including Luther, Zwingli, and Calvin. They also reject compromise with the state and military service, which put them in opposition to a state church and the political positions of Zwingli and Calvin. These positions led to their persecution by both Roman Catholics and the magisterial Reformers.

Anabaptist beliefs are stated in the *Schleitheim Confession* adopted by the Swiss Brethren Conference February 24, 1527. This is not a "confession of faith" in a dogmatic or normative sense, but an outline of the shape of the "obedient" church in relation to the problems of the time. Regarding the doctrine of baptism, the document states:

> Baptism shall be given to all those who have learned repentance and amendment of life, and who believe truly that their sins are taken away by Christ, and to all those who walk in the resurrection of Jesus Christ, and wish to be buried with Him in death, so that they may be resurrected with Him and to all those who with this significance request it (baptism) of us and demand it for themselves. This excludes all infant baptism, the highest and chief abomination of the Pope. In this you have the foundation and testimony of the apostles. Matt. 28, Mark 16, Acts 2, 8, 16, 19. This we wish to hold simply, yet firmly and with assurance.

[50] This is John Howard Yoder's assessment in *Anabaptism and Reformation in Switzerland: An Historical and Theological Analysis of the Dialogues Between Anabaptists and Reformers* (Kitchener, Ontario: Pandora Press, 2004), 121.

The Anabaptists confessed three kinds of baptism: "that of the Spirit given internally in faith; that of water given externally through the oral confession of faith before the church; and that of blood in martyrdom or on the deathbed."[51] The Anabaptist interpretation of the scriptural text "Go therefore and make disciples of all nations, baptizing them . . ." (Matt 28:19) was that teaching should precede rather than follow baptism. The slogan was "first faith and then baptism." Grebel taught that baptism does not save, increase faith, or give very great comfort. Nor is it a final refuge on the deathbed. His position was also that children are saved without faith.[52] According to the Anabaptist Balthasar Hubmaier, "outward baptism is nothing but an open witness of the inward commitment with which man publicly testifies before everyone that he is a sinner and that he regards himself as guilty."[53] Thus it is "an outward and public testimony to the inward baptism of the spirit."[54] Baptism is not "the true reality by which man is made righteous, but is only a sign, a covenant, a likeness, and a memorial of one's dedication, which [sign] reminds one daily to expect the true baptism, called by Christ 'the water of all tribulations.'"[55] The church administers the sign of baptism, but God gives the true baptism through the water of all tribulation and in the comfort of the Holy Spirit.[56]

Baptism is also enrollment in the fellowship of believers. Baptism had an important role in shaping the Anabaptist community by externally defining the boundaries of the community and in the confession of an obligation to holiness.[57] Grebel came to believe that holiness of life was only to be found in separation from nonbelievers. A believer's baptism demarcated the community marked by the rule of Christ from the wider society. Baptism indicated acceptance of the discipline of the community. The community's identity as a pure community separate from the world

[51] Balthasar Hubmaier, "A Short Justification" (1526), cited in Walter Klaassen, ed., *Anabaptism in Outline: Selected Primary Sources* (Scottsdale, PA: Herald Press, 1981), 166.

[52] Conrad Grebel, "Letter to Münster" (1524), cited in Klaassen, ed., *Anabaptism in Outline*, 164.

[53] Balthasar Hubmaier, "The Sum of a Christian Life" (1525), cited in Klaassen, ed., *Anabaptism in Outline*, 164.

[54] Balthasar Hubmaier, "A Christian Instruction" (1526–27), cited in Klaassen, ed., *Anabaptism in Outline*, 167.

[55] Hans Hut, "The Mystery of Baptism," cited in Klaassen, ed., *Anabaptism in Outline*, 170.

[56] Ibid.

[57] See John Howard Yoder, *Anabaptism and Reformation in Switzerland*, 72.

was reinforced by the practices of the ban and excommunication. According to the *Schleitheim Articles*, the ban and baptism were symbols of the true church.

The Reformed Tradition

The Reformed tradition has a varied theological heritage, with both the sacramental theology of John Calvin and that of Ulrich Zwingli being authentic Reformed options, not to mention the considerable development within the nineteenth and twentieth centuries. William B. Evans comments: "Few doubt that a Zwinglian conception of the sacraments has tended to predominate in American Reformed Christianity, especially since the nineteenth century, and that revivalist, low-church Presbyterianism has been more the rule than the exception among conservative Presbyterians."[58] Since Reformed sacramental theology will tend toward either a more Zwinglian or a more Calvinistic interpretation, it will be necessary to compare these two Reformed theologians before examining the confessional documents. The theology of the earlier Reformers is much more discursive than what is formalized in confessions and catechisms, so a detailed look at their theology will help flesh out the spirit and intent of the confessional statements.

Ulrich Zwingli

Ulrich Zwingli (1484–1531) parted ways with Luther's sacramental realism on the one hand, and engaged in a vigorous dispute with the Anabaptists on the other hand. Zwingli held a spiritual understanding of Christ's presence that reflected his understanding, in his sacramental theology, of the relationship between the sign and that which was signified. Zwingli situates his sacramental theology in opposition to the

---

[58] William B. Evans, "'Really Exhibited and Conferred . . . In his Appointed Time': Baptism and the New Reformed Sacramentalism," *Presbyterion* 31, no. 2 (2005): 72–88, at 73. For studies of baptism in these Reformed confessions and creeds see Geoffrey W. Bromiley, "Baptism in the Reformed Confessions and Catechisms," in *Baptism, the New Testament and the Church: Historical and Contemporary Studies in Honour of R.E.O. White*, ed. Stanley E. Porter and Anthony R. Cross, 402–18 (Sheffield: Sheffield University Press, 1999), and Cornelis P. Venema, "Sacraments and Baptism in the Reformed Confessions," *Mid-America Journal of Theology* 11 (2000): 21–86.

Catholics, Luther and his followers, and the Anabaptists. In response to both Catholics and Luther, Zwingli denies that sacraments are "signs of such a kind that, when they are applied to a man, the thing signified by the sacraments at once takes place within him," for this would violate the liberty of the Spirit.[59] In Zwingli's view the Creator and the Spirit are not bound by the material agency of the sacraments since the divine Spirit distributes itself to individuals as it will—to whom it will, when it will, where it will.[60] The separation between the external rite and the action of the Holy Spirit is evident in Zwingli's statement: "What men can give is only outward baptism, either by external teaching or pouring or dipping in water." Only God can give the baptism of the Spirit "and he himself chooses how and when and to whom that baptism will be administered."[61]

For Zwingli there is no salvation in external baptism, nor does it justify or wash away sin, and neither does it confirm faith.[62] Even if someone "had been deluged with the whole Jordan and a sacred formula been repeated a thousand times," this cannot assure a person of his sins being forgiven. For Zwingli, if signs "are the things which they signify they are no longer signs, for sign and thing signified cannot be the same thing."[63] It is simply a covenant sign, indicating that all who receive it are willing to amend their lives and to follow Christ.[64] As an initiatory sign he compares it to the cowl, the habit given to a monastic novice. He also sees no difference between Christ's baptism and John the Baptist's baptism, since both mark off those who pledge themselves to a life of repentance.[65]

Zwingli also opposes the Anabaptists, who teach "that the sacraments are signs which make a man sure of the thing that has been accomplished

[59] Ulrich Zwingli, *Commentary on True and False Religion* (March, 1525), ed. Samuel Macauley Jackson and Clarence Nevin Heller (repr. Durham: The Labyrinth Press, 1981 [copyright American Society of Church History, 1929]) §15, p.183. Translation of *De vera et falsa religione commentarius*, originally published in *The Latin Words and the Correspondence of Huldreich Zwingli*, vol. 3, reissued under the title: *The Latin Works of Huldreich Zwingli* (Philadelphia: Heidelberg Press, 1929).
[60] Ibid., 182.
[61] Ulrich Zwingli, "Of Baptism" (May 27, 1525), in *Zwingli and Bullinger*, vol. 24. Library of Christian Classics, Selected Translations with Introduction and notes by G. W. Bromiley (Philadelphia: Westminster Press, 1953), 133.
[62] Ibid., 138, 153.
[63] Ibid., 131.
[64] Ibid., 141; Zwingli, *Commentary on True and False Religion*, 185–86.
[65] "Of Baptism," 149, 164; *Commentary on True and False Religion*, 189–92.

within him" and "refuse baptism to all who have not previously so well learned and confessed the faith that they can respond to all its articles."[66] He also disagrees with those who insist that teaching precedes rather than follows baptism.[67] For Zwingli sacraments are not "signs given for the confirmation of an existing faith in that which we have already learned and to which we are pledged."[68] He advocated the baptism of children, holding that the children of Christians were God's own as the children of the Israelites were God's own. Therefore, just as the children of the Israelites were circumcised, so are the children of Christians eligible for baptism.[69] Both are children of the covenant.[70]

For Zwingli "a sacrament is nothing else than an initiatory ceremony or a pledging," so that "those who are initiated by sacraments bind and pledge themselves, and as it were, seal a contract not to draw back."[71] This draws the criticism of G. W. Bromiley, who thinks that Zwingli overemphasizes what we ought to do rather than what God has already done for us, noting that a covenant is two sided, involving a pledge from both parties.

For Zwingli sacraments also have a cognitive function: "These most friendly elements and signs, water and wine and bread, have been given to us in order that by the outward signs we may know the grace and loving-kindness of the New Testament, that we are no longer under the Law—the shedding of blood has therefore been abrogated by the blood of Christ—but under grace."[72] The sign of the sacrament is given not for the person who receives it, but for the benefit of other believers so that they will see that the baptized has bound himself to a new life and will confess Christ.[73] Baptism, for example, is simply "a mark or pledge by which those who receive it are dedicated to God,"[74] a mark or seal of an inclusion in the community of faith. The sign of baptism identifies the

[66] Ibid., 182.
[67] "Of Baptism," 146.
[68] Ibid., 138.
[69] *Commentary on True and False Religion*, 23–24.
[70] See Ulrich Zwingli, "Refutation of the Tricks of the Catabaptists" (1527), in *Ulrich Zwingli (1484–1531): Selected Works*, ed. Samuel Macauley Jackson (Philadelphia: University of Pennsylvania Press, 1901), esp. 219–47.
[71] *Commentary on True and False Religion*, 181.
[72] Ibid., 132.
[73] Ibid., 137, 197.
[74] Ibid., 146. James F. White comments that Zwingli may be the first to interpret baptism in this way. *The Sacraments in Protestant Practice and Faith* (Nashville: Abingdon Press, 1999), 37.

Christian community and builds it up much as circumcision identified the covenant community of the Old Testament. Baptism is a sign and seal of community, not an efficacious sign of grace or forgiveness of sin. Even though we are given knowledge of the grace of Christ through the sacramental sign, baptism and faith need not be concurrent.[75]

Zwingli draws the criticisms of Catholics for not having a theology of an efficacious sign, since he draws too much of a distinction between the sign and the thing signified. Calvin's theology faults Zwingli for not having enough connection between the external sacrament and the internal sacrament.

John Calvin

John Calvin (1509–64) defines a sacrament in the *Institutes of the Christian Religion* as "an outward sign by which the Lord seals on our consciences the promises of his good will toward us in order to sustain the weakness of our faith; and we in turn attest our piety toward him in the presence of the Lord and of his angels and before men."[76] The *Catechism of the Church of Geneva*, written by Calvin, defines it as "an outward attestation of the divine benevolence towards us, which, by a visible sign, figures spiritual grace, to seal the promises of God on our hearts, and thereby better confirm their truth to us."[77] Thus for Calvin sacraments are seals, involve both God's actions toward us and our response, and teach the truth of God's promises.

Calvin wanted to avoid subjectivizing the sacraments and to retain the objectivity of the promise, but he also did not want to detach the objective promise from its connection with faith. He wanted to maintain a middle course between the Papists, who in his view conflated the reality and the sign, and Zwingli who separated the sign from the reality it

[75] "Of Baptism," 136.

[76] John Calvin, *Institutes of the Christian Religion*. XXI, Library of Christian Classics, ed. John T. McNeill, trans. Ford Lewis Battles (Philadelphia: Westminster Press, 1960), chap. 4.1, p. 1277.

[77] John Calvin, *Catechism of the Church of Geneva*, in *Selected Works of John Calvin: Tracts and Letters*. vol. 2, *Tracts*, part 2, ed. Henry Beveridge and Jules Bonnet (Grand Rapids: Baker Book House; Edinburgh: Calvin Translation Society, 1846; repr. 1983), 83–84.

signified.[78] In his view sacraments were instituted to establish and increase faith.[79] They did this by setting God's promises before our eyes and by being a seal[80] and guarantee of these promises to us.[81] Faith does not reside in the sacrament, but rises up to God, the author of the sacraments. Because of our embodied human nature and our need for visual signs, sacraments represent the promises of God to us as if they were "painted in a picture from life."[82] The purpose of the sacraments is "to bring us to communion with Christ." They are "helps and means by which we are either engrafted into the body of Christ, or being engrafted, are drawn closer and closer, until he makes us altogether one with himself in the heavenly life."[83]

The theme of "covenant" figures strongly in Calvin's sacramental theology, as it did in Zwingli's, and he identifies sacraments as "tokens of the covenants," also identified with God's word of promise.[84] The two sacraments, baptism and the Lord's Supper, correspond to the two great covenantal signs of the Old Testament, circumcision and the Passover. Covenant, in Calvin's theology, also means election. He posits a double covenant: a general election given to Abraham and his descendants and a secret election to those counted among the elect according to God's predestination to salvation. The problem this poses to his baptismal theology is the uncertainty of ever knowing a baptism to be efficacious, since it is only truly efficacious for the elect, and these are unknown to all apart from God.[85]

Other Reformed theologians offer alternative explanations of covenant and election, with corresponding implications for their baptismal theology. For example, Heinrich Bullinger (1504–75), a contemporary of Calvin, posits only one covenant from Abraham through Christ. He stresses the continuity of the old and new covenants, the covenant sign changing from circumcision to baptism. Bullinger said that infants should

---

[78] See Ronald. S. Wallace, *Calvin's Doctrine of the Word and Sacrament* (London: Oliver and Boyd, 1953), 165.

[79] Calvin, *Institutes*, IV, xiv, 9.

[80] Ibid., 5.

[81] Ibid., 12.

[82] Ibid., 5–6.

[83] "Exposition of the Heads of Agreement," in *Tracts*, part 2 (see n. 77 above), 222–23.

[84] *Institutes*, IV, xiv, 6.

[85] John W. Riggs, *Baptism in the Reformed Tradition* (Louisville: Westminster John Knox, 2002), 103.

be baptized as a sign of their adoption into God's family, just as the "children of old" received circumcision to mark their membership "in the eternal covenant of God."[86] For a much later theologian, Karl Barth (1886–1968), predestination takes place in Jesus Christ alone. God's eternal choice was the incarnation of his Son in Jesus Christ and in him the "non-rejection of man."[87] Jesus Christ is both the electing God and the elected human being.[88] In response, the person of faith is called to discipleship and thanksgiving. Barth opposes the practice of infant baptism because an infant is incapable of discipleship. In his mature work he no longer considers baptism to be a sacrament, since Christ is the only sacrament. He considers baptism a human liturgical work in recognition of what God has done for us in Christ and in obedience to the commission given us to baptize.[89]

Baptism is not only a sign of the covenant, it is a seal of the promise of the covenant and its fulfillment in Jesus Christ.[90] As a seal, baptism is directed toward the object of faith, God's activity in us through Christ in the power of the Spirit, rather than being an act of personal faith and confession. We acknowledge this work in us when we confess our faith. Baptism is not a seal of personal faith, but a seal of God's promises to strengthen our faith.[91] The addition of "seal" to "sign" ensures that the sign is not a mere illustration, for it offers and conveys Christ to the

---

[86] Riggs, *Baptism in the Reformed Tradition*, 37, citing "De sancto baptismo," in *Catechesis*, 63-65b: "in aeterno dei foedere."

[87] See Karl Barth, *Church Dogmatics*, II.2, *The Doctrine of God*, trans. G. W. Bromiley, et al. (Edinburgh: T&T Clark, 1957), 117, 167.

[88] Ibid., 94–145.

[89] Barth's early work was *The Teaching of the Church Regarding Baptism*, trans. Ernest A. Payne (London: CSM Press, 1948). In his preface to his later treatment of the topic, *Church Dogmatics*, IV.4 (Edinburgh: T&T Clark, 1969), ix, he says that this earlier work is outdated since he has come to a different view of the matter. He does not want it to be quoted as his last word on the subject.

[90] Calvin, *Institutes*, IV, 14, 3 and 9.

[91] See Geoffrey W. Bromiley, "The Meaning and Scope of Baptism," in *Major Themes in the Reformed Tradition*, ed. Donald K. McKim, 234–38 (Grand Rapids: Eerdmans, 1992). See also G. C. Berkouwer, "The Sacraments as Sign and Seals," 217–33 in the same volume. Although it is beyond the scope of the present study, we can say the same for the sacrament of confirmation, which is all too often considered a personal ratification of faith by the adolescent whose baptism as an infant was not of his or her own choosing.

believer.[92] Properly speaking, the Spirit is the seal.[93] In conveying the covenant promise the seal conveys Christ, for Christ is the substance of the promise. Baptism is efficacious, since in baptism we truly encounter Christ and his benefits.

This effect, however, depends both on the faith with which it is received[94] and whether the person baptized is numbered among the elect. Calvin says: "For nothing ought to be expected from it [baptism] apart from the promise but the promise no less threatens wrath to unbelievers than offers grace to believers. Hence any man is deceived who thinks anything more is conferred upon him through the sacraments than what is offered by God's Word and received by him in true faith."[95] The efficacy consists in truly conveying the promise, that is, the Word, through the materiality of the sign. Sacraments do not bestow any grace of themselves, but the efficacy lies in God truly executing whatever he promises and represents in signs and in our receiving the promise—offered to us through the material instrumentality of a sacramental sign—with faith.[96] The cause of justification and the power of the Spirit are not enclosed within the elements of the sacrament, but the elements as sign and seal attest to the work of God as promised. That work is only perceived and received in faith. The gift of the sacrament is offered to all—so the sacraments always retain their efficacy—but not everyone is capable of receiving Christ and his gifts, which can only be received according to the measure of faith.[97] In his polemics against Rome, Calvin thought that Catholics believed the sacraments to have a magical power efficacious without faith.[98] The relationship between baptism and faith will be examined more closely in a later chapter.

How a sacrament is efficacious and the relationship between God's Word and the sacramental sign become clear with Calvin's own example

[92] Calvin, *Institutes*, IV, xiv, 14, 16 and IV, xiv, 7–13.

[93] "Heads of Agreement," in *Mutual Consent in Regard to the Sacraments; Between the Ministers of the Church of Zürich and John Calvin, Minister of the Church of Geneva,* in *Selected Works of John Calvin. Tracts and Letters*, vol. 2, *Tracts*, part 2, no. 15, p. 216.

[94] Calvin, *Institutes*, IV, xiv, 7.

[95] Ibid., 14.

[96] Ibid., 17.

[97] "Heads of Agreement," (see n. 93 above), no. 18, p. 217.

[98] "Canons and Decrees of the Council of Trent, with the Antidote, M.D.XLVII," in *Selected Works of John Calvin, Tracts and Letters*, vol. 3, 174. Volume 3 is a reproduction of *Tracts*, vol. 3, *Containing: Antidote to the Council of Trent . . .* (Edinburgh: Calvin Translation Society, 1851).

of the rainbow as a sign of the covenant with Noah: "God set the rainbow for Noah and his descendants, as a token that he would not destroy the earth with a flood [Gen]. Noah regarded this as a sacrament . . . the rainbow (which is but a reflection of the sun's rays upon the clouds opposite) could [not] be effective in holding back the waters; but because [it] had a mark engraved upon [it] as God's Words, so that [it was a] proof and seal of his covenants."[99] The rainbow began to be what it was not previously, namely, a witness of the covenant that the Lord made with Noah. We now read the promise of God in it, that the earth will never again be destroyed by a flood. The rainbow in itself does not cause anything to happen, but the rainbow as a sign of something other than itself brings to mind God's promise, and it is the promise that is efficacious.

However, Calvin taught that the grace of the sacrament is only received by the elect. Citing Augustine, he says: "In the elect alone the sacraments effect what they represent."[100] The sign of baptism and what is signified, that is, the promise embodied in Christ himself, are not so linked that they cannot be separated, since the grace of baptism is conditioned by God's sovereign decree of election.

Calvin's teaching about the efficacy of baptism is directed against the scholastic teaching that the sacraments confer grace *ex opere operato*, that is, "by the very fact of the action's being performed," by the valid administration of the sacrament unless an obstacle is placed in its way.[101] There are two issues here: first, a correct understanding of *ex opere operato*, and second, an accurate assessment of Roman Catholic teaching regarding the kind of obstacle that obstructs the efficacy of baptism.

The scholastic teaching of *ex opere operato* has its roots in Augustine and was developed in the twelfth and thirteenth centuries by Peter Lombard, Alexander of Hales, Thomas Aquinas, and others. Unfortunately, the Reformed interpretation of *ex opere operato* is often an idea of a magical or mechanistic functioning of baptism that takes place apart from faith.[102] Calvin insists that "the elements become sacraments only when the word

---

[99] Calvin, *Institutes*, IV, xiv, 18.

[100] Ibid., 15, citing Augustine, *John's Gospel* xxvi. 11, 12, 15 (MPL 35. 1611–1614; tr. NPNF VII. 171ff.); *De catechizandis rudibus* xxvi. 50 (MPL 40. 344; tr. ACW II. 82).

[101] Ibid., 26. For Roman Catholic teaching see the Council of Trent, Session VII, Canons on the Sacraments in General, canons 6, 8.

[102] "Canons and Decrees of the Council of Trent, with the Antidote, M.D.XLVII," in Calvin, *Selected Works*, vol. 3 (see n. 98 above), 174.

is added, not because it is pronounced, but because it is believed."[103] However, the Roman Catholic intention in the affirmation of sacramental efficacy *ex opere operato* is not to deny the necessity of faith, but to teach that "the sacrament is not wrought by the righteousness of either the celebrant or the recipient, but by the power of God."[104] When the sacrament is celebrated with the intention of the church, the power of Christ and his Spirit acts in and through it independently of the holiness of the minister. Calvin agrees that baptism is not affected by the worthiness or unworthiness of the minister. Nor do erroneous beliefs invalidate the sacrament. Thus he thought it unnecessary to rebaptize those who were baptized under the papacy.[105] However, although the Reformers interpreted the principle to mean that the sacrament operated independently of the objective activity of Christ and the subjective faith of the recipient, the actual intent of the principle was to stress that Christ and the Spirit are the principal actors (principal cause) in the sacrament through the agency of the sacrament (instrumental cause).

The principle of *ex opere operato* refers to the objective validity of the sacrament. Its correlative principle, *ex opere operantis*, that is, "by the work of the person working or receiving the sacrament," means that the fruitfulness of the sacraments, whether a person actually receives grace, depends on the disposition of the one who receives them. This disposition includes faith as well as charity. This correlation of the Roman Catholic principles of *ex opere operato* and *ex opere operantis* is really not very different from what William B. Evans identifies as the pattern of objective offer and subjective reception: the grace objectively offered in baptism must be subjectively received by faith.[106] Both are means of distinguishing sacramental validity from sacramental efficacy. G. W. Bromiley admits that *ex opere operato* "is not quite so mechanical as it sounds, or as it is sometimes represented in Protestant polemics" since some measure of repentance and faith are required before the sacrament can have its effect.[107] The exception would be the baptism of infants, for whom Bromiley sees the sacramental effect as something wholly automatic

[103] "Heads of Agreement" (see n. 93 above), 228.
[104] Aquinas, ST III, q. 68, a. 8, cited in *Catechism* (1994), 1128.
[105] Calvin, *Institutes*, IV, 15, 16.
[106] Evans, "Really Exhibited and Conferred," 78. Evans finds indications of this pattern in *Institutes* IV. 15. 15; IV. 14. 14, 16, 17; and IV. 15. 5, 15, 17.
[107] G. W. Bromiley, *Sacramental Teaching and Practice in the Reformation Churches* (Grand Rapids: Eerdmans, 1957), 45.

since infants are incapable of an obstacle such as insincerity.[108] Perhaps we can conclude that *ex opere operato* has been something of a red herring in ecumenical relations, not representing as significant a difference between traditions as has sometimes been thought. As a principle it was largely misunderstood because it was taken out of the context of its correlation with the principle of *ex opere operantis.*

Bromiley puts his finger on the real difference between Roman Catholic and Reformed doctrine, which is the theological anthropology of the baptismal effect reflecting the differing doctrines of justification. He interprets the medieval teaching on justification as inherently subjectivisitic as a work done in rather than for the individual, namely, regeneration, rebirth, interior renewal. Bromiley represents the Reformed positions this way:

> The true work of baptism is the work which is done for us, not in us. It is not we who literally die and rise again, but Jesus Christ, the One for the many, and we by faith in Him. It is not we who are righteous, but we are counted righteous in Jesus Christ, being righteous only because the life which we now live by the faith of Christ, and faith in Him is our reality before God and therefore in truth. Once this is grasped, then the whole emphasis on a subjective work is seen to be false, and the notion of a causal operation drops away of itself, being replaced by that of grace, and the word of grace, and the grateful response of penitence and faith . . . the real work of baptism is not a subjective work in us; it is the objective work accomplished in Christ for us.[109]

A central ecumenical problem regarding baptism is the doctrine of justification, which divides Catholics from Reformed perhaps more than any other doctrine. The centrality of the doctrine of justification is such that it has repercussions for other doctrines. Here it affects not the *fact* of sacramental efficacy, something Calvin was at pains to uphold in the face of adversaries such as Zwingli and the Anabaptists, but the *manner* in which baptism is efficacious. More will be said about justification in a later chapter.

The second misconception about Roman Catholic theology encountered among Reformed theologians concerns the obstacle impeding the reception of baptismal grace. The importance of a correct understanding

[108] Ibid., 45–46.
[109] Ibid., 46–47.

is underlined in Calvin's comment, "If we were agreed as to what constitutes a legitimate disposition, there would be no further disputes as to efficacy."[110] In his response to the Council of Trent, Calvin cites unbelief as the obstacle to baptismal efficacy.[111]

The baptism of infants poses certain difficulties for a baptismal theology. Calvin, like Luther and Zwingli, defended the practice of baptizing infants and engaged in vehement polemics against the Anabaptists with the argument that just as infants were not excluded from the covenant sign of circumcision, neither should they be excluded from baptism since they are already part of the covenant:

> . . . baptism is not administered to infants that they might become sons and heirs of God; but, because they *already are reckoned* by God to that place and rank, the grace of adoption is sealed in their flesh by baptism. Otherwise the Anabaptists would correctly exclude them from baptism. For unless the truth of the external sign can belong to them, it will be mere profaneness to call them to participation in the sign itself. Nevertheless, if anyone would deny them baptism, we have an instant reply: they are already in Christ's flock and God's family, since the covenant of salvation which God contracts with the faithful, is also common to their children. Just as the words say, "I will be your God, and the God of your seed."[112]

Calvin responds to the Anabaptist objection that confession of faith must precede baptism by saying that "it is not necessary that faith and repentance should always precede baptism, for they are only required of those whose age makes them capable of both. It will be sufficient, then, if, after infants have grown up, they exhibit the power of their baptism."[113] Infants are baptized into *future* repentance and faith, the

---

[110] "Canons and Decrees of the Council of Trent, with the Antidote, M.D.XLVII," Antidote to the Seventh Session, canon 7.

[111] Ibid., canon 6. However, as we have seen in the previous chapter, in the Exposition of the Heads of Agreement Calvin names mortal sin as an obstacle to the efficacy of the sacraments.

[112] Riggs, *Baptism in the Reformed Tradition*, 64, citing John Calvin to John Clauberger (June 24, 1556), in C. O. 16.203–07, especially 206 (no. 2484). Italics added by Riggs.

[113] *Catechism of the Church of Geneva* in *Selected Works of John Calvin*, vol. 2, *Tracts*, part 2 (see n. 77 above), 87–88. Volume 2 is a reproduction of *Tracts*, vol. 2, *Containing Treatises on the Sacraments . . .* (Edinburgh: Calvin Translation Society, 1849). Interestingly, Thomas Aquinas (ST III, q. 69, a. 6, reply) comments that "certain authors in the past maintained that grace and virtues are not given to children in baptism but the character of Christ is impressed upon them in virtue of which, when they come

seed of which lies concealed in them.[114] Thus efficacy of baptism is not tied to the actual moment when it is administered. Only later, when they are able, do infants appropriate the promise of God that baptism proclaims. Nevertheless, according to Calvin's doctrine of predestination not all those born into the covenant or who receive the visible sign of baptism necessarily receive the effect of the sacrament.

Reformed Confessions and Catechisms

Having neither a central teaching office as do Catholics nor an official document such as the *Book of Concord* of the Lutherans that articulates official doctrine, the Reformed tradition relies on a dynamic tradition of confessional statements adopted to articulate faith at very particular places and historical times. These statements represent a spectrum of Reformed theological positions, and their authoritative weight depends on the particular church receiving them as part of its tradition. This study refers to *The Book of Confessions*, part 1 of the *Constitution of the Presbyterian Church (U.S.A.)*.[115] Even though there are nuances and developments represented in the various confessions, for the purposes of identifying Reformed baptismal doctrine the approach here will be simply to identify the main elements of Reformed baptismal theology as articulated in these authoritative documents.

The *Heidelberg Catechism* (1563) defines sacraments as "visible, holy signs and seals instituted by God in order that by their use he may the

---

to maturity, they receive grace and virtues," citing Peter Lombard, IV *Sent.* 4, 7 and Peter of Poitiers (*Pictaviensis*), V *Sent.*, PL 211, 1232; *antique*, pre-thirteenth-century medievals.

[114] Calvin, *Institutes*, IV, 16, 20.

[115] *Book of Confessions*. Study Edition (Louisville: Geneva Press, 1996). The pertinent Confessions and Catechisms consulted include: the *Scots Confession*, the *Heidelberg Catechism*, the *Second Helvetic Confession*, the *Westminster Standards* including the *Westminster Confession of Faith*, the *Shorter Catechism*, and the *Larger Catechism*, and the *Confession* of 1967. Other confessions in the Reformed tradition not contained in the *Book of Confessions* of the Presbyterian Church (U.S.A.) include the *First Helvetic Confession* of 1536, the *French (Gallican) Confession* of 1559, the *Belgic Confession* of 1561, the Anglican *Thirty-Nine Articles* of 1571, the *Irish Articles* of 1615, the *Geneva Catechism* of 1615 (included here in the discussion of Calvin's theology), or the *Consensus Zigurinus* of 1549. These are available in Philip Schaff, *Bibliotheca symbolica ecclesiae universalis. The Creeds of Christendom, with a History and Critical Notes* (Grand Rapids: Baker Book House, 1966).

more fully disclose and seal to us the promise of the gospel, namely, that because of the one sacrifice of Christ accomplished on the cross he graciously grants us the forgiveness of sins and eternal life."[116] Created to mediate doctrinal disputes at the time, it almost completely avoids the issues of predestination and election that figure in much of Reformed baptismal theology. The *Westminster Confession of Faith* defines sacraments as "holy signs and seals of the covenant of grace, immediately instituted by God to represent Christ and his benefits, and to confirm our interest in him: as also to put a visible difference between those that belong unto the church, and the rest of the world; and solemnly to engage them to the service of God in Christ, according to his Word."[117] The *Larger Catechism* (1647), compiled to give preachers guidance in explaining the doctrines of the *Westminster Confession*, has this definition: "A sacrament is an holy ordinance instituted by Christ in his Church to signify, seal and exhibit unto those that are within the covenant of grace, the benefits of his mediation; to strengthen and increase their faith and all other graces; to oblige them to obedience; to testify and cherish their love and communion one with another, and to distinguish them from those that are without."[118] The catechism identifies two parts of a sacrament: "an outward and sensible sign used according to Christ's own appointment," and "an inward and spiritual grace thereby signified."[119] A comparison of the definition of the *Catechism* with both the Westminster Standards and the theology of John Calvin shows that sacraments really communicate what they symbolize.

These documents recognize baptism as a sacrament along with the Lord's Supper.[120] The church baptizes in obedience to Matthew 28:19.[121] The most comprehensive definition of baptism is given in the *Larger Catechism*:

---

[116] The *Heidelberg Catechism*, q. 66. Brought to Manhattan Island in 1609, the *Heidelberg Catechism* was the first Reformed confession in the North American colonies.

[117] The *Westminster Confession of Faith*, XXVII.1. The Westminster Standards developed in the context of the English Reformation.

[118] *Larger Catechism*, q. 162. The *Larger Catechism* states the policy of the church, while the *Shorter Catechism* functions as a statement of personal religion (*The Book of Confessions*, Study Edition, 167–68).

[119] *Larger Catechism*, q. 164.

[120] *Second Helvetic Confession*, XIX; *Scots Confession*, XXI; *Heidelberg Catechism*, q. 68; *Larger Catechism*, q. 164.

[121] *Second Helvetic Confession*, XX; *Heidelberg Catechism*, q. 71.

> Baptism is a sacrament of the New Testament, wherein Christ hath
> ordained the washing with water in the name of the Father, and of
> the Son, and of the Holy Ghost, to be a sign and seal of ingrafting
> into himself, of remission of sins by his blood, and regeneration by
> his Spirit; of adoption, and resurrection unto everlasting life; and
> whereby the parties baptized are solemnly admitted into the visible
> Church, and enter in an open and professed engagement to be
> wholly and only the Lord's.[122]

Baptism is a covenant sign corresponding to the event of the Passover
and the sign of circumcision.[123] The sacraments seal God's promises to
us by presenting them to our senses and by signifying God's word of
promise.[124] They are added to God's word as a confirmation of it.[125] Their
purpose is to confirm God's promise to us, to strengthen our faith, and
to distinguish "betwixt God's people and those that were without his
league."[126] In turn, those baptized obligate themselves to God "for obedience, mortification of the flesh, and newness of life."[127]

The signs are not bare signs. They effect what they signify, but they
do this through the activity of the Holy Spirit when they are received in
faith.[128] They graft us into Christ Jesus and make us partakers of his
righteousness by which our sins are remitted.[129] The forgiveness of sins
occurs through the action of Jesus Christ and the Spirit and not merely
through the outward washing with water.[130]

Infants are baptized because they are included in God's covenant.[131]
Baptism becomes efficacious when they become able to respond in faith.
Thus the efficacy of baptism is not tied to the moment of its administration even though the sacrament really offers, exhibits, and confers grace
by the Holy Spirit to be received later in repentance and faith. Those
who are not part of the covenant of promise through their parents must
wait for baptism until they can profess their faith in Christ and commit
to obedience to him.

---

[122] *Larger Catechism*, q. 165.
[123] *Heidelberg Catechism*, q. 74.
[124] *Second Helvetic Confession*, XIX; *Heidelberg Catechism*, q. 66.
[125] *Second Helvetic Confession*, XIX.
[126] *Scots Confession*, XXI. See also *Second Helvetic Confession*, XX.
[127] *Second Helvetic Confession*, XX.
[128] *Scots Confession*, XXI; *Heidelberg Catechism*, q. 72.
[129] *Scots Confession*, XXI; *Heidelberg Catechism*, qq. 69, 70, 71, 72, 73.
[130] *Heidelberg Catechism*, q. 72.
[131] *Second Helvetic Confession*, XX; *Heidelberg Catechism*, q. 74; *Larger Catechism*, q. 166.

The doctrines of the sovereignty of God and God's election govern the relationship between baptism and salvation. On the one hand, grace and salvation are not so inseparably connected to baptism that no person can be saved without baptism. On the other hand, not all the baptized are necessarily regenerated.[132]

Baptism must be administered by lawful ministers using the words of Matthew 28:19 and can be received only once.[133] Since Calvin opposed baptism by women, the confessions prohibit baptism by midwives in the belief that baptism is not necessary for salvation for one already within the covenant. Therefore baptism should await administration by an authorized minister.[134] The minister's faults cannot affect the validity of the sacraments.[135] Furthermore, additional rites used by the Roman Catholic Church, such as lights, oil, salt, and spittle, are prohibited.[136]

Importantly for ecumenism, G. W. Bromiley notes that erroneous beliefs about baptism are not grounds for rebaptism: "It is for this reason that in spite of the erroneous beliefs of Romanism, the baptism which it administers can be accepted as true baptism, and the retention of the sacrament regarded as a mark of the persistence of the true church through all the errors and superstitions."[137]

This understanding of baptism raises two questions for a Roman Catholic: What is the anthropology of baptismal regeneration, given the Reformed doctrine of imputed righteousness? What is the anthropology of being grafted into Christ? For example, the *Second Helvetic Confession* states: "inwardly we are regenerated, purified, and renewed by God through the Holy Spirit; and outwardly we receive the assurance of the greatest gifts in the water, by which also those great benefits are represented, and, as it were, set before our eyes to be beheld."[138] In Reformed theology the focus of attention is on the work done by Christ on behalf of the baptized rather than on the work done in the baptized. Also, the

---

[132] *Westminster Confession of Faith*, XXX.5.
[133] *Scots Confession*, XXII; *Second Helvetic Confession*, XIX; *Westminster Confession of Faith*, XXX.2, 7.
[134] *Second Helvetic Confession*, XX; *Scots Confession*, XII.
[135] *Second Helvetic Confession*, XIX.
[136] *Second Helvetic Confession*, XX; *Scots Confession*, XXII.
[137] Bromiley, *Sacramental Teaching*, 42.
[138] *Second Helvetic Confession*, XX. It is difficult to reconcile this reference to regeneration with the statement by Cornelis P. Venema that "the Reformed confessions do not teach baptismal regeneration" ("Sacraments and Baptism in the Reformed Confessions," 80).

imputation of righteousness is not associated with regeneration. Nevertheless, "regenerate" and "regeneration" are words associated with baptism in Reformed documents. Baptism not only pardons sin; it offers regeneration understood as newness of life.[139] Thus there seems to be a tension between a theology of baptismal regeneration and a forensic theology of justification in spite of Reformed insistence on the work of Christ for us rather than in us.

The Baptist Tradition

Baptists are historically divided into two groups. The "General" Baptists originated in England in 1611 and believed in the universal character of Christ's redemption. The "Particular" Baptists originated in Holland in 1638–41 and maintained that Christ's redemption was intended for the elect alone. The "General" Baptists were influenced by the Dutch theologian Jacob Arminius, while the "Particular" Baptists reflect the Calvinist theology of the *Westminster Confession*. Most Baptists in the United States today are Calvinist Baptists.[140] Baptists' relationship to the earlier Anabaptists remains a debated issue today.

The Baptist tradition is not "confessional" in the sense of giving regulative authority to written statements. Although there are Baptist confessions of faith that have been used to distinguish Baptist groups from one another and from other Protestants, to show kinship between Baptist groups and other groups, as instructional aids, as a means of refuting heresy, and as guides to the study of the Bible,[141] nevertheless a Baptist confession of faith does not have binding authority. Nor do these statements speak for all Baptists, since they represent a consensus of belief

[139] See *Catechisms of the Church of Geneva* (n. 77 above), 87.

[140] This, however, is not without its own history. An older Calvinism broke down in the 1800s with the "Manifest Destiny" movement. H. Leon McBeth (*The Baptist Heritage* [Nashville: Broadman Press, 1987], 699) reports a resurgence of Calvinistic theology among the Southern Baptists by the 1980s, seeking to stem what were perceived as Arminian tendencies in the Southern Baptist Convention. There has long been a tension between "invitation" evangelism and the Calvinist form of predestination.

[141] James E. Carter, "A Review of Confessions of Faith Adopted by Major Baptist Bodies in the United States," *Baptist History and Heritage* 12 (April 1977): 75–91, at 75, referring to William H. Lumpkin, *Baptist Confessions of Faith* (Philadelphia: Judson Press, 1959), 16–17.

only of those who issue the statement. Baptist confessional statements serve to express doctrinal consensus at particular times and to illustrate Baptist history.[142]

Mark Heim, however, comments that there is an implicit confessional basis for Baptists, since Baptists read Scripture through tradition, particularly the received tradition of the first four centuries.[143] He notes that Baptist confessions "inherited" the content of the Nicene Creed through the *Westminster Confession*. Thus Baptist confessions and church life assumed the basic propositions regarding the Trinity, human sin, and Christology, although they have tended to use them as practical criteria for judging and shaping experience rather than as propositions requiring intellectual assent in the manner of a creed.[144] Heim concludes that "a firm but inchoate 'confession' has undergirded Baptist life."[145] A lively conversation continues between Fundamentalist Baptists and Modernists as to whether Baptists should have explicit confessional statements.[146]

Scripture "interpreted by the Holy Spirit through the community of regenerated believers" is the confessional standard of Baptists.[147] Any other confessional statement is understood as an interpretation of Scripture. The confessional unity of Baptists, however, lies more in commonly recognized practices such as the specific acts of preparation for baptism, acceptance for baptism, admittance to church membership, selection for ordination, and participation in the Lord's Supper.[148] Thus, although there may be confessional statements that give some guidance, the most reliable sources for ascertaining what a Baptist believes about baptism are the texts of Scripture and Baptist practices.

James E. Carter identifies the confessions of faith important for Baptists in America as the *Philadelphia Confession of Faith* (1742), the *New Hampshire Declaration of Faith* (1833), and the *Southern Baptist Statement on Baptist Faith and Message* (1925, revised 1963 and 2000). The *Philadelphia Confession of Faith* identifies baptism as an ordinance of the New Testament, ordained by Jesus Christ, which is a sign to the baptized person of his

---

[142] Carter, "Review of Confessions of Faith," 75.

[143] S. Mark Heim, "Challenged to Confess: Can Baptists Cope with Ecumenical Progress? *American Baptist Quarterly* 4 (December 1985): 327–39, at 336.

[144] Ibid.

[145] Ibid.

[146] For examples see the bibliography listed in Steve Baker, "Baptist Confessions of Faith: A Bibliography," *Baptist History and Heritage* 27 (1992): 44–55.

[147] Heim, "Challenged to Confess," 333.

[148] Ibid., 337.

or her fellowship with Christ in His death and resurrection, of being engrafted into Him, of the remission of sins, and of his or her giving up unto God, through Jesus Christ, to live and walk in newness of life. Only those who actually profess repentance toward God and faith in and obedience to the Lord Jesus are the proper subjects of this ordinance. The outward element to be used in this ordinance is water, in which the party is to be baptized in the name of the Father, and of the Son, and of the Holy Spirit. Immersion, or dipping of the person in water, is necessary to the due administration of this ordinance.[149] The proper ministers of baptism are only those who are qualified and called by the commission of Christ.[150]

The *New Hampshire Declaration of Faith* states:

> Of Baptism and the Lord's Supper We believe that Christian Baptism is the immersion in water of a believer, into the name of the Father, and Son, and Holy Ghost; to show forth, in a solemn and beautiful emblem, our faith in the crucified, buried, and risen Saviour, with its effect in our death to sin and resurrection to a new life; that it is prerequisite to the privileges of a Church relation; and to the Lord's Supper, in which the members of the Church, by the sacred use of bread and wine, are to commemorate together the dying love of Christ; preceded always by solemn self-examination.[151]

The Southern Baptist document *Statement on Baptist Faith and Message* (2000) states: "Christian baptism is the immersion of a believer in water in the name of the Father, the Son, and the Holy Spirit. It is an act of obedience symbolizing the believer's faith in a crucified, buried, and risen Saviour, the believer's death to sin, the burial of the old life, and the resurrection to walk in newness of life in Christ Jesus. It is a testimony to his faith in the final resurrection of the dead. Being a church ordinance, it is prerequisite to the privileges of church membership and to the Lord's Supper."[152] This statement on baptism is exactly as it appears in the 1963 version of the *Statement on Baptist Faith and Message* and is only a slight expansion of the 1925 statement, which merely says that baptism is an immersion of a believer in the name of the Father, Son, and Spirit, that

---

[149] *Philadelphia Confession of Faith* (1742), chap. 30.
[150] Ibid., chap. 29.
[151] *New Hampshire Declaration of Faith* (ca. 1833), no. 14.
[152] *Statement on Baptist Faith and Message* (2000), VII.

this act is a symbol of our faith, and that it is prerequisite to the privileges of a church relation and the Lord's Supper.

The common elements in the doctrine and practice of baptism according to these statements are: (1) Baptism is done in obedience to Christ's imperative in Matthew 28:19 and is administered using the biblical formula of the trinitarian name; (2) Baptism is administered only to believers and is a symbol of an act of faith that has already been made; (3) Baptism is a church ordinance requisite for the privileges of church membership and admission to the Lord's Supper; (4) Baptism is a sign of a Christian's fellowship with Christ in his death and resurrection; (5) The form of baptism is immersion; (6) The proper minister of baptism is an authorized minister of the church. Baptism by immersion was seen as required by the New Testament and the Baptist theology of baptism. Particular Baptists restored the practice of immersion in 1640–41. Immersion did not become customary among General Baptists until a generation after John Smyth, with no proof of immersion before 1660, even though it was probably practiced in mid-century.[153]

Thorwald Lorenzen offers this summary of the generally accepted Baptist practice of baptism:

> When a person in the context of the Christian community "hears" the story of Jesus as the story of God's love and "responds" to it, we may speak of a faith-event. The believer experiences the forgiveness of sins, divine acceptance and conversion. Faith, however, always seeks public confession in word and deed. This act of public confession includes the public celebration of baptism, whereby the believer by immersion is baptized in the name of the Father, and the Son and the Holy Spirit (or in the name of Jesus). This is often connected with the first participation in the Lord's Supper. And as such the whole service concretely expresses commitment to Christian discipleship and entry into full communicant membership of the local Baptist church.[154]

Southern Baptists have had problems with what they call "alien baptism," that is, baptisms they do not consider as valid because not coming from a true church. Some Southern Baptist churches insist on Baptist baptism alone, considering all others as alien. Others accept the immersion

[153] McBeth, *The Baptist Heritage*, 37, 44.
[154] Thorwald Lorenzen, "Baptists and Ecumenicity with Special Reference to Baptism," *Review and Expositor* 77 (2004): 21–46, at 22.

of believers upon a profession of faith, whether or not these baptisms were performed by Baptists. Some consider non-Baptist immersion irregular but not invalid.[155] The origins of this controversy regarding "alien baptism" lie in the Landmark movement in the nineteenth century, which considered Baptists to be the only true church. Since Baptists consider baptism, the Lord's Supper, and preaching as churchly acts committed by Christ to his church, only Baptist churches can validly perform them.[156] The Southern Baptist Convention remains divided on the issue.

Baptists have engaged a number of different traditions in dialogue on the subject of baptism.[157] These ecumenical agreements affirm that baptism imparts what it promises: "the forgiveness of sins, union with Christ in his death and resurrection, regeneration, elevation to the status of sonship, membership in the church, the body of Christ, new life in the Spirit, the earnest of the resurrection of the body."[158] Here, though, Baptists are divided among themselves, some holding that baptism is a sign of what has previously been accomplished in a profession of faith and the reception of the Holy Spirit and other Baptists professing a more sacramental view.[159] The controverted topics in these discussions are: the baptism of infants; the necessity of professed faith by the person being baptized; whether baptism is best described as a sacrament, sign, symbol,

---

[155] McBeth, *The Baptist Heritage*, 697.

[156] Ibid., 452.

[157] See Lorenzen, "Baptists and Ecumenicity," 21–46; Baptist-Lutheran Dialogue, "A Message to our Churches," in *Growth in Agreement II: Reports and Agreed Statements of Ecumenical Conversations on a World Level, 1982–1998*, ed. Jeffrey Gros, Harding Meyer, and William G. Rusch, 155–75 (Grand Rapids: Eerdmans, 2000); Baptist-Reformed Dialogue, "Report of Theological Conversations Sponsored by the World Alliance of Reformed Churches and the Baptist World Alliance, 1977," in *Growth in Agreement I: Reports and Agreed Statements of Ecumenical Conversations on a World Level*, ed. Harding Meyer and Lukas Vischer, 132–51 (New York: Paulist Press; Geneva: World Council of Churches, 1984); and Baptist-Roman Catholic Dialogue, "Growth in Understanding: A Progress Report on American Baptist-Roman Catholic Dialogue," in *Building Unity: Ecumenical Dialogues with Roman Catholic Participation in the United States*, ed. Joseph A. Burgess and Jeffrey Gros, 39–51 (New York: Paulist Press, 1989).

[158] "Report of Theological Conversations Sponsored by the World Alliance of Reformed Churches and the Baptist World Alliance, 1977," §21. Although this is an agreed statement of the Reformed-Baptist conversation, these effects of baptism are also accepted by Lutherans and Catholics.

[159] See Stanley K. Fowler, *More Than a Symbol: The British Baptist Recovery of Baptismal Sacramentalism*. Studies in Baptist History and Thought, vol. 2 (Carlisle, Cumbria; Waynesboro, GA: Paternoster Press, 2002).

or an ordinance; and whether baptism is necessary for church member-ship or even for being a Christian.[160]

Generally these conversations agree on the intimate relationship be-tween faith, baptism, and discipleship, on God's initiative in offering grace, and on the role of the Holy Spirit in enabling a human response to that offer. The difficulty arises in agreeing on how faith relates to baptism. For Baptists this must be a personal, conscious faith prior to baptism. For the Reformed, faith must also be personal and conscious, but may come after baptism provided the person is surrounded and upheld by the faith of the church and the family. Lutherans and the Reformed emphasize that baptism confers and manifests prevenient grace. Baptists see prevenient grace manifested in the cross and resur-rection and appropriated through faith by baptism. The Baptists in their dialogue with the Reformed acknowledge baptism as "a powerful sign and an effective means of grace" and affirm "the unity of the rite and the spiritual reality which it signifies."[161] This formulation sounds very Catholic, but the dialogue emphasized that this statement must be read in light of the next paragraph in the document. The Baptist view is that baptism is an effective sign only through personal response.[162] However, the Baptist inability to acknowledge the baptism of infants as Christian baptism causes Lutherans in their dialogue to question whether Baptists really do understand baptism as a means of grace.[163] A final area of dis-agreement is whether the complex of elements comprised of profession of faith, water baptism, and communion occur contemporaneously with the act of believer's baptism, or whether they can occur over a period of time.

Baptismal doctrine is closely aligned with the views of the church. For example, John Smyth (ca. 1570–1612), an early leader of the General Baptists who founded the first identifiable Baptist church of modern times in Holland about 1609, decided that baptism should be adminis-tered only to believers and that this voluntary confession/baptism should

---

[160] An excellent survey of the state of these questions in Britain is Anthony R. Cross, *Baptism and the Baptists* (Carlisle, Cumbria; Waynesboro, GA: Paternoster Press, 2000); see also *Baptist Sacramentalism*, eds. Anthony R. Cross and Philip E. Thompson. Studies in Baptist History and Thought, vol. 5 (Carlisle, Cumbria; Waynesboro, GA: Pater-noster Press, 2003).

[161] "Report of Theological Conversations Sponsored by the World Alliance of Re-formed Churches and the Baptist World Alliance, 1977," §§14, 21.

[162] Ibid., §22.

[163] Lorenzen, "A Message to our Churches," §34.

form the basis of the church. H. Leon McBeth suggests that Smyth's most basic concern may not have been for baptism but for a pure church. Since such a church must be comprised only of true Christians, baptism must be given only to professed believers.[164] For Baptists the decisive issue is not baptism as such, but "the living Church of confessing Christians."[165]

Since this would also be true of the Mennonites, it can certainly be asked whether sacramental practices in general arise from ecclesiology. Often this ecclesiology is shaped by a group's self-definition with respect to the dominant culture. The more sectarian the group, the more stringent are the requirements for baptism, which delineates the boundaries of the church. For example, Augustine, who had a universal view of the church as a hospital for sinners, had the most open theology of baptism regarding who could administer it (anyone in case of emergency) and the age at which it is conferred (infants). The English Separatists, who wanted to take the Bible seriously and order their lives by its teachings, also wanted a church made up of the "redeemed." Although early Separatists did not practice believer's baptism, some of the views of the Separatists were adopted by later groups who took the Separatists' ecclesiology to its logical conclusion by adopting the practice of believer's baptism, thereby earning the name "Baptist." These groups also espoused religious liberty and the separation of church and state.

The Roman Catholic Response to the Reformers in the Council of Trent

The Roman Catholic Church responded to the baptismal theology of the Reformers in its canons on baptism from the Council of Trent.[166] In response to the Reformers limiting sacraments to two, baptism and the Lord's Supper, the council defined the seven sacraments (c. 1), although it acknowledged that some sacraments are more excellent than others (c. 3). It also affirmed a difference between the sacraments of the Old Law and those of the New Law. It denied that sacraments are instituted for the nourishment of faith alone (c. 5) in order to affirm that they are also instituted to confer grace (c. 7) on all those who place no obstacles

---

[164] McBeth, *The Baptist Heritage*, 35.

[165] Lorenzen, "Baptists and Ecumenicity," 22.

[166] Council of Trent, Session VII (3 March 1547). The canons cited in this paragraph are the canons on the sacraments in general.

in their way (c. 6). Here the council is refuting the position that sacraments are only outward signs of grace or justice received through faith. Trent taught that the sacraments of baptism, confirmation, and orders imprint a character on the soul and therefore cannot be repeated. The moral character of a minister does not obstruct the efficaciousness of a sacrament (c. 12), but the minister must have the intention of doing what the church does (c. 11). The Reformers had criticized the Roman church for introducing elements such as salt and oil with accompanying rituals to the baptismal rite in addition to the use of water. Trent decreed that these could not be despised or omitted by pastors (c. 13).

Trent denied that faith in the divine promise alone is sufficient to obtain grace, but affirmed that the sacraments confer grace *ex opere operato* (c. 8). Here it seems to be denying a subjective basis of grace in the person believing in order to affirm the objective nature of grace as a work of Christ. This raises the question whether the Reformers and Trent were interpreting the relationship between faith and sacramental efficacy in the same way. For the Reformers the stress was on the divine promise, which was perceived to be objective. This promise could only be received by faith. Trent was concerned to maintain the independence of the sacrament in such a way that its validity depended neither on the qualities of the minister (c. 12) nor on the subjective disposition of the recipient. However, faith was required for the fruitfulness of the sacrament, this being supplied by the faith of the church in the case of infants.

Canon 1, which was "warmly discussed" by the council fathers, teaches that the baptism of John did not have the same effect as the baptism of Christ, as Calvin taught. Canon 3 simply affirms that the Roman Catholic Church has the true doctrine concerning the sacrament of baptism. Canons 2, 4, and 5 restate traditional baptismal doctrine by mandating the use of "natural" water, affirming the validity of baptisms performed by heretics when given in the name of the Trinity with the intention of doing what the church does, and stating the necessity of baptism for salvation. Canons 6–10 are directed against the Lutheran teaching on baptism as a perpetual sacrament, meaning that baptismal grace cannot be lost and that sins committed after baptism are remitted by the renewal of the faith of one's baptism.[167] These canons teach that with baptism we undertake the obligation not only to believe, but to keep God's commandments and to fulfill the whole law of Christ. Canons 11–13 are

---

[167] See also the Decree on Justification, Session VI (13 January 1547), canon 29.

directed against Anabaptist teaching about the necessity of rebaptism after apostasy, the age of baptism, and the rebaptism of those baptized in infancy. Canon 14 counters the teaching of Erasmus that those baptized as children should be asked to ratify what their sponsors promised in their name.[168]

A more positive teaching on baptism occurs within a discussion of the differences between the sacrament of penance and that of baptism.[169] The council identifies the fruits of baptism as putting on Christ, being made an entirely new creature in Christ, and the full and complete remission of all sins. It calls penance "a laborious kind of baptism," comparing the necessity of penance for those who have fallen after baptism to the necessity of baptism for those who have not yet been regenerated.

Clearly, the Council of Trent did not develop a comprehensive theology of baptism. Its goal was not to explain in detail each particular doctrine, but to indicate the boundaries of the doctrine. Jedin comments: "The canons rested on the theological foundations laid by scholasticism, but in themselves they were not scholasticism but definitions of things that must be believed; and this is what they were meant to be."[170] Perhaps importantly for ecumenical theology, Trent refused to decide on the question of sacramental causality.

Clarifications

It would be incorrect to say that in Roman Catholic baptismal theology the power of baptism resides "in" the water, or that the rite confers baptism "magically" or "mechanically" by the mere fact of being performed. Nor can we say that sacraments contain grace as a bottle contains medicine.[171] However, church teaching says that sacraments contain

---

[168] Hubert Jedin, *A History of the Council of Trent*, trans. Dom Ernest Graf, vol. 2 (New York: Thomas Nelson, 1961), 390. For the origins of the canons on the sacraments see Ferdinand Cavellera, "Le décret du Concile de Trente sur les sacrements en général," *Bulletin de Littérature ecclésiastique* 6 (1914): 361–77, 401–25; 7 (1915): 17–33, 66–88; 9 (1918): 161–81. See Albert Michel, *Les décrets du Concile de Trente* (Paris: Letouzey, 1938), 166–236, and the article "Sacrements" in *Dictionnaire de Théologie Catholique* 14, part 1 (1939), 485–644, especially 596ff.

[169] Council of Trent, Session XIV (25 November 1551), chap. 2.

[170] Jedin, *History of the Council of Trent*, 391.

[171] Hugh of St. Victor (end of 11th century–1141) developed an analogy wherein God was the physician, the human the sick person, the priest the minister or messenger,

grace. For example, the *Decree for the Armenians* as well as the Council of Trent state that sacraments truly contain grace and confer it "on those who worthily receive it."[172] The Reformers were quite critical of this, for it seemed to separate the causality of the sacraments from the promise of Christ. The expression also unfortunately contributes to a reified notion of grace as a "thing" that can actually exist in a container and is quantifiable rather than being God's very self dwelling in us (uncreated grace) or the effects on our human nature of our participation in the life of God. Grace is not a supernatural substance.

Hence it is very important, first of all, to understand what is meant by "sacraments contain grace." There are actually two problems here: an understanding of sacraments as containers and an understanding of grace as a substance that can be contained. To accurately interpret the notion of sacraments "containing" grace we must interpret the phrase within the original polemic in which this concept developed. The purpose of saying that the sacraments of the New Law contain and confer grace was to contrast them with the sacraments of the Old Law, which prefigured and prepared for the sacraments of the New Law but did not bestow grace.[173] The notion of "containing" differentiated the sacraments of the New Law from those of the Old Law as to their efficacy, but was never an explanation for how that efficacy occurred. To the extent that the Reformers were reacting against a mechanical notion of "containing," their response is understandable. However, there were also differing interpretations between Roman Catholics and some Reformers on the difference between the sacraments of the Old Law and those of the New Law. For example, Calvin thought that circumcision accomplished the same things as baptism.

Second, the grace of the sacraments does not exist apart from the word. The relationship between word and sacrament has received a different emphasis and interpretation in Roman Catholic sacramental theology, although sacramental symbolic action has always been accompanied by words. Within a scholastic interpretation the formula or words of the

---

grace the antidote, and the sacrament the vessel. He also speaks of the sacraments "containing" grace. *On the Sacraments of the Christian Faith (De Sacramentis)*, trans. Roy J. Deferrari (Cambridge, MA: Mediaeval Academy of America, 1951), book 1, part 9, III; see esp. 157. See also Peter Lombard, IV *Sent.* dist. I, n. 2.

[172] Council of Trent, Session VII (3 March 1547), Canons on the Sacraments in General, canon 6. Hugh of St. Victor speaks of sacraments "containing" grace in *On the Sacraments of the Christian Faith*, book 1, part 9, III, 157.

[173] ST III, q. 61, a. 4; III, q. 70, a. 1.

sacrament constitute the "form" of the sacrament, while the material elements or sign of the sacrament constitute the "matter" of the sacrament. The Council of Trent did not address the role of the word in the sacraments. The Second Vatican Council urged that the administration of every sacrament include Scripture readings and a word of explanation with pastoral application, in effect a short homily by the sacramental minister.[174] This Liturgy of the Word, precisely as liturgy, forms part of the ritual action of the sacrament. Neither of these treatments of "word" explicitly connects either to the word of institution nor to the Word, Jesus Christ, although post–Vatican II sacramental theology does so.[175]

The role of word *within* a sacrament (and not merely word *and* sacrament) has been enhanced in contemporary theology through reflection on the entirety of the sacramental economy of salvation[176] and the identification of the church's mission as proclamation of the word. Within this enriched understanding of both the sacramentality of the word and the word within a sacramental economy of salvation, the word event within the sacrament cannot be restricted to the sacramental formula or even to a Scripture reading within the sacramental ritual.[177] A sacrament itself becomes "the highest and most compressed form of the Church's word of proclamation."[178]

Significantly, the Catholic understanding of grace and justification by faith and through grace in the *Joint Declaration on the Doctrine of Justification* incorporates a theology of the word: "Persons are justified through baptism as hearers of the word and believers in it."[179] Such a statement distances justification through baptism from any possibility of a mechanistic understanding of sacramentality. It evokes the relationship between proclamation of the word and reception of the word in faith, which can only occur as a personal encounter with Christ. Most importantly, it seamlessly joins a theology of justification through baptism and justification by faith.

Third, Thomas Aquinas in his commentary on Matthew explicitly states that the sacrament of baptism does not consist in the blessing of the water, but in its infusion. We only receive grace by receiving the sacra-

---

[174] Vatican II, SC, 35.

[175] Karl Rahner, "What Is a Sacrament?" *Theological Investigations*, vol. 14, trans. David Bourke (London: Darton, Longman & Todd, 1976), 135–60.

[176] Herbert Vorgrimler, *Sacramental Theology* (Collegeville, MN: Liturgical Press, 1992), 77.

[177] Vatican II, *Ad Gentes*, 1.

[178] Vorgrimler, *Sacramental Theology*, 77.

[179] *JDDJ*, 27.

ment. "Oil and water, because they are inanimate objects, do not contain grace. Sacraments only contain grace because they contain that one who is the fullness of grace."[180] Peter Lombard distinguishes, with regard to the Eucharist, between what is contained and signified and what is signified and not contained. The first is what scholastics would call the *res et sacramentum*, the second the *res*: "The thing contained and signified is the flesh of Christ which he received from the Virgin and the blood which he shed for us. The thing signified and not contained is the unity of the Church in those who are predestined, called, justified, and glorified."[181] Now, if baptism and the Eucharist are two different modalities of the same mystery, that is to say, the death and resurrection of Jesus Christ, we may ask: what is contained and signified (the *res et sacramentum*) in baptism? Paul gives us the answer: the death and resurrection of Christ. The scholastic response was to say that the *res et sacramentum* is the sacramental character, which is participation in the priesthood of Christ. But this priesthood is none other than the death of Christ in his self-offering to his Father. Thus what is present in the sacrament of baptism is the death and resurrection of Christ. Luther saw this in his sacramental realism, although he did not use the sacramental categories of the scholastics. What is present is not just the promise of forgiveness of sin, but the very christological event itself offered for the forgiveness of sin. When we receive the sacrament of baptism we participate in that event and thus die and rise with Christ to new life in grace. This participation is not possible unless the event of Christ's dying and rising is also present in the sacrament.

What flows from this participation is that which is contained, but not signified. As with the Eucharist, the first effect is the unity of the church as the ecclesial body of Christ. This is what we really mean when we say that we become members of the church through baptism. We are not members of the church as we are members of organizations or clubs; we are members of the church as members of the body of Christ, the body dead and risen, both signified and contained in the sacrament. Second, as members of this body we receive the sanctifying grace that is the life of this body; the Holy Spirit, who is the bond of unity of the body; and

[180] Thomas Aquinas, *Super. Mt.*, chap. 26, 1.3: *In aliis etiam sacramentis non percipitur sacramentum in benedictione, sed in infusione; quia olem et aqua, cum sint inanimate, non continent gratiam: unde cum gratia sit finis sacramenti, non potest inferri nisi per susceptionem sacramenti. Set in isto sacramento continetur ille qui est plenitude gratiae.*

[181] Peter Lombard, *The Four Books of Sentences*, IV (ca. 1152), Distinction VIII, 7. Translation in James White, *Documents of Christian Worship: Descriptive and Interpretive Sources* (Louisville: Westminster John Knox, 1992), 124.

forgiveness of sin, the consequence of union with the sinless one. Ultimately, the grace "contained" in the sacrament is none other than Christ himself.

The Reformers were correct when they said that Christ is our justification and our righteousness. From a Roman Catholic point of view, however, they were incorrect in separating too radically our condition and Christ's righteousness. Christ does not merely substitute his righteousness for our lack of righteousness and sinfulness. By being grafted into Christ in baptism through participation in his body dead and risen, we ourselves are renewed through this incorporation into Christ.

Sacraments are not things any more than grace is a substance. If anything, sacraments are encounters with Christ, an offering and a receiving, which is to say that they are actions involving Christ, as one who gives himself in the encounter, and us, who receive him in faith.[182] Sacraments create a dynamic relationship; they are not static holy things. Unfortunately, language such as "contain" and even "receive" is less than adequate in communicating what happens in sacraments. "Signify," the verb, is actually much better than "sign," the noun. "Confer grace" is better than "contain grace," although the expression still limps since it makes grace into an object. Grace is either a modification of human nature empowering us for acts of faith, hope, and charity that are beyond the powers of human nature without this help, or God's presence with us in our very being.

Major Convergences and Differences in Baptismal Doctrine

Catholics profit greatly from conversations with their ecumenical partners. As has already been mentioned, contemporary Roman Catholic theology has retrieved a more substantial theology of the word. A robust theology sees sacraments as visible words and the word of God as sacramental. Luther's theology of the word and his theology of baptism as embodying God's promise are certainly compatible with Catholic theology. Likewise, Calvin's emphasis on baptism as a covenant reminds Catholics of the connection between baptism and Eucharist, the sacrament most often associated with the New Covenant. However, both

---

[182] This is the thesis of Edward Schillebeeckx, *Christ the Sacrament of the Encounter with God* (Kansas City: Sheed and Ward, 1963).

baptism and Eucharist are sacraments of the death and resurrection of Jesus Christ, whose Passover establishes the New Covenant. Baptist practice underscores the need for conversion in a baptismal life, an emphasis given more attention in the Catholic Rite of Christian Initiation of Adults implemented after Vatican II.

Significant similarities exist among the faith traditions examined in this chapter. All of them baptize in obedience to Christ's command in Matthew 28:19-20. All baptize in the triune name of Father, Son, and Spirit. All baptize with water. Most importantly, all the traditions examined here share an implicit or explicit Christology as articulated in the early ecumenical creeds. They believe Jesus Christ to be truly human and truly divine, the son of God, and the second person of the Trinity. The doxological confession contained in the act of baptism proclaims and acclaims a trinitarian pattern of Christian life and worship centered in the revelation of Jesus Christ. This belief constitutes the basis of Christian unity. Baptism is both a sign of faith and a profession of faith in this triune God.

Baptism is also an acceptance of the obligations of Christian discipleship. In the pattern of Christian living expressed by Paul in Romans 6, death and resurrection not only point to an eschatological expectation of the resurrection of the dead and eternal life; they define the character of Christian life, which is a dying to sin and a rising to life in Christ. In baptism the Christian is no longer a slave to sin, but lives in grace.

Nevertheless, significant differences divide the baptismal doctrine of the traditions summarized in this chapter. This chapter has examined the definitions of baptism and the relationship between the sign of baptism and its referent, and asked the question whether baptism effects anything. According to this investigation, the traditions studied can be situated along this continuum:

Catholics → Lutherans → Reformed (Calvin → Zwingli) → Baptists

The traditions at the left end of the continuum have the closest relationship between sacramental sign and referent; those to the right have the loosest. A common theme in Catholic, Lutheran, and Reformed baptismal theology, although they express this differently, is that there is both an objective and a subjective aspect to the sacrament, the objective aspect being related to the validity of the sacrament and the subjective aspect being related to the reception of grace. Sacramental activity involves both the work of God and human response to that work. Catholics express this as the relationship between the principles of sacramental efficacy *ex opere operato* (according to the work worked) and *ex opere operantis* (according to the person working or the disposition of the recipient). Luther expressed this in terms of God's promise and human response to that promise in faith. Calvin affirmed the Lutheran position regarding promise and faith, but added the concept of covenant and election. Since, for Calvin, baptism is only truly efficacious for the elect, either faith is only truly possible for the elect or the sacrament of baptism is only valid for the elect. In either case, the relationship between the sacrament and its effect is weakened since a third condition, namely, election, is added to the equation. In all three of these traditions baptism is the work of Christ and the minister is only his instrument.

The most profound difference in baptismal theology lies between these traditions, on the one hand, and, on the other hand, Zwingli and those Baptists for whom baptism is a human act performed in obedience to the divine command. As we have seen, Zwingli separated the sign from what it signifies and the external rite from the action of the Holy Spirit, denying any causal relationship or identity between them. For Zwingli baptism is a sign of that to which we pledge ourselves and a sign that identifies the community of those dedicated to God. In opposition to the Anabaptists who thought that baptism was a sign that confirmed an existing faith, Zwingli advocated the baptism of infants, comparing the children of Christians to the children of the Israelites who were included in the sign of the covenant through circumcision.

For many Baptists, baptism is a sign of previous faith and conversion. It is a human act, even though in obedience to God's institution. The Baptists further part company with the other traditions over the practice of infant baptism, only admitting professed believers to baptism.

The most significant differences among the various traditions are anthropological and soteriological: Does baptism effect regeneration? Does it justify? These are really two different questions, the first inquiring into the anthropology of baptism and justification, the second probing the relationship between baptism and justification by faith. Although some initial indications of differences between the traditions have been given here, these questions will be examined more closely in chapter 6, which discusses the relationship between baptism, faith, and justification.

Chapter Four

Baptism and Patterns of Initiation: Catholics and Orthodox

When the search for a common doctrine of baptism reached a certain impasse, the ecumenical movement sought a wider context of commonality, appealing not to a common event or theology of baptism but rather to a common process or pattern of initiation in which baptism is one moment.[1] This wider context has been ecumenically and theologically fruitful, demonstrating that baptism incorporates rites and patterns of life as well as doctrine. For example, the consultation on the role of worship in the search for Christian unity held in Ditchingham, England in 1994 emphasized the ecumenical significance of the pattern of eucharistic celebration and also suggested that baptism has an order and pattern that is meaningful, ancient, and increasingly recognized in the churches.[2]

The subsequent consultation on baptism in Fauverges, France in 1997 took up the Ditchingham emphasis on order and pattern, developing its

---

[1] Paul Fiddes makes the helpful point that we are looking for a process of initiation, of which baptism is one moment, rather than a process of baptism. Then confirmation and Eucharist are not seen as completions of baptism, as if baptism were incomplete in itself, but as completions of initiation. "Baptism and the Process of Initiation," *The Ecumenical Review* 54 (2002): 48–65, at 60.

[2] The report is in Thomas F. Best and Dagmar Heller, eds., *So We Believe, So We Pray: Towards Koinonia in Worship*. Faith and Order Paper No. 171 (Geneva: World Council of Churches, 1995), 4–26.

application to baptism.[3] This emphasis on *ordo* is not a comparison of liturgical rites, although it certainly takes account of them, but rather a comparison of deeper structures of initiation, including such elements as proclamation/evangelization, conversion, profession of faith, water bath, meal, and Christian formation/life in community.[4] In this *ordo* word leads to sacrament, and sacrament leads to Christian living. In short, it is the process of making Christians and the path of discipleship.

The Fauverges consultation points out that the *ordo* of baptism is discernable in Acts 2, where baptisms follow Peter's preaching and lead those who are baptized to life in community where "they devoted themselves to the apostles' teaching and fellowship, to the breaking of bread and the prayers" (2:42) as well as to the distribution of goods to those in need (2:45).[5] Similarly, in 1 Peter, which may well represent a baptismal pattern, the proclamation of the resurrection and teaching about new life (1:2–2:1) lead to purification and new birth, eating and drinking God's food (2:2-3), and participation in community as the royal priesthood, the new temple, and the people of God (2:4-10).[6]

Similarly baptism, a broader process of initiation, and baptismal life are related to each other as a threefold series of recapitulations involving the more restricted baptismal rite, the larger *ordo* of Christian initiation, and the general pattern of Christian living. The briefer form becomes a shorthand for the next expanded form, the sacramental rite indicating symbolically what is lived in day-to-day Christian living:

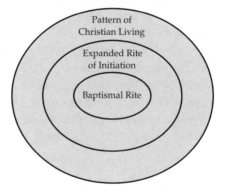

Pattern of
Christian Living

Expanded Rite
of Initiation

Baptismal Rite

Figure 4

---

[3] "Report of the Consultation," in *Becoming Christian: The Ecumenical Implications of Our Common Baptism*, ed. Thomas F. Best and Dagmar Heller. Faith and Order Paper No. 184 (Geneva: World Council of Churches, 1999), §10.

[4] Ibid., §4, §§19-20.

[5] Ibid., §20.

[6] Ibid.

The baptismal rite itself recapitulates the larger pattern of initiation, which in turn recapitulates a larger pattern of Christian living. Thus the renunciations of evil and the recitation of the creed in the baptismal rite summarize the work of conversion in the catechumenate within an expanded rite of initiation and the ongoing penitential life of Christian discipleship. Likewise, the first Eucharist of the expanded rite of initiation anticipates the whole of the Christian life.[7] Participation in the Eucharist not only involves full participation in the liturgical assembly, but also signifies participation in the life of the community through suffering witness in the world in the pattern of Christ's suffering on behalf of many.[8] The larger pattern of Christian initiation recapitulates the pattern of Christian living with its immersion in the word of God, its repeated reconciliations, and the lifelong process of growth in life in Christ. The consultation summarizes this pattern thus: "By means of God's continuing grace and presence baptism is *process* and once-for-all eschatological event and *pattern* for all of life."[9]

This report notes, however, that the various elements of catechesis, water bath, admission to the Eucharist, and community life have been separated one from the other. Baptism has been separated from the gift of the Spirit, from the Eucharist, and from perceived responsibility for an ethical life. Different traditions stress different aspects of this *ordo* to varying degrees, some emphasizing teaching and the making of disciples, others embodying a rich tradition of liturgical symbolism, and still others nurturing postbaptismal life in very intentional ways. The report of the consultation suggests to the churches that a renewed appreciation of this *ordo* of Christian initiation is a source for interpreting and renewing their own practices and for aiding in the recognition of the baptismal practices of other churches.

Following the suggestion of the consultation, this chapter compares the pattern and theology of initiation embedded in three groupings of ecclesial traditions: the practices of Catholics and the Orthodox, who base their theology and practice of baptism on ancient rites of initiation; those of Protestant churches, which in recent years have retrieved many of the elements of the catechumenate; and those of the Christian churches that exclusively practice believer's baptism.

---

[7] Ibid., §22.

[8] See Gordon Lathrop, "Water that Speaks: The *Ordo* of Baptism and its Ecumenical Implications," 13–29, in *Becoming Christian: The Ecumenical Implications of Our Common Baptism*, at 17.

[9] "Report of the Consultation," §22.

Catholics and Orthodox:
Heirs of Catechumenal Rites of Initiation

Although the baptismal liturgies of the Catholics and Orthodox differ in significant ways, they share in common the heritage of Christian initiation of the patristic period. Even though these two traditions share a common heritage, their differences have resulted in Orthodox churches at times rebaptizing Roman Catholics who enter the Orthodox Church. In 1987 the Joint International Commission for Theological Dialogue between the Roman Catholic Church and the Orthodox Church identified similarities of doctrine and differences in practice between the two traditions in a statement, "Faith, Sacraments, and the Unity of the Church," also known as the Bari Statement.[10]

According to this common statement the essential points of the doctrine of baptism on which the two churches are agreed include:

1. the necessity of baptism for salvation;

2. the effects of baptism, particularly new life in Christ and liberation from original sin;

3. incorporation into the church by baptism;

4. the relation of baptism to the mystery of the Trinity;

5. the essential link between baptism and the death and resurrection of the Lord;

6. the role of the Holy Spirit in baptism;

7. the necessity of water, which manifests the character of baptism as the bath of new birth.[11]

Differences regarding baptism identified in the document were:

1. the Catholic Church, while recognizing the primordial importance of baptism by immersion, ordinarily practices baptism by infusion, while the Orthodox Church practices immersion;

---

[10] Joint International Commission for Theological Dialogue between the Roman Catholic Church and the Orthodox Church, "Faith, Sacraments, and the Unity of the Church," *Greek Orthodox Theological Review* 34, no. 2 (1989): 153–64. The statement is the result of the meeting of the Commission that took place from June 9–16 at the Oasi Sancta Maria, Cassano delle Murge, near Bari, Italy. This was a continuation of a meeting held at the same location in 1986.

[11] "Faith, Sacraments, and the Unity of the Church," 49.

2. in the Catholic Church a deacon can be the ordinary minister of baptism;[12]

3. the Catholic Church admits to first communion "baptized persons who have not yet received confirmation, even though the disciplinary directives which called for the traditional order of the sacraments of Christian initiation have never been abrogated";[13]

4. in the Catholic Church baptism is not celebrated along with chrismation and the Eucharist.

According to this document the areas of agreement are all doctrinal, while the areas of difference concern the practice of baptism, including the order of the sacraments of initiation, the manner of baptism (immersion or infusion), and the minister of baptism. Significantly for an ecumenical document, the statement says nothing about a real mutual recognition of baptism.[14] Jean-Marie Tillard interprets this as an indication that the Commission could not honestly affirm the truth and validity of Roman Catholic baptism.[15] Orthodox evaluations of Roman Catholic baptism are not uniform. The strictest opinions hold that Roman Catholics receive grace in baptism and are consequently true Christians, but according to the Orthodox principle of economy, meaning that even though the rite is deficient, it is not a void ceremony or empty rite because God's grace compensates for what is deficient.

---

[12] Ibid., 50.

[13] Ibid., 51. This provokes objections or reservations by Roman Catholics as well as the Orthodox. This inversion of the sacraments of initiation is occasioned by delaying the sacrament of confirmation. The practice of the Roman Catholic Church is to admit persons to first communion after catechesis and the attainment of the age of reason, usually identified as about seven years of age. Confirmation, except for those admitted into the church with a unified rite of initiation at the Easter Vigil, typically occurs after first communion, most frequently in early adolescence.

[14] However, an agreed statement of the North American Orthodox-Catholic Theological Consultation, "Baptism and 'Sacramental Economy'" (June 3, 1999) does state: "The Orthodox and Catholic members of our Consultation acknowledge, in both of our traditions, a common teaching and a common faith in one baptism, despite some variations in practice which, we believe, do not affect the substance of the mystery. We are therefore moved to declare that we also recognize each other's baptism as one and the same" (4). Accessed from http://www.usccb.org/seia/agreed.shtml (September 17, 2008).

[15] J.-M. R. Tillard, "Baptism: New Problems and New Questions," *Ecumenical Trends* 17, no. 2 (1988): 17–20, at 17.

Tillard aptly identifies the source of the difficulty of the recognition of Roman Catholic baptism as not simply the ritual practices, but the ecclesiology underlying the ritual practices. For the Orthodox the only true, authentic initiation is the one celebrated according to the faith and ritual of the only true, authentic church, namely the Orthodox Church.[16] Only those who are baptized in the Orthodox Church are truly baptized. Tillard concludes that the mutual recognition of baptism between Roman Catholics and the Orthodox must begin with recognition of the ecclesiastical character of a community. This, of course, raises the ecumenical "chicken and egg" dilemma: does mutual recognition of sacraments lead to mutual recognition of churches, or does mutual recognition of churches lead to the mutual recognition of the sacramental practices within these churches? Ecumenical discussion must necessarily proceed on both fronts simultaneously.

A 1999 agreed statement of the North American Orthodox-Catholic Theological Consultation, "Baptism and 'Sacramental Economy,'" moves in this direction. It states: "The Orthodox and Catholic members of our Consultation acknowledge, in both of our traditions, a common teaching and a common faith in one baptism, despite some variations in practice which, we believe, do not affect the substance of the mystery. We are therefore moved to declare that we also recognize each other's baptism as one and the same."[17] It connects this agreement on baptism with steps toward a mutual recognition of each other's ecclesial reality in the statement: "The fact that our churches share and practice this same faith and teaching requires that we recognize in each other the same baptism and thus also recognize in each other, however 'imperfectly,' the present reality of the same Church. By God's gift we are each, in St. Basil's words, 'of the Church.'"[18] Here the statement argues from a common baptism to recognition of ecclesiality, although it stops short of affirming a mutual recognition of each other as churches. The Catholic Church recognizes the Orthodox as being truly churches, although in imperfect communion with the Roman Catholic Church,[19] in which the church of Christ subsists in its fullness.[20] The Orthodox, as we have seen, consider themselves to

---

[16] Ibid., 18.
[17] North American Orthodox-Catholic Theological Consultation, "Baptism and 'Sacramental Economy,'" I, A, 4.
[18] Ibid., III, A, 3.
[19] Vatican II, UR, 13–18.
[20] Vatican II, LG, 8.

be the truly authentic church. The North American Consultation recommends that the International Commission begin anew where the Bari Statement came to an abrupt conclusion and that it "proceed to reaffirm explicitly and clearly, with full explanation, the theological grounds for mutual recognition by both churches of each other's baptism."[21]

Catechumenal Heritage

Recent historical studies of early initiation rites have uncovered a great diversity among them. One historian, Paul Bradshaw, concludes that "we cannot really talk of a standard or normative pattern of early initiation practice in primitive Christianity. Nor can we simply classify the various rites as being fundamentally either Eastern or Western in shape."[22] Thus any attempt in ecumenical circles to establish mutual recognition of baptism on the basis of a common pattern must tread very lightly and paint with very broad strokes. That being said, the first full direct description of this process is given in Justin's first *Apology* (ca. 160 CE):

> Lest we be judged unfair in this exposition, we will not fail to explain how we consecrated ourselves to God when we were regenerated through Christ. Those who are convinced and believe what we say and teach is the truth, and pledge themselves to be able to live accordingly are taught in prayer and fasting to ask God to forgive their past sins, while we pray and fast with them. Then we lead them to a place where there is water, and they are regenerated in the same manner in which we ourselves were regenerated. In the name of God, the Father and Lord of all, and of our Saviour, Jesus Christ, and of the Holy Spirit, they then receive the washing with water. For Christ said: "Unless you be born again, you shall not enter the kingdom of heaven" (John 3.5). . . . There is invoked over the one who wishes to be regenerated, and who is repentant of his sins, the name of God, the Father and Lord of all. . . . This washing is called illumination, since they who learn these things become baptized in the name of Jesus Christ, who was crucified under Pontius Pilate, and in the name of the Holy Spirit, who predicted through the prophets everything concerning Jesus.

---

[21] "Baptism and 'Sacramental Economy,'" III, B, 1.

[22] Paul F. Bradshaw, *The Search for the Origins of Christian Worship: Sources and Methods for the Study of Early Liturgy* (New York: Oxford University Press, 2002), 169.

> After thus baptizing those who have believed and given their
> assent, we escort them to the place where are assembled those whom
> we call brothers and sisters, to offer up sincere prayers in common
> for ourselves, for the newly baptized, and for all other persons wher-
> ever they may be, in order that, since we have found the truth, we
> may be deemed fit through our actions to be esteemed as good citi-
> zens and observers of the law, and thus attain eternal salvation. At
> the conclusion of prayers we greet one another with a kiss. Then,
> bread and chalice containing wine mixed with water are presented
> to the one presiding over the brothers and sisters. [An account of
> the Eucharist follows as well as an account of sending communion
> to those who are absent, and food and support to the poor.][23]

Gordon Lathrop identifies the following pattern in this account:

- Teaching the faith and enquiry about conduct

- Praying and fasting of candidates and the community

- Procession to the water

- Washing

- Procession to the place of community prayer

- Eucharist

- Continual reminding, in Sunday Eucharist and in care of the poor[24]

Reference to baptism in the trinitarian name of Father, Son, and Spirit
is conspicuously absent in Lathrop's account of this *ordo*, although it is
present in Justin's report of the baptismal process. This absence masks
a potential ecumenical difficulty for the mutual recognition of baptism
should various traditions choose to adopt a trinitarian formula other
than Father, Son, and Spirit. The Roman Catholic Church, for example,
considers the use of alternative formulations such as Creator, Redeemer,
and Sanctifier grounds for declaring a baptism invalid.[25]

---

[23] English text in *Documents of the Baptismal Liturgy*, ed. E. C. Whitaker, revised and
expanded by Maxwell E. Johnson, 3rd ed. (Collegeville, MN: Liturgical Press, 2003), 3.

[24] Lathrop, "Water that Speaks," 19.

[25] On February 1, 2008, the Congregation for the Doctrine of the Faith issued a
response to the question whether baptisms with the formulas "I baptize you in the
name of the Creator, and of the Redeemer, and of the Sanctifier" or "I baptize you in
the name of the Creator, of the Liberator, and of the Sustainer" are valid. It replied,
"negative" to this question and "affirmative" to the question whether persons baptized
with these formulas must be baptized *in forma absoluta*. Pope Benedict XVI approved

Although the Vatican does not provide a theological rationale for its judgment, the reason lies in the biblical text, in the tradition of the church, and in trinitarian theology. Alternative formulas deviate from the biblical imperative. Although some recent scholarship questions the prescriptive force of Matthew's formula, its use is firmly embedded in the larger tradition of the church even if its use in actual baptisms cannot be traced to the first century and even though historical-critical scholarship does not identify the formula as *ipsissima verba Domini*, but rather interprets it as an allusion to later ecclesiastical practice.[26]

Furthermore, some of these formulations reflect an unorthodox trinitarian theology. For example, Creator, Redeemer, Sanctifier is modalistic, insufficiently distinguishing between Father, Son, and Spirit. Such a formula also fails to acknowledge that all three persons of the Trinity are involved in the divine acts of creation, redemption, and sanctification. Salvation is not one undifferentiated act, but an interrelated act of Father, Son, and Spirit. The Father is reconciled to humankind through the reconciling activity of the Son in the power of the Spirit. It is in the economy of salvation that the distinctions in God appear.[27] Finally, this particular substitution loses its relational and Christocentric center. The Father is the Father of the Son and the Spirit is the Spirit of the Son.

Thus baptism is not simply a washing, but an insertion into trinitarian life, what we call grace. This trinitarian confession of faith is particularly important, given the fact that even though traditions vary considerably in their doctrine of baptism, christological and trinitarian confession as defined in the councils of Nicea and Constantinople really constitutes the basis for mutual recognition of baptismal doctrine. This needs to be reflected in any mutual recognition of baptismal *ordo*.

Lathrop also discerns this pattern in the early writing called the *Didache*, generally considered to be a Syrian document of the late first to

---

these responses and ordered their publication. http://www.vatican.va/roman_curia/congregations/cfaith/documents/rc_con_cfaith_doc_20080201_validity-baptism_en.html (accessed May 22, 2008).

[26] See, however, Richard A. Norris Jr., "Confessional and Catechetical Formulas in First- and Early-Second-Century Christian Literature," in *One Lord, One Faith, One Baptism: Studies in Christian Ecclesiality and Ecumenism in Honor of J. Robert Wright*, ed. Marsha L. Dutton and Patrick Terrell Gray, 14–28 (Grand Rapids: Eerdmans, 2006). Norris argues that although Matthew 28:19 undoubtedly contributed the structure of baptismal formulas that became prevalent in the churches, it cannot be considered as prescriptive since the practice they seem to inculcate is not obvious in any of the records of the first-century Christian movement (24).

[27] Nicholas Cabasilas, *The Life in Christ*, trans. Carmino J. deCatanzaro (New York: St. Vladimir's Seminar Press, 1974), 74.

early second century. The pattern becomes even more evident in the "order of the catechumenate" that was developed in Rome about the year 180 and was still evident in the third century, but that, for all practical purposes, no longer existed during the Middle Ages. The catechumenate is testimony to the normativity of initiation proceeding in stages. This *ordo* is clearly about Christian discipleship, the formation of Christians as well as the formation of the Christian community.

Today the Catholic and Orthodox churches use rites based on the ancient catechumenate, and many Protestant churches are retrieving elements of it in their processes of initiation. Rites more closely derived from the ancient order of initiation clearly incorporate the *ordo* identified by the World Council of Churches consultations. These more expanded rites exhibit a more complex theology when compared to a rite of baptism restricted to immersion or infusion in the name of the Trinity. The euchology of these rites reaches farther back into a theology of creation and farther forward into eschatology. The rites are indicative not only of a manner of Christian discipleship but also of a Christian anthropology. In sum, they can be characterized as cosmic in scope, transformational in their anthropology, eucharistic in meaning, ecclesiological in context, and eschatological in orientation.

Catholic Rite of Christian Initiation of Adults

The Constitution on the Sacred Liturgy (*Sacrosanctum Concilium*) from Vatican II stipulated that the catechumenate was to be renewed and broken up into several stages. The time of the catechumenate was to be sanctified through liturgical rites to be celebrated at a series of points throughout this time of preparation for baptism.[28] Furthermore, both rites of adult baptism, the simpler one and the more elaborate one, were to be revised, the latter with reference to the renewed catechumenate. A special Mass, "For the Conferring of Baptism," was to be put into the Roman Missal.[29] The Rite of Christian Initiation of Adults (RCIA) was published by the Sacred Congregation for Divine Worship in January 1972.

---

[28] SC 64.
[29] SC 66.

The RCIA comprises a process of conversion involving the participation of a faith community and culminating in a unified rite of initiation including baptism, confirmation, and Eucharist at the Easter Vigil. The National Conference of Catholic Bishops approved national statutes for the catechumenate in the United States in 1986, and, beginning on September 1, 1988, the Rite of Christian Initiation of Adults was mandated for use whenever an adult or anyone of catechetical age is prepared for baptism in the United States.

This rite is now normative for our understanding of baptism, even though most Roman Catholics are baptized as infants. The norm is established not by the frequency with which a certain form of baptism is administered, but by the form that determines the meaning of baptism.[30] In this case it is full, conscious, faithful participation in the baptismal rite by an adult that constitutes the norm. We are still exploring the impact of the rite on the life of the church, on our ecclesiology, and on our understanding of the individual sacraments.

The first stage of the RCIA consists of inquiry on the part of the candidates and an initial conversion leading to the desire to become Christians. It ends with the rite of acceptance into the order of catechumens.

The next stage is the catechumenate proper, which begins with the rite of acceptance into the order of catechumens and may last for several years. It is a period of catechesis in which there is both doctrinal formation in the faith of the church and formation in a Christian way of life assisted by sponsors, godparents, and the local community of faith. The names of the catechumens, who henceforth are regarded as Christians, are inscribed in the register of catechumens. Nevertheless, even though "Christian," they are not yet "of the faithful" and not yet deputed for the public worship of the church. Thus they are normally dismissed from the eucharistic assembly before the prayer of the faithful and preparation of the gifts. The catechumens give witness to the church of the conversion required of the whole church.[31] This stage ends with the rite of election, signifying that the elect are ready to enter proximate preparation for the sacraments of initiation. This rite is called "election" because the acceptance of the catechumen by the church is founded on election by God, in whose name the church acts.[32]

[30] Kavanagh, *The Shape of Baptism*, 108–9.
[31] Ibid., 130.
[32] RCIA, 119.

A time of enlightenment and purification, which ordinarily coincides with Lent, involves the elect in a more intense spiritual preparation for the sacraments of initiation. The rites of this period include the scrutinies and exorcisms, which consist of silent prayer, intercessions, prayer of exorcism, and the imposition of hands in the presence of the assembled community. Their purpose is to make the elect more aware of their sinfulness and to strengthen their resolve to turn from evil and follow Christ. This stage also includes formal presentations of the Creed and the Lord's Prayer.

On the morning of Holy Saturday, a day of prayer, reflection, and fasting, the elect "give back" the Creed and the Lord's Prayer by reciting and briefly explaining them. Other rites that may be celebrated as immediate preparation for the sacraments of initiation include the ephphatha rite (the unstopping of the ears and mouth), the choosing of a baptismal name, and anointing with the oil of catechumens.

The elect are pardoned for all their sins, admitted into the people of God, graced with adoption as children of God, and led by the Holy Spirit into the promised fullness of time begun in Christ through the celebration of the sacraments of baptism, confirmation, and Eucharist. The usual time for the celebration of these sacraments of initiation is the Easter Vigil, the celebration of Christ's paschal victory over sin and death. The church keeps vigil through prayer and Scripture readings that recall creation and the history of God's salvation. The baptismal liturgy begins after the homily with the presentation of the elect, the Litany of the Saints, and the blessing of the water. The elect renounce sin, profess their faith, and are baptized. The baptized are then clothed with a white garment, representing new creation and new life in Christ, and given a lighted candle representing Christ, the light of the world. Confirmation by prayer to the Holy Spirit, the imposition of hands, and anointing with the oil of chrism follows. At the conclusion of the rite the celebrant offers the greeting of peace as a sign of welcome into the church. At this point the eucharistic liturgy continues and the neophytes receive the Eucharist for the first time with the congregation.

The Rite of Christian Initiation of Adults concludes with a period of postbaptismal catechesis called "mystagogia." The neophytes meet for prayer and additional catechesis on the rites they have just experienced. They take their place in the Christian assembly and live out their commitment in the life and mission of the church.

The outline of the stages of the restored catechumenate is:

Period of Evangelization and Precatechumenate
First Step: Rite of Acceptance into the Order of Catechumens

Receiving the Candidates
   Candidates' First Acceptance of the Gospel
   Affirmation by the Sponsors and the Assembly
   Signing of the Candidates with the Cross
   Invitation to the Celebration of the Word of God

Optional Rites
   Exorcism and Renunciation of False Worship
   Giving of a New Name
   Presentation of a Cross

Period of the Catechumenate

Rites Belonging to the Period of the Catechumenate
   Celebrations of the Word of God
   Minor Exorcisms
   Blessing of the Catechumens
   Anointing of the Catechumens
   Presentations (optional): Creed and the Lord's Prayer
   Sending of the Catechumens for Election (optional)

Second Step: Election or Enrollment of Names

Liturgy of the Word
   Homily
   Presentation of the Catechumens
   Affirmation of the Godparents and the Assembly
   Act of Admission or Election
   Intercessions for the Elect
   Prayer over the Elect
   Dismissal of the Elect

Liturgy of the Eucharist

Period of Purification and Enlightenment
   Rites: The Scrutinies (Third, Fourth, and Fifth Sundays of Lent)
      Presentations: Creed (Third Week of Lent), Lord's Prayer (Fifth
      Week of Lent)
   Preparation Rites on Holy Saturday: Recitation of the Creed, Ephphatha
      Rite, Choosing a Baptismal Name (optional), Concluding Rites

Third Step: Celebration of the Sacraments of Initiation
   Celebration of Baptism
      Presentation of the Candidates
      Invitation to Prayer

        Litany of the Saints
        Prayer over the Water
        Profession of Faith
            1. Renunciation of Sin
            2. Profession of Faith
        Baptism
        Explanatory Rites
            1. Anointing after Baptism
            2. Clothing with a Baptismal Garment
            3. Presentation of a Lighted Candle
    Celebration of Confirmation
        Invitation
        Laying on of Hands
        Anointing with Chrism
    Period of Postbaptismal Catechesis or Mystagogy

Catholic Rite of Baptism for Children

Even though the Rite of Christian Initiation of Adults is normative for a Roman Catholic understanding of the theology of baptism, it is helpful to also give the Roman Catholic rite for infants, which is more comparable to the Orthodox rite:

Reception of the Child

Liturgy of the Word
    Scriptural Readings and Homily
    Intercessions (Prayer of the Faithful)
    Prayer of Exorcism and Anointing before Baptism

Celebration of the Sacrament
    Blessing and Invocation of God over Baptismal Water
    Renunciation of Sin and Profession of Faith
    Baptism

Explanatory Rites
    Anointing after Baptism
    Clothing with the White Garment
    Lighted Candle
    Ephphatha or Prayer over Ears and Mouth

Conclusion of the Rite
    Lord's Prayer
    Blessing and Dismissal

In the rite of reception of children the minister inquires of the parents and godparents what they ask of God's church for the baptized. The answer is "baptism," although alternate possible responses include: faith, the grace of Christ, entrance into the church, or eternal life. The celebrant also asks what name is to be given to the children. He then instructs the parents in their responsibility to train the children in the practice of the faith. He signs each child by the sign of the cross and invites the parents and godparents to do the same.

The intercessory prayers indicate the effects of baptism when they ask that God bathe the children in light, give them the new life of baptism, and welcome them into God's holy church. Other prayers ask that through baptism and confirmation the children may be made faithful followers and witnesses to the Gospel and that God will lead them by a holy life to the joys of God's kingdom. Prayers then follow that the lives of their parents and godparents may be examples of faith to inspire these children. Their families are commended to God's love, and the minister prays that the grace of baptism in each one present may be renewed. An abbreviated Litany of the Saints concludes the intercessory prayers.

The prayer of exorcism asks God to cast out the power of Satan and to set these children free from original sin. This is the only place in the rite that mentions original sin, which is not named in the Rite of Christian Initiation of Adults. The blessing and invocation of God over the baptismal water is the same as in the rite for adults and will be given below. In the name of the children, the parents and godparents reject Satan, all his works and empty promises, sin, and the glamor of evil. They then also profess faith in Father, Son, and Holy Spirit by a threefold response to an interrogatory creed. The celebrant then indicates that the infant is baptized into the faith of the church by proclaiming: "This is our faith. This is the faith of the church. We are proud to profess it, in Christ Jesus our Lord."

The celebrant asks the parents and godparents whether it is their will that the child should be baptized in the faith of the church, which all assembled have professed with them. Upon ascertaining their will to do so, he baptizes the child, saying: "I baptize you in the name of the Father, and of the Son, and of the Holy Spirit." With each invocation of a trinitarian name he immerses or pours water on the child.

The explanatory rites express in symbolism the meaning of the sacrament. The anointing after baptism with the chrism of salvation identifies the child as a member of Christ, who is Priest, Prophet, and King. The clothing with a white baptismal garment symbolizes incorruption, new creation, and being clothed in Christ. The color white signifies that the Christian already participates in the glory of the resurrection, white being the color of the clothing of God in Daniel 7:9, of Christ in his transfiguration revealing the glory of the resurrection (Mark 9:3), of the twenty-four elders seated round the throne in the book of Revelation (Rev 4:4), and of the crowd of the elect (Rev 7:9, 13).[33] The presentation of a lighted candle signifies enlightenment by Christ, the light of the world, and the flame of faith.

Orthodox

The Orthodox Order of Holy Baptism is a unified rite of initiation inclusive of baptism and chrismation, but is administered to infants. Infants are communed at the first Divine Liturgy they attend after baptism. It incorporates rituals from the ancient liturgies of baptism. Even though its theology is thoroughly paschal, it may also occur at various times throughout the liturgical year. The Order of Baptism in the rite for the Orthodox Church of America follows this structure:

Reception into the Catechumenate
> Three Exorcisms
> Recitation of the Symbol of Faith

Holy Baptism
> The Great Litany
> The Blessing of the Baptismal Water
> The Blessing of the Oil of Catechumens
> The Anointing
> The Baptism

The Order of Holy Chrismation
> Rites of Ablution and Tonsure
> The Churching of the Child

The Dismissal[34]

---

[33] A. G. Martimort, *L'Église en Prière: Introduction à la Liturgie* (Paris: Desclée, 1961), 546–47.

[34] Rite of the Orthodox Church in America, introduction and text written and edited by Paul Lazor, *Baptism* (New York: Department of Religious Education, The Orthodox Church in America, 1983).

The Orthodox rite, even though written for a child, contains numerous vestiges of the ancient rite of initiation. It begins with reception into the catechumenate. The priest goes to the vestibule of the church, where the sponsors, with the child, await him. He breathes gently in the face of the child, a nonverbal echo of the ephphatha rite. He makes the sign of the cross over the child, an action also from the Rite of Acceptance into the Order of Catechumens, and then lays his hand on the child's head, indicating that the person will henceforth belong to God, and prays for the person to be baptized.

The three exorcisms are prayers that the devil may be banned from any influence over the person to be baptized. A fourth prayer asks that the eyes of understanding of the person to be baptized may be opened that the illumination of the Gospel may shine brightly in him (her). The priest then breathes gently in the form of a cross over the mouth, brow, and breast of the child, asking that every evil and unclean spirit may be expelled. The sponsors, with the one to be baptized, face the West and renounce Satan and all his works in a threefold affirmation. They then turn to the East and in a threefold affirmation state that they unite themselves to Christ. The recitation of the Nicene Creed follows immediately. The prayer concluding this section of the liturgy asks for holy illumination and the grace of holy baptism. It contains imagery of putting off the old man and renewal unto life everlasting in the plentitude of the power of the Holy Spirit in the unity of Christ.

The priest then leads the sponsors and the one to be baptized in procession to the baptismal font. The very movement of the procession is symbolic of movement from death to life and from the world to God's kingdom. Lighted candles are given to the sponsors, indicating illumination by Christ, the light of the world. The baptismal font is incensed, and the Great Litany follows.

The Great Litany is not the Litany of the Saints, but begins with general prayers of intercession for the world, those present, the ministers of the church, the president, civil authorities, and the armed forces. It continues with prayers that the water may be sanctified with the power and effectual operation and descent of the Holy Spirit, that there may be sent down into it the grace of redemption, the blessing of Jordan, that there may come upon this water the purifying operation of the supersubstantial Trinity, and that the water may prove effectual for the adverting of every snare of visible and invisible enemies. Invocations for the person to be baptized follow: that this person be made worthy of the kingdom, be a child of the light and an heir of eternal good things, a member and partaker of the death and resurrection of Christ. Prayers continue for the preservation of the baptized and that the water may be a laver of regeneration unto the remission of sins, and a garment of incorruption. The litany concludes with a prayer for the worthiness of the minister and a final prayer that the image of Christ may be created in the person to be baptized and that this person may be built up on the foundation of the apostles and prophets and may be implanted as a plant of truth in God's holy, catholic, and apostolic church. It ends with a prayer that as the baptized increases in godliness the all-holy name of the Father, Son, and Spirit may be glorified.

The blessing of the baptismal waters follows, the cosmic dimensions of which will be discussed in more detail later. The oil of catechumens is then blessed and the one to be baptized is anointed on the forehead, breast, and shoulders, ears, hands, and feet. It is important to note that this first anointing is not chrismation, which is the second anointing after baptism. Oil signifies healing and light, as it was used as a salve and for light in lanterns and oil lamps.

The baptismal rite stipulates a triple immersion, each immersion following the name of the Father, Son, and Holy Spirit. Immersion is considered to be the method of baptism most adequate to the meaning of the sacrament since it represents death and resurrection. The triple immersion symbolizes life in the Holy Trinity. The officiating bishop or priest uses the formula: "The servant of God (*name*) is baptized in the name of the Father. Amen. And the Son. Amen. And the Holy Spirit. Amen." The baptized is given a Christian name taken from the Orthodox calendar of saints. Then a white baptismal garment is placed on the baptized, signifying righteousness. The Troparion sung while the baptized is being clothed is "Grant unto me the robe of light, O Most Merciful Christ our God, who dost clothe thyself with light as with a garment." This carries forward the theme of illumination that figures so prominently in the Orthodox baptismal rite.

The Order of Holy Chrismation follows, with an anointing of the baptized in the sign of the cross on the eyes, the nostrils, the lips, the ears, the breast, and the hands and feet. With each anointing the priest says: "The seal of the gift of the Holy Spirit." The chrismation concludes with a circular procession around the baptismal font. This is followed by two mystagogical readings of biblical texts explaining the meaning of the rite, Romans 6:3-11 and Matthew 28:16-20.

The catechetical materials of the Greek Orthodox Church in America explain the relationship between baptism and chrismation thus: "Baptism is birth to new life. Chrismation is the bestowing of a new power by which this life can be lived."[35] Furthermore, "baptism is the personal Easter while Chrismation is the personal Pentecost of each member of the Church."[36] "Christ" means "the Anointed one." Thus Christians are persons anointed with the Holy Spirit as Christ was anointed.

In the Rite of Ablution the priest sprinkles the baptized, with words reflective of the Orthodox interpretation of the effect of baptism: "You are justified. You are illumined. You are sanctified. You are washed: in the Name of our Lord, Jesus Christ, and by the Spirit of our God." When he washes the oil and chrism from the baptized he says, "You are baptized. You are illumined. You have been chrismated. You are sanctified. You are washed: in the Name of the Father, and of the Son, and of the Holy Spirit.

The tonsure, the cutting of the hair of the newly baptized in four places, signifies the offering to God of the baptized.

The baptismal rite is followed by the Churching of the Child. The mother and child retire to the vestibule, where they are met by the priest who takes the child, signs it with the cross and carries it into the church. In the middle of the church he pronounces the formula: "The servant of God (name) is churched: In the name of the Father, and the Son, and the Holy Spirit. Amen. In the midst of the church shall he (she) sing praises to Thee." If a child is male, the priest carries him through the Sanctuary. If the child is female, she is brought only to the Royal Doors. Then the priest says the prayer of St. Simeon (Luke 2:29-32). The liturgy ends with the dismissal.

Both the Roman Catholic rite for the baptism of infants and the Orthodox rites retain the following elements from the Rite of Christian Initiation of Adults, but in a more compressed form: exorcisms, explicit renouncement of Satan, intercessory prayers, anointing of the baptized, confession of a creed (Nicene for the Orthodox and either the Apostles' Creed or the Nicene Creed for Roman Catholics), blessing of the baptismal water, and the anointing of the person to be baptized with the oil of catechumens. The major difference in the Orthodox rite is that the baptism of a child is immediately followed by chrismation. This is then followed in turn by rites of ablution and tonsure and the churching of the child, all absent from the Roman rite.

[35] Lazor, *Baptism*, 11.
[36] Ibid., 12.

As already mentioned, the rites of those traditions most closely associated with the ancient rite of initiation are cosmic in scope, transformational in their anthropology, eucharistic in meaning, ecclesiological in context, and eschatological in orientation. The following pages will develop each of these characteristics.

The Cosmic Dimension of the Baptismal Rite

The cosmic dimension of the baptismal rite lies in the relationship of a theology of new creation to the first creation. This cosmic perspective prevents baptism from being an event associated in an exclusive way with the salvation of an individual and protects against a narrow ecclesiocentrism wherein baptism is seen exclusively as the door to church membership. The new creation achieved in baptism is a new relationship of God not only to the person baptized, but to the world.[37] The association with the natural universe is made through the medium of the baptismal water, which as the most elemental matter becomes the symbol of all matter and thus of the world and even the cosmos.[38] When human beings are finally restored to their full destiny in Christ, the whole cosmos shares in this release from bondage to decay and in the freedom of the glory of the children of God (Rom 8:20). Water's symbolism is multivalent: the amniotic fluid of the womb, purification and cleansing, refreshment, life fluid, but also chaos, death, and destruction. The water of baptism recalls the moment of creation when God's Spirit breathed on the waters, making them the wellspring of all holiness. The Orthodox tradition also interprets Christ's baptism in the Jordan as sanctifying those waters. The Jordan, river of repentance and renewal, was the ancient boundary between the wilderness and the Promised Land.[39] Baptism is also the place of passage and the locus of liberation, as it evokes the passage through the Red Sea. Henceforth water becomes a symbol of deliverance and a recurring element in salvation history that is personal, communal, and cosmic.

---

[37] See Alexander Schmemann, *The World as Sacrament* (London: Darton, Longman & Todd, 1965), 82, and idem, *Of Water and the Spirit: A Liturgical Study of Baptism* (New York: St. Vladimir's Seminary Press, 1974), chap. 2.

[38] Ibid.

[39] John E. Burkhart, "Have All the Seas Gone Dry?" *Reformed Liturgy and Music* 15 (1981): 172–77.

This history is recounted in the prayer in the Roman Catholic rite for blessing the water:

Father,
you give us grace through sacramental signs,
which tell us of the wonders of your unseen power.

In baptism we use your gift of water,
which you have made a rich symbol of the grace
you give us in this sacrament.

At the very dawn of creation
your Spirit breathed on the waters,
making them the wellspring of all holiness.

The waters of the great flood
you made a sign of the waters of baptism
that make an end of sin
and a new beginning of goodness.

Through the waters of the Red Sea
you led Israel out of slavery
to be an image of God's holy people,
set free from sin by baptism.

In the waters of the Jordan
your Son was baptized by John
and anointed with the Spirit.

Your Son willed that water and blood should flow from his side
as he hung upon the cross.

After the resurrection he told his disciples:
"Go out and teach all nations,
baptizing them in the name of the Father, and of the Son, and of the
Holy Spirit."

Father,
look now with love upon your church
and unseal for it the fountain of baptism.

By the power of the Holy Spirit
give to this water the grace of your Son,
so that in the sacrament of baptism
all those whom you have created in your likeness
may be cleansed from sin

and arise to a new birth of innocence
by water and the Holy Spirit.

We ask you, Father, with your Son
to send the Holy Spirit upon the waters of this font.
May all who are buried with Christ in the death of baptism
rise also with him to newness of life.

We ask this through Christ our Lord.[40]

From an ecumenical perspective it is worth noting, in addition to this prayer's recounting of the role of water in the history of salvation, not only its rich use of scriptural allusions, but the manner in which Scripture is used. The prayer is an example of a canonical reading of Scripture in which texts from different books of the Bible mutually interpret each other. It is also a typological reading of Scripture whereby, for example, the blood and water flowing from the pierced side of Christ are interpreted as types of the sacraments of Eucharist and baptism. Similarly, the passage through the Red Sea is a type of Christ's passage through death to life and the Christian's passage from sin to grace and from death to life in baptism.

The structure of the prayer is that of a eucharistic anaphora: anamnesis, epiclesis, and a concluding doxology. In replicating the structure of eucharistic prayer, it evokes both the grammar and the purpose of liturgical prayer. The purpose of liturgy is twofold: the sanctification of women and men and worship of God. The dynamic of liturgical prayer is doxological and trinitarian. We give thanks and praise to the Father, we remember the Son, and we invoke the Holy Spirit. This dynamic movement is most evident in the celebration of the Eucharist, which commemorates the great *exitus-reditus* wherein we recognize the Father as the creator and giver of gifts that are transformed in the power of the Holy Spirit into the body of Christ and returned in offering to the Father. The sacrament is given for the glorification of God through Christ's self-gift to the Father and through our transformation into Christ and incorporation in that same self-gift.

The baptismal prayer explicitly identifies water as the Father's gift, a symbol of the grace of the sacrament. The anamnesis recalls the events of salvation through the agency of water, culminating in Jesus' baptism in the Jordan and his salvific death on the cross. The epiclesis invokes

---

[40] Rite of Christian Initiation of Adults, 222A.

the Holy Spirit to give to the water the grace of the Son so that those created in the Father's likeness may be cleansed from sin to be born to new innocence by water and the Holy Spirit. The *exitus* is a departure from sin and death, and the *reditus* is resurrection in newness of life with Christ. In baptism Christians are sanctified and give glory to God.

The Orthodox blessing of the water expresses this cosmic participation in the saving mystery of baptism in the blessing of the water in even more detail than the Roman Catholic rite:

> Great art thou, O Lord, and marvelous are thy works, and there is no word which suffices to hymn thy wonders. (three times) For thou, of thine own good will, hast brought into being all things which before were not, and by thy might thou dost uphold creation, and by thy providence thou dost order the world. When thou hadst joined together the universe out of four elements, thou didst crown the circle of the year with four seasons. Before thee tremble all the Powers endowed with intelligence. The sun sings unto thee. The moon glorifies thee. The stars meet together before thy presence. The light obeys thee. The deeps tremble before thee. The water-springs are subject unto thee. Thou hast spread out the heavens like a curtain. Thou hast established the earth upon the waters. Thou hast set round about the sea barriers of sand. Thou hast shed abroad the air for breathing. The Angelic Powers serve thee. The Choirs of the Archangels fall down in adoration before thee. The many-eyed Cherubim and the six-winged Seraphim as they stand round about and fly, veil their faces in awe before thine ineffable glory. For thou, who art God inexpressible, existing uncreated before the ages, and ineffable, didst descend upon earth, and didst take on the semblance of a servant, and wast made in the likeness of man: for, because of the tender compassion of thy mercy, O Master, thou couldst not endure to behold mankind oppressed by the Devil; but thou didst come, and didst save us. We confess thy grace. We proclaim thy mercy. We conceal not thy gracious acts. Thou hast delivered the generation of our mortal nature. By thy birth thou didst save us. We confess thy grace. We proclaim thy mercy. We conceal not thy gracious acts. Thou hast delivered the generation of our mortal nature. By thy birth thou didst sanctify a Virgin's womb. All creation magnifies thee, who hast revealed thyself. For thou, O our God, hast revealed thyself upon earth, and hast dwelt among men. Thou didst hallow the streams of Jordan, sending down upon them from heaven thy Holy Spirit and didst crush the heads of the dragons who lurked there.

Wherefore, O King who lovest mankind, come thou now and sanctify this water, by the indwelling of thy Holy Spirit. (three times) And grant unto it the grace of redemption, the blessing of Jordan. Make it the fountain of incorruption, the gift of sanctification, the remission of sins, the remedy of infirmities, the final destruction of demons, unassailable by hostile powers, filled with angelic might. Let those who would ensnare thy creature flee far from it. For we have called upon thy Name, O Lord, and it is wonderful, and glorious, and awesome unto adversaries.

The priest then blesses the water by dipping the fingers of his right hand into it and tracing the Sign of the Cross three times. He breathes on the water and says:

Let all adverse powers be crushed beneath the sign of the image of thy Cross. (three times) We pray thee, O God, that every aerial and obscure phantom may withdraw itself from us, and that no demon of darkness may conceal himself in this water, and that no evil spirit which instills darkening of intentions and rebelliousness of thought may descend into it with him (her) who is about to be baptized.

But do thou, O Master of all, show this water to be the water of redemption, the water of sanctification, the purification of flesh and spirit, the loosing of bonds, the remission of sins, the illumination of the soul, the laver of regeneration, the renewal of the Spirit, the gift of adoption to sonship, the garment of incorruption, the fountain of life. For thou hast said, O Lord: Wash and be clean; put away evil things from your souls. Thou hast bestowed upon us from on high a new birth through water and the Spirit. Wherefore, O Lord, manifest thyself in this water, and grant that he (she) who is baptized therein may be transformed; that he (she) may put away from him (her) the old man, which is corrupt through the lusts of the flesh, and that he (she) may, in like manner, be a partaker of thy Resurrection; and having preserved the gift of thy Holy Spirit, and increased the measure of grace committed unto him (her), he (she) may receive the prize of his (her) high calling, and be numbered with the first born whose names are written in heaven, in thee, our God and Lord, Jesus Christ.

For unto thee are due glory, dominion, honour, and worship, together with thy Father, who is from everlasting, and thine all-holy, and good, and life-giving Spirit, now and ever, and unto ages of ages.

The prayer begins with praise to God for his mighty works. The references to creation in this prayer are not only reminiscent of the Genesis account of creation but also contain other rich biblical allusions to God's power with respect to the natural world, as in the wisdom literature, especially the book of Job, chapters 38–39. The cosmology reflects an ordered universe extending from the four elements of the earth to the angelic powers, here echoing the eschatological material in the book of Revelation, especially the fourth chapter. Between creation and final consummation lies the incarnation, wherein God is revealed, dwells among us, and sanctifies the waters of the Jordan. As sacrament of the new creation, the sacrament of baptism is situated between creation and creation's eschatological completion. In contrast to the prayer blessing the water in other traditions, aside from references to creation the prayer is inspired primarily by New Testament imagery, especially Jesus' baptism in the Jordan. This imagery is more explicitly trinitarian in contrast to the almost exclusively christological emphasis in traditions that make no reference to Jesus' own baptism, which have no epiclesis over the baptismal water or anoint with a prayer referencing the Spirit. There are no references to Noah or to the passage through the Red Sea. The prayer identifies the effects of baptism: transformation of the baptized through grace from corruption to incorruption, sharing in Christ's resurrection, the gift of the Holy Spirit, remission of sins, the remedy of infirmities, and the final destruction of demons. It concludes with a doxology.

Baptism as Transformative and Regenerative

Both Catholics and Orthodox share an interpretation of baptism as transformative of human nature. This is evident in the language of new creation and regeneration. The Catholic conviction is that "through the Holy Spirit, Baptism is a bath that purifies, justifies, and sanctifies."[41] This is by the efficacy of the Holy Spirit through the "imperishable seed" of the Word of God producing its life-giving effect.[42] The Orthodox rite is filled with similar language of purification, illumination, regeneration, new birth, incorruption, and renewal.

The pattern of life changes to one of discipleship and identification with Christ. The signing of the cross on the senses indicates that the catechumens take on the way of Christ. Even though in the Catholic rite the signing of the cross may be limited to the forehead, the signing of the other senses being optional, the head signifies the whole body: hearing

[41] *Catechism* 1227, referencing 2 Cor 6:11; 12:13.
[42] *Catechism* 1228.

the voice of the Lord, seeing the glory of God, responding to the word of God, having Christ dwell in their hearts through faith, bearing the gentle yoke of Christ on their shoulders, having Christ be known in the work of their hands, and walking in the way of Christ. Baptism signifies conversion in its most literal sense: a turning from sin to Christ, a renouncing of sin and evil, and an embrace of the cross of Christ, from darkness to light, from unbelief to faith, from death to life.

However, human nature is also changed, which is the full meaning of "new creation." This is not simply an extrinsic change or a change of life, but a regeneration that occurs by being grafted into Christ. The baptized literally "put on Christ."[43] A new relationship by virtue of participation in Christ generates a new nature, although the language of the liturgy is more existential than ontological. For example, the conclusion of the prayer for the blessing of water in the Catholic rite asks that "all those whom you [the Father] have created in your likeness may be cleansed from sin and rise to a new birth of innocence by water and the Holy Spirit." The rationale for regeneration is not philosophical, but biblical, as the catechism notes in citing Titus 3:5 and John 3:5: "This sacrament is also called 'the washing of regeneration and renewal by the Holy Spirit,' for it signifies and actually brings about the birth of water and the Spirit without which no one 'can enter the kingdom of God.'"[44] This emphasis on birth imagery along with Jesus' baptism in the Jordan comprised the dominant interpretation and paradigm of initiation prior to the fourth-century Nicene context, after which an emphasis on baptism as death and resurrection in Christ (Rom 6) became prominent.[45]

Baptism as Eucharistic in Orientation and Meaning

For both Catholics and the Orthodox, baptism is eucharistic in orientation and meaning. In Latin and Eastern rites the Christian initiation of adults reaches its culmination in a single liturgical celebration of the three sacraments of initiation: baptism, chrismation/confirmation, and Eucharist. In the Eastern rites infants receive chrismation and Eucharist immediately after baptism, although in the Roman rite years of catechesis

[43] Gal 3:27.
[44] *Catechism* 1215.
[45] Maxwell E. Johnson, "The Shape of Christian Initiation in the Lutheran Churches: Liturgical Texts and Future Directions," *Studia Liturgica* 27 (1997): 33–60, at 42.

intervene before confirmation and the Eucharist.[46] Thus the Eucharist is the summit of Christian initiation.[47]

Baptism makes Christians into a priestly community deputed for the church's eucharistic worship. As early as the *Didache* (ca. 160), baptism was a prerequisite for reception of the Eucharist: "But let no one eat or drink of your eucharist but such as have been baptized in the name of the Lord."[48] The baptized have the right and the responsibility of participating in the eucharistic liturgy. This is why catechumens participating in the Rite of Christian Initiation of Adults are dismissed after the Liturgy of the Word in Catholic churches. They have not yet received this deputation. In this sense we are baptized into the Eucharist. This relationship is most evident in a unified rite of initiation as practiced in the Rite of Christian Initiation of Adults and by the Orthodox.

Just as the Rite of Christian Initiation makes adult baptism at the Easter Vigil the norm for understanding baptism, the Eucharist at the Easter Vigil is where the Eucharist is most itself in public and the "standard that defines the meaning of everything else—cross and sacrifice, memorial and presence, ministry and priesthood, intercession and prayer, participation and communion."[49] The Eucharist is the culmination of initiation because it is there that the communion of believers with one another and with Christ is sacramentally visible in the sacrament of God's presence with us. Aidan Kavanagh eloquently describes the relationship between baptism and the Eucharist when he articulates the principle on which the rite's norm of baptism rests:

> That baptism is inadequately perceptible apart from the eucharist; that the eucharist is not wholly knowable without reference to conversion in faith; that conversion is abortive if it does not issue in sacramental illumination by incorporation into the Church; that the Church is only an inept corporation without steady access to Sunday, Lent, and the Easter Vigil; that evangelization is mere noise and catechesis only a syllabus apart from conversion and initiation into a robust ecclesial environment of faith shared. In baptism the eucharist begins, and in the eucharist baptism is sustained. From this premier sacramental union flows all the Church's life.[50]

---

[46] *Catechism* 1233.

[47] Ibid.

[48] *Didache* 7, 1–3; 9, 5.

[49] Nathan D. Mitchell, *Forum Essays: Eucharist as Sacrament of Initiation* (Chicago: Liturgy Training Publications, 1994), 109–10.

[50] Kavanagh, *The Shape of Baptism*, 122.

Both baptism and the Eucharist sacramentalize an individual's participation in the paschal mystery and an individual's incorporation in the church. According to the introduction to the Rite of Christian Initiation of Adults, the whole initiation bears a "markedly paschal character, since the initiation of Christians is the first sacramental sharing in Christ's dying and rising and since, in addition, the period of purification and enlightenment ordinarily coincides with Lent and the period of post-baptismal catechesis or mystagogy with the Easter season."[51] Thus both the content and timing of the rite are paschal. The one mystery of Jesus Christ dead and risen subsists under both the sacramental mode of baptism and the sacramental mode of Eucharist. In baptism the sacramental sign is immersion into the death and resurrection of Christ in the waters of baptism. In the Eucharist the sign is the body and blood of Christ crucified and risen. Baptism is the once-for-all, never repeatable sacrament of the immersion of Christians into the paschal event. The Eucharist is the repeatable sacrament by which we are associated with the paschal mystery. Both sacraments incorporate Christians into the body of Christ, for in baptism we become members of the church, and the Eucharist builds up the church as one body by virtue of our communing in the one bread of Christ (1 Cor 10:16-17).

Baptism as Ecclesiological

Baptism is ecclesiological in context. For both Catholics and Orthodox, a person enters the church through the door of baptism. Thus in many churches the baptismal font is located near the door of the church, reminding us that we enter the church through baptism. However, baptism is more than a mere ritual of membership in an organization; it is truly incorporation. The baptized is literally "embodied" into the church, which is the ecclesial body of Christ. In being united with Christ a person is by that fact united with Christ's ecclesial body, the church: "For just as the body is one and has many members, and all the members of the body, though many, are one body, so it is with Christ. For in the one Spirit we were all baptized into one body—Jews or Greeks, slaves or free—and we were all made to drink of one Spirit" (1 Cor 12:12-13). Thus baptism

---

[51] *The Rites of the Catholic Church*, vol. 1 (New York: Pueblo, 1990), §8.

is entrance into the one, holy, catholic church of Christ, and not simply a membership rite for a particular denomination.

Nevertheless, incorporation into Christ and his church is not merely a spiritualized reality. It is necessarily achieved through incorporation into a visible local community of Christians.[52] This leads immediately to the paradox of unity in the one church of Jesus Christ and the disunity experienced through membership in a particular church not in communion with other particular churches.[53] Mutual recognition of baptism will be dependent on churches' recognizing each other as particular, even if imperfect or partial, realizations of the one body of Christ. We are not one church because we share a common baptism. We share a common baptism because we are one church. The ecclesial reality determines the sacramental reality.

The ecclesial context of baptism carries the implication that baptism should normally be administered by an ordained minister in the presence of a faith community assembled for its public worship. Baptism is not a private event attended by family and friends in an otherwise empty church. The faith community bears the responsibility of receiving and nurturing the newly baptized. Because we enter the one church through baptism, baptism is not repeatable even if a Christian baptized in infancy should profoundly experience a renewed conversion to Jesus Christ later in life or change denominations.

Baptism as Eschatological in Orientation

Baptism is eschatological in its orientation. This flows directly from the intimate connection with the Eucharist, whose association with a messianic banquet is sign of the ultimate and final union to which we are called and that will be completed only in the eschatological end time. Baptism is also eschatological as a participation in the resurrection of Jesus Christ. According to the theology of Romans 6:3-11, those who have been buried with Christ through baptism into death will also be

---

[52] This is one of the principles identified in the Report of the British Council of Churches Working Party in *Christian Initiation and Church Membership* (London: British Council of Churches, 1988), 23.

[53] See Susan K. Wood, "Baptism and the Foundations of Communion," in *Baptism and the Unity of the Church*, 37–60 (Grand Rapids: Eerdmans, 1998).

united with Christ in a resurrection like his. Baptism by immersion signifies this rising in a way that infusion cannot. Finally, baptism is eschatological because it effects a communion with Christ and with the Christian community that is only definitive eschatologically.

Chapter Five

Baptism and Patterns of Initiation: Protestant Traditions

Protestant rites of initiation need to be understood against the rites of the medieval West.[1] In that period infants were baptized as soon as possible in a privatized rite rather than in the context of the public prayer of the church. Infant initiation had been reduced to infant baptism. A unified rite of initiation incorporating baptism, postbaptismal chrismation, and Eucharist had become a sequence of four sacraments celebrated over a number of years: baptism in infancy with postbaptismal anointing with chrism given by a presbyter, first confession in preparation for first communion, first communion, and confirmation by a bishop at age seven or later.[2] The catechumenate and extended rite of initiation had been compressed into a single rite. Maxwell Johnson summarizes the situation thus:

> On the Eve of the Reformation, then, baptism itself had become a rite administered almost exclusively to infants as a precautionary

[1] See Maxwell E. Johnson, *The Rites of Christian Initiation: Their Evolution and Interpretation*, rev. ed. (Collegeville, MN: Liturgical Press, 2007), chap. 6.

[2] See J. D. C. Fisher, *Christian Initiation: Baptism in the Medieval West* (London: SPCK, 1965) for an account of the disintegration of the primitive rite of initiation.

step, i.e., a rite for the dying, designed to rescue the candidate from the power of original sin and death; a rite filled with exorcisms designed to snatch the infant away from the grasp of Satan; a self-contained rite with no necessary relationship to the public liturgical life of the Church; a rite in which catechesis proper had been replaced by the exorcisms themselves; a rite leading to a process of catechetical formation which was limited to the memorization of a few texts; and a rite increasingly narrowed by scholastic theology to the categories of matter, form, intention, and dominical institution. Such is the rite and its interpretation inherited by both Protestants and Roman Catholics in the sixteenth century.[3]

These rites and interpretations of baptism remained rather constant in the Roman Catholic Church into the twentieth century. However, they were the subject of criticism by the sixteenth-century Reformers. J. D. C. Fisher lists five objections:

(1) Since it could be shown from Scripture that by divine appointment baptism must be administered with water in the name of the Trinity, nothing else was essential to the rite; the blessing of the font and the use of oil, candles, salt and spittle being therefore unnecessary additions introduced by men. (2) These additions gave rise to superstition. (3) The prevalent custom of baptizing children at any time in an almost empty church detracted from the honour due to a holy sacrament, and obscured the ecclesial element in baptism. (4) Not enough care was given to choose suitable godparents. (5) The service was not meaningful because it was in Latin.[4]

Beginning with Luther's 1526 Order of Baptism, the explanatory rites were dropped from Protestant services. The theology and practice of baptism focused on the dominical command of Matthew 28:18-20. Anything additional was not considered to be biblical. This leads to the conjecture that a significant difference between traditions heavily influenced by the ancient catechumenate and many Protestant rites lies in their different approach to Scripture. The ancient catechumenal rites

---

[3] Maxwell E. Johnson, *The Rites of Christian Initiation: Their Evolution and Interpretation* (Collegeville, MN: Liturgical Press, 1999), 233. This summary does not occur in the 2007 revised and expanded edition (see n. 1 above).

[4] J. D. C. Fisher, "Lutheran, Anglican, and Reformed Rites," in *The Study of Liturgy*, rev. ed., ed. Cheslyn Jones, Geoffrey Wainwright, Edward Yarnold, and Paul Bradshaw, 120–32 (London: SPCK; New York: Oxford University Press, 1992), 155.

have biblical allusions, but they range throughout the canon of Scripture, from the spittle Jesus uses to heal the man born blind (John 9:6) to the white garments of those inscribed in the Book of Life (Rev 3:5) or the armies in heaven in Revelation 19:14. This typological approach to Scripture was characteristic of the patristic period, which coincided with the ancient catechumenate. Even though Luther's Flood Prayer is typological in its references to the waters of creation, the Flood, and the crossing of the sea out of slavery to freedom, the Protestant reform of the baptismal rites focused on the command and promise in Matthew, eliminating most typological allusions. The charge that extraneous rites are not biblical and therefore are of human invention must be understood from the perspective of this focus on the dominical command and a kind of biblical literalism with respect to it.

The theology and rituals of Lutheran initiation lie between Catholic and Orthodox initiation on the one hand and strictly Reformed patterns and theology on the other, and so share some of the characteristics of both groups. Maxwell Johnson points out that the Lutheran Reformation was "a 'conservative' movement, both theologically and liturgically, valuing highly and retaining much of the Western Latin liturgical tradition in its own reforms of the sacramental rites of the Church."[5] Nevertheless, a significant difference is that Lutheran theology, in company with other Protestant traditions, has always insisted that baptism constituted full initiation.[6] Lutherans do not consider postbaptismal chrismation, which became known as confirmation, to be a sacrament, and do not identify the Eucharist as a sacrament of *initiation*. Nevertheless, Luther had little quarrel with baptism as practiced in the Roman Catholic

[5] Johnson, *Rites of Christian Initiation*, 317.

[6] Maxwell Johnson notes the Reformation tendency to view confirmation not as a sacrament, gift, seal, or pneumatic completion of baptismal initiation into Christ and the church but, rather, as an independent rite of adult maturity according to which the Reformers sought to "reform" confirmation according to a catechetical, educational model (*The Rites of Christian Initiation* [2007], 456). The document, "Christian Initiation in the Anglican Communion: The Toronto Statement 'Walk in Newness of Life,'" makes the unequivocal claim that "baptism is complete sacramental initiation and leads to participation in the eucharist." It affirms the rite of confirmation as having a continuing pastoral role as means of "renewal of faith" among the baptized, or a reaffirmation of the baptismal covenant (cf. 3.19–20), but it is not to be seen in any way as a "completion of baptism." *Christian Initiation in the Anglican Communion. The Toronto Statement "Walk in Newness of Life": The Findings of the Fourth International Anglican Consultation, Toronto 1991*, ed. David R. Holeton. Grove Worship Series, no. 118 (Bramcote, UK: Grove Books, 1991).

Church, as is evident in his comments in "The Babylonian Captivity of the Church":

> Blessed Be God and the Father of our Lord Jesus Christ, who according to the riches of his mercy [Eph. 1:3, 7] has preserved in his church this sacrament at least, untouched and untainted by the ordinances of men, and has made it free to all nations and classes of mankind, and has not permitted it to be oppressed by the filthy and godless monsters of greed and superstition.[7]

Luther's *Little Book of Baptism (Taufbüchlein)* (1523), written in German, was a minor simplification of the Latin Magdeburg Rite of 1497, retaining the prebaptismal ceremonies of exsufflation, the giving of salt, exorcisms with signings of the cross, the *effete* (ephphatha) with the use of spittle, the threefold renunciation of Satan, profession of faith, and anointing. New elements added to the Latin rite include a prayer of Luther's own composition, the *Sindflutgebet* or Flood Prayer, and the directions to dip the child in the font. Luther produced a second *Little Book of Baptism* in 1526 that omitted what some considered to be "human ceremonies," such as the exsufflation, the giving of salt, the *effete*, the pre- and post-baptismal anointings, and the presentation of the lighted baptismal candle. He further reduced the number of exorcisms. Thus a comparison of Martin Luther's two baptismal rites of 1523 and 1526 shows a progressive simplification and elimination of elements from the medieval rite in use during his time. This also represents a growing departure from the rituals accompanying a more extended rite of initiation.

Having indicated the earliest departures from the Roman Catholic practice, the present study passes over the development of Protestant rites in the sixteenth century, there being ample and excellent historical studies of these,[8] and examines contemporary baptismal rites in the interest of tracing ecumenical convergences and divergences and comparing the rites with the baptismal theologies of these traditions.

---

[7] Martin Luther, *Three Treatises*, "The Babylonian Captivity of the Church" (Philadelphia: Fortress Press, 1970), 178. (*Werke*, 36, 37.)

[8] See. J. D. C. Fisher, *Christian Initiation: The Reformation Period* (London: SPCK, 1970); Johnson, *Rites of Christian Initiation*, rev. ed. (see n. 1 above), 309–73; Hugh Oliphant Old, *The Shaping of the Reformed Baptismal Rite in the Sixteenth Century* (Grand Rapids: Eerdmans, 1992); Bryan Spinks, *Reformation and Modern Rituals and Theologies of Baptism: From Luther to Contemporary Practices* (Aldershot and Burlington: Ashgate, 2006), 1–100.

In addition to the restoration of the catechumenate model in Roman Catholicism in the Rite of Christian Initiation of Adults, recently there has also been a retrieval of the catechumenal process in Protestant churches. In 1982 the basic structure of Christian initiation was delineated in the notes on the first order in *Occasional Services: A Companion to the Lutheran Book of Worship,* "Enrollment of Candidates for Baptism."[9] The Evangelical Lutheran Church in Canada developed an adult catechumenate process in its *Living Witnesses* series in 1992 and the Evangelical Lutheran Church in America also did so with its *Welcome to Christ* resources in 1997.[10] The Office of Evangelism Ministries of the Episcopal Church in the United States of America published *The Catechumenal Process: Adult Initiation and Formation for Christian Life and Ministry* in 1990.[11] Methodists and Presbyterians have also produced similar rites of initiation.[12] As society becomes less Christian, churches are finding that more adults are seeking Christian initiation, thus creating a need for churches to develop catechumenal processes for adults. As patterns of the catechumenate become more common among Christian churches, the theologies of baptism may converge more closely as doctrine develops to reflect baptismal practice.

Lutheran Tradition: The Flood Prayer

The Flood Prayer is a ritual element retained in the Lutheran traditions with strong resonances with the catechumenal tradition. It is an element that presents the theology of baptism within the traditions that incorporate it and is thus worthy of study from that perspective even though it is not essential to the act of baptism. To underline the continuity of Luther's theology of baptism with the Roman Catholic rite, it is instructive to note

[9] *Occasional Services: A Companion to the Lutheran Book of Worship* (Minneapolis: Augsburg; Philadelphia: Board of Publication, Lutheran Church in America, 1982), cited in Frank Senn, *Christian Liturgy* (Minneapolis: Fortress Press, 1997), 663.

[10] The bibliographical information for these resources is given in Senn, *Christian Liturgy,* 663, n. 86.

[11] *The Catechumenal Process: Adult Initiation and Formation for Christian Life and Ministry* (New York: The Church Hymnal Corporation, 1990).

[12] *The United Methodist Hymnal* (Nashville: United Methodist Publishing House, 1990), 32–54; and Presbyterian Church (USA), *Book of Common Worship,* prepared by the Theology and Worship Ministry Unit for the Presbyterian Church (USA) and the Cumberland Presbyterian Church (Louisville: Westminster John Knox, 1993), 403–88.

the resemblance of Luther's Flood Prayer to the blessing over the water at the Easter Vigil:

> Almighty eternal God, who according to thy righteous judgment didst condemn the unbelieving world through the flood and in thy great mercy didst preserve believing Noah and his family, and who didst drown hardhearted Pharaoh with all his host in the Red Sea and didst lead thy people Israel through the same on dry ground, thereby prefiguring this bath of thy baptism, and who through the baptism of thy dear Child, our Lord Jesus Christ, hast consecrated and set apart the Jordan and all water as a salutary flood and a rich and full washing away of sins: We pray through the same thy groundless mercy that thou wilt graciously behold this N. and bless him with true faith in the Spirit so that by means of this saving flood all that has been born in him from Adam and which he himself has added thereto may be drowned in him and engulfed, and that he may be sundered from the number of the unbelieving, preserved dry and secure in the holy ark of Christendom, serve thy name at all times fervent in sprit and joyful in hope, so that with all believers he may be made worthy to attain eternal life according to thy promise; through Jesus Christ our Lord. Amen.[13]

The prayer continues with a prayer of exorcism, that the devil may acknowledge God's judgment, give glory to the three divine persons, and depart from the person being baptized, who is signed with the cross.

The Flood Prayer is notable in its use of typology of the flood in Noah's time and of the Red Sea to prefigure baptism. All represent saving events. By Jesus' baptism in the Jordan all water is consecrated. The effect of baptism is a full washing away of sins, a drowning of the old Adam. Furthermore, the prayer contains a petition that the baptized may be blessed with true faith in the Spirit and thus be separated from unbelievers and preserved in the ark of Christendom and thus attain eternal life. This emphasizes the Lutheran doctrine of justification by faith. The Catholic prayer does not include this prayer for faith. However, both it and the Orthodox prayer contain an epiclesis invoking the Spirit to bless the baptismal water, not present in Luther's prayer, although it asks for true faith in the Spirit. The Catholic prayer also refers to the water and blood flowing from Christ's side on the cross, traditionally seen as types of baptism and the Eucharist. The reference to the devil in the prayer immediately following the Flood Prayer does not have a direct corre-

[13] *Werke*, vol. 53, 97–98.

spondence in the Catholic rite, but is closer to the Orthodox rite, which includes rich references to angels and demons. However, the Orthodox prayer does not include typology from the Old Testament. Although, as we have seen, the Orthodox prayer is the most cosmological of all, the Catholic and Orthodox prayers begin with a reference to creation, absent from Luther's prayer but present in contemporary Lutheran texts. Both the Lutheran and the Orthodox prayers end with a doxology.

The Thanksgiving Prayer in the 1978 *Lutheran Book of Worship* of the ELCA adapted Luther's Flood Prayer to more closely resemble the Catholic prayer at the Easter Vigil and is also influenced by the thanksgiving over the water in the *Book of Common Prayer*.[14] It begins with a reference to the Spirit moving over the waters at creation. Interestingly, it omits the references to faith that are present in Luther's original text. It refers to the effects of baptism as being both freedom from bondage to sin and also rebirth. In both the 1978 and 2006 rites the epiclesis does not evoke the Spirit explicitly to sanctify the water, but is directed to those who are washed in the waters of baptism, asking that they may be given new life. Thus the Lutheran rite distances itself from any suggestion that a power or sanctification resides in the water and remains close to Luther's Flood Prayer and to his reservations about a power in the water discussed in chapter 3.

The 2006 revision in *Evangelical Lutheran Worship* eliminates the reference to the condemnation of the wicked by the waters of the flood. The 1978 statement about water as a sign of the kingdom and of cleansing and rebirth is also omitted, although a reference to new life remains. The statement that baptism is done in obedience to Christ's command is also omitted. One wonders what the principles of revision were for the 2006 text other than to simplify the prayer, since the revisions do not make it more faithful to the Lutheran tradition.

The rite for baptism in *Lutheran Worship* (LC-MS, 1982) does not include any version of the Flood Prayer, but allows the possibility of a baptismal garment and lighted candle. Its revision, *Lutheran Service Book* (LC-MS, 2006), does include the Flood Prayer, which occurs immediately after the sign of the cross has been made on the forehead and heart of each candidate. It follows Luther's prayer rather closely, but changes "Christendom" to "Christian Church." As with Luther's prayer, it does not begin with a reference to creation and does not include an epiclesis. It also

---

[14] *The Book of Common Prayer and Administration of the Sacraments and Other Rites and Ceremonies of the Church According to the Use of the Episcopal Church* (New York: Church Hymnal Corporation and Seabury Press, 1977), 306–7.

follows Luther's prayer in that it does not have the form of a thanksgiving preface, omitting any reference to thanksgiving. *Christian Worship* (WELS, 1993) does not include the Flood Prayer or have any provision for a baptismal garment or candle within the rite. Its rite reflects the concern not to add any elements to the dominical command.

The services of baptism according to the use of the Episcopal Church USA (ECUSA, 1979),[15] the United Methodist Church (1992),[16] and the Presbyterian Church (USA) (1993)[17] include a thanksgiving over the water that has a reference to creation and an epiclesis over the water. The Presbyterian rite includes double epiclesis over the water and on those washed in the waters.[18] Whether or not a tradition's rite includes a thanksgiving over the water is indicative of how influenced it is by the catechetical and liturgical tradition or how focused it is on not adding anything to the dominical command.

Baptismal Rites for Children

Some rites for the baptism of children are a compressed form of the catechumenate, with prayers of exorcism, anointing before baptism, the prayer over the water, postbaptismal anointing, clothing with a white garment, and the gift of a lighted candle, while others eliminate most if not all what the Roman Catholic church calls "explanatory rites" or what the ELCA refers to as "symbolic" rites. Arguably, the more a rite for infants departs from a catechumenal model, originally developed for the initiation of adults, the more explicitly the norm for an understanding of baptism shifts to the rite for children.

This shift is evident in the inclusion of Mark 10:13-16, a "proof-text" for the baptism of infants in some rites: *The Lutheran Agenda* (1941), *Lutheran Service Book* (LC-MS, 2006), *Christian Worship* (WELS, 1993). This is also an optional text in the Roman Catholic rite for children, although John 3:1-6; Matthew 28:18-20; Mark 1:9-11 are also recommended and Exodus 17:3-7; Ezekiel 36:24-28; Ezekiel 47:1-9, 12; Romans 6:3-6; Romans

---

[15] *The Book of Common Prayer and Administration of the Sacraments and Other Rites and Ceremonies of the Church According to the Use of The Episcopal Church* (New York: Church Hymnal Corporation and Seabury Press, 1977).

[16] *The United Methodist Book of Worship* (Nashville: United Methodist Publishing House, 1992), 90.

[17] Presbyterian Church (USA), *Book of Common Worship* (Louisville: Westminster John Knox, 1993), 410–12.

[18] Ibid., 412.

8:28-32; 1 Corinthians 12:12-13; Galatians 3:26-28; Ephesians 4:1-6; and 1 Peter 2:4-5, 9-10 are listed as possible texts. The ELCA rite does not contain any Scripture reading, due to the fact that the presumption is that the rite takes place within a service already containing Scripture readings. From a theological and liturgical point of view it is preferable that the readings present a theology of baptism rather than offer an apologetic for the one being baptized. Consequently, even in the baptism of infants the choice of Mark 10:13-16 is regrettable.

The shift to the baptism of infants has led to including an exhortation to parents and godparents concerning their catechetical responsibilities. Thus *Evangelical Lutheran Worship* (ELCA, 2006) instructs the parents:

> As you bring your children to receive the gift of baptism, you are entrusted with responsibilities:
> To live with them among God's faithful people,
> bring them to the word of God and the holy supper,
> teach them the Lord's prayer, the Creed, and the Ten Commandments,
> place in their hands the holy scriptures,
> and nurture them in faith and prayer,
> so that your children may learn to trust God,
> proclaim Christ through word and deed,
> care for others and the world God made,
> and work for justice and peace.

The minister then elicits a promise from the parents and sponsors to help the children grow in the Christian faith. The *Lutheran Service Book* (LC-MS, 2006) contains a similar exhortation, while the rite of the Wisconsin Synod does not. The Roman Catholic rite also includes an instruction concerning the parents' responsibility to train the children in the practice of the faith. This occurs before the actual baptism, thus raising at least two questions.

Many traditions consider these instructions to be problematic for different reasons. For traditions indebted to the catechumenal tradition these instructions and exhortations appear to be misplaced insofar as they relate to mystagogia, the instruction in the sacramental mysteries that traditionally occurred after baptism. As an instruction for the mystagogia that is to follow baptism, these instructions should follow the sacrament. For Protestant traditions these instructions seem to place a human requirement on God's gracious free gift of baptism. Despite these objections, the intent of including such an exhortation is to emphasize the nature of baptism as a sacrament of faith and to show that baptism cannot proceed apart from an affirmation that the infant will be brought up in the faith of the church. Indiscriminate baptisms of infants for whom there is no assurance of being raised in the faith are to be avoided.

Protestant Criticisms of the Adoption of Catechumenal Elements

The adoption by Protestants of baptismal rites incorporating elements of a catechumenate is not without critics. For example, a member of the Lutheran Church-Missouri Synod criticizes the catechumenate process as a process of progressively evidenced sanctification, as introducing human elements that detract from baptism being entirely God's action, and as quantifying and fractionalizing the grace and gifts of baptism:

> The system had danger of fractionalizing the gifts of Baptism and spreading them separately over a process of sanctification, with Baptism at the end doing the remainder. . . . When Baptism came to be regarded as partial—an initiation, part of a process, a beginning with subsequent quantitative stages and accompanying gifts that brought one to final perfection, and so to fitness to be loved by God—then grace, gifts, and Holy Spirit were quantified and fractionalized. Then the whole lot is not given in Baptism. The Gospel is the whole lot the Law measures and quantifies.[19]

This criticism identifies baptism as a process rather than distinguishing it from initiation as a process culminating in baptism. Behind this criticism also lies an anthropology of complete human passivity with respect to the reception of God's gifts.

Another critic, John W. Riggs, speaking from the perspective of the Reformed tradition, questions whether the methods and theological perspectives of the liturgical movement, inclusive of the retrieval of the Rite of Christian Initiation of Adults, fit with Protestant worship practices or theological perspectives.[20] In his opinion, if "Christian worship reen-

---

[19] Norman E. Nagel, "Holy Baptism," in *Lutheran Worship: History and Practice*, ed. Fred L. Precht, authorized by the Commission on Worship of the Lutheran Church—Missouri Synod (St. Louis: Concordia Publishing House, 1993), 269.

[20] Riggs, *Baptism in the Reformed Tradition*, 1.

acts the central datum of the community's life,"[21] then he finds inconsistency and incongruity between the Rite of Christian Initiation and Reformation principles. He cites ecclesiology, specifically the difference between the Catholic emphasis on the liturgy as constitutive of the church and its view of the visible, historical church as the body of Christ engrafted into the paschal mystery and continuing the mission of Christ in the world, contrasted with the Reformation emphasis on an invisible church as the body of Christ in general and Calvin's emphasis on God's election as constitutive of the church, as a fundamental difference.

Regarding baptism, Riggs's critique of the ELCA's *Lutheran Book of Worship* would also apply to its successor, *Evangelical Lutheran Worship*, and is also extended to the Presbyterian Church (USA)'s *Book of Common Worship*, whose rite of baptism affects the largest number of Reformed Christians in the United States. In his opinion both depart from the emphasis on fiduciary faith he finds dominant in Luther's baptism rites of 1523 and 1526.[22] In all of these worship books, the Thanksgiving Prayer over the water adapted from Luther's Flood Prayer includes a reference to creation that is missing in Luther's version.[23] Where Luther describes the people in the flood story as "believing" or "unbelieving," the *Lutheran Book of Worship* describes them as "chosen" or "wicked." *Evangelical Lutheran Worship* uses no description at all, simply emphasizing the themes of deliverance and passage from slavery into freedom. The *Book of Common Worship* speaks of righteousness being given a new beginning in the destruction of evil by the waters of the flood. However, here God's sovereign activity seems to be linked to water rather than to the covenant.[24]

Another difference noted by Riggs is that whereas in Luther's rites the minister first addresses the one being baptized, reenacting God's initiative, the more recent rites begin with the minister addressing the community about the meaning of baptism.[25] Similarly, he finds that the language of the Thanksgiving Prayer "diffuses the personal divine address and human response by referring to divine activity with matter (water), which we must then interpret."[26]

---

[21] Ibid, 11.

[22] Ibid., 11–15.

[23] The second option in the Presbyterian *Book of Common Worship* omits the reference to creation, but also does not include references to belief and unbelief.

[24] Riggs, *Baptism in the Reformed Tradition*, 114.

[25] Ibid., 15.

[26] Ibid., 111.

James F. Kay is quite critical of the renunciations of evil. Because, according to Reformed theology, the children of believing parents are included in the covenant, renunciations are "contrary to scripture because the children of a believer are not 'unclean' (1 Cor 7:14) or under the sway of Satan, but are 'federally holy before Baptism, and therefore are they Baptized.'"[27] For the same reason neither the parents nor the congregation take vicarious vows as proxies for children in the baptismal promises. The theological weight of these promises in the Reformed tradition is that "the parents confess with the congregation the apostolic faith of the Church catholic into which the children are being baptized."[28] The promise to teach the faith to the child is an acknowledgment that the baptized and subsequently catechized children are expected to acknowledge the covenant through their own future profession of faith. In addition, he observes that the renunciation in the *Book of Common Worship*, "Do you renounce the ways of sin that separate you from the love of God?" is heretical since nothing, in fact, can separate us from God's love (Rom 8:39).

Kay criticizes the introduction of charismatic signation into a Reformed liturgy on the basis that no promise is attached to this sign and the Lord himself was not anointed with oil, but with the Holy Spirit at his baptism.[29] For Kay this represents the most egregious example of the harvest of the post–Vatican II ecumenical liturgical renewal movement.[30] Kay suspects that the adoption of the fruits of this movement represents an agenda of "a wholesale repeal of the Reformation."[31] A stronger negative assessment cannot be made of what might be considered in other circles as a positive ecumenical rapprochement.

Finally, both Riggs and Kay observe the rare occurrence of covenant language in the rite, where it is required only at the beginning of the section of the Profession of Faith.[32] Here Riggs notes that it is not clear whether baptism effects one's entrance into the covenant or whether

---

[27] James F. Kay, "The New Rites of Baptism: A Dogmatic Assessment," in *To Glorify God*, ed. Bryan Spinks and Iain Torrance, 201–12 (Edinburgh: T&T Clark, 1999), at 205.

[28] Ibid., 204.

[29] Ibid., 211.

[30] He cites Calvin's *Forme des prières*: "But it is certain that the chrism, candle and other such pomps are not of God's ordinance, but have been added by men: and finally they have come to this, that people are more attracted by them and hold them in greater esteem than the ordinances of Jesus Christ" (ibid., 212).

[31] Ibid.

[32] Ibid., 203, 212.

baptism is the seal of the covenant already established. Although Reformed theology holds the latter, the language is ambiguous. According to Reformed theology baptism does not enact the covenant, but is a means by which a person appropriates the covenant by which he is already embraced. Since the divine initiative of election to the covenant occurs prior to baptism, this appears to rob baptism of divine initiative and action only to turn it into a human action of response. Riggs says as much: "Only from the human side could one call baptism initiation into the covenant."[33] Divine offer and human response seem no longer to be united within the sacrament.

The Reformed answer to this is that in response to the Reformation radicals, Reformed theology stressed the validity of baptism, which meant that baptism truly offers God's grace. Baptism effects regeneration through the single event of God's offer of grace and its reception in faithful trust. Nevertheless, an underlying inconsistency in the Reformed position seems to be that baptism is ultimately effective only for the elect, for those incorporated into the covenant, a covenant into which baptism itself does not initiate. Historically, the Reformed theology of baptism was caught between two conversation partners: late medieval piety, for which it stressed faithful appropriation, and the Reformation's radicals, for whom it stressed the validity of baptism.[34] The challenge is to convince the heirs of the medieval piety of its continuing claim to efficaciousness when the doctrine of baptism is subordinated to a doctrine of election of particular individuals.

These observant criticisms of the inclusion of catechumenal elements in Protestant rites of initiation underscore the direct link between liturgical prayer and doctrine. If the principle of *lex orandi, lex credendi*, that we believe according to how we pray, holds true, the liturgical convergence in the retrieval of the catechumenate will eventually lead to a doctrinal convergence, at least in the implicit assumptions of those who participate in it. In this case ecumenical unity is fostered through a convergence in patterns of initiation. However, if this doctrinal convergence resulting from liturgical convergence is not considered to be faithful to Reformation principles, then ecumenical conversation must return to those principles and once again take up the doctrinal issues.

In the meantime these traditions must ask themselves why they are retrieving these catechumenal elements. They do not represent the

---

[33] Riggs, *Baptism in the Reformed Tradition*, 120.
[34] Ibid.

medieval church, the immediate object of the Reformation, but a more
ancient form of initiation closer to Christian origins. The question is not
whether this ancient form is compatible or not with Reformation principles, but whether this liturgical form is compatible with the Scripture
and tradition of the apostolic church. At this level the ecumenical and
liturgical question may revolve around scriptural hermeneutics, the
Reformation and Catholic uses of Scripture differing, one being more
typological and far ranging across the canon and the other more literal
and focused with respect to the liturgy of initiation.

Baptism and Postbaptismal Anointing

A thorny problem that cannot be addressed in detail in the present
study is the relationship between baptism and the postbaptismal anointing that came to be known as confirmation. When a catechumenate that
culminated in the reception of all three sacraments of initiation fell out
of use due to the baptism of infants becoming the dominant practice, it
eventually followed that the order of baptism followed by confirmation,
then Eucharist, no longer represented pastoral practice. The sacraments
of initiation were first received over a period of time separated by years,
and then in an entirely different sequence.[35] In the United States within
Roman Catholicism the order in which a child receives the sacraments
is presently: baptism shortly after birth, followed by first penance before
first Eucharist at about age seven. Confirmation occurs sometime during
adolescence when the bishop visits the local parish. As Aidan Kavanagh
has observed:

> Confirmation in adolescence or early adulthood as the sacrament
> peculiar to one's mature assumption of public responsibilities in
> Church and society had the effect of reinforcing the presumption
> that baptism was the sacrament peculiar to birth and infancy. In that
> position, baptism was the wholly necessary exorcism of original sin
> and the occasion of the infants being lent sufficient faith by the
> Church, through the good office of godparents and parents, to see

[35] See Johnson, *Rites of Christian Initiation*, 381–91 for the history of this shift. He cites
numerous ecclesiastical documents that legislated the proper order of the sacraments
despite continuing pastoral practice to the contrary: the preparatory document for
the First Vatican Council (1870), *De Administratione sacramentorum*; the 1917 Code of
Canon Law; and a 1932 statement of the Sacred Congregation for the Sacraments.

it through to the critical stage when, as an individual on the verge of "maturity," that faith could be appropriated by the former infant in his or her own right—namely in confirmation.[36]

The separation of confirmation from baptism reinforced the idea that the baptism of infants was primarily for the removal of original sin rather than being a participation in the paschal mystery of Christ according to the theology of Romans 6, or preparation for ministry and Christian life according to the theology of Christ's baptism and anointing by the Spirit in the Jordan. It also had the unfortunate effect of shifting the emphasis in confirmation to a human act, namely, personal affirmation of baptism, rather than keeping the emphasis on God's activity on our behalf in the sacraments.

In this light, then, the imposition of hands and the prayer accompanying the postbaptismal anointing in the ELCA's rites, both in the 1979 *Lutheran Book of Worship* and the 2006 *Evangelical Lutheran Worship*, and in the Presbyterian Church (USA)'s *Book of Common Worship* are significant. Both traditions incorporate a prayer for the sevenfold gift of the Spirit, an imposition of hands, and an anointing with oil with a prayer for the seal of the Holy Spirit. In the ELCA rite the minister, laying both hands on the head of each of the newly baptized, prays: "Sustain (name) with the gift of your Holy Spirit; the spirit of wisdom and understanding, the spirit of counsel and might, the spirit of knowledge and the fear of the Lord, the spirit of joy in your presence, both now and forever." The presiding minister then marks the sign of the cross on the forehead of each of the baptized with oil saying, "(Name), child of God, you have been sealed by the Holy Spirit and marked with the cross of Christ forever." The prayer for the Spirit is based on the sixth-century Gelasian sacramentary, itself derived from the early-third-century *Apostolic Tradition*, traditionally attributed to Hippolytus. Maxwell Johnson comments that the prayer for the gifts of the Spirit can be interpreted as an explicit conferral of the Holy Spirit, although it is not absolutely clear whether baptism or the handlaying prayer constitutes the "seal" of the Spirit.[37]

This anointing, the imposition of hands, the announcement of the seal of the Spirit, and the prayer for the gifts of the Spirit represent what Roman Catholics understand to be a confirmation rite in everything but

---

[36] Aidan Kavanagh, *The Shape of Baptism: The Rite of Christian Initiation* (New York: Pueblo, 1978), 86.

[37] Johnson, *Rites of Christian Initiation*, 427.

name. It does not carry the same meaning as the postbaptismal anointing in Catholicism, which is christological in meaning rather than pneumatological: "He now anoints you with the chrism of salvation, so that, united with his people, you may remain for ever a member of Christ who is Priest, Prophet, and King."

In 1971, Pope Paul VI decreed in his Apostolic Constitution on the Sacrament of Confirmation: "The Sacrament of Confirmation is conferred through the anointing with chrism on the forehead, which is done by the laying on of the hand, and through the words: ¨Be sealed with the gift of the Holy Spirit."[38] Immediately before this, however, the bishop and priests who administer the sacrament with him lay hands upon all the candidates (by extending their hands over them) and say a prayer that closely corresponds to the handlaying and prayer in the ELCA rite:

> All-powerful God, Father of our Lord Jesus Christ,
> by water and the Holy Spirit
> you freed your sons and daughters from sin
> and gave them new life.
> Send your Holy Spirit upon them
> to be their helper and Guide.
> Give them the spirit of wisdom and understanding,
> the spirit of right judgment and courage,
> the spirit of knowledge and reverence.
> Fill them with the spirit of wonder and awe in your presence.
> We ask this through Christ our Lord.

Paul VI comments that "the laying of hands on the elect, carried out with the prescribed prayer before the anointing, is still to be regarded as very important, even if it is not of the essence of the sacramental rite: it contributes to the complete perfection of the rite and to a more thorough understanding of the sacrament."[39]

The resemblance between the current Lutheran rite and the Roman Catholic rite of confirmation is even more remarkable when this prayer for the gifts of the Spirit is compared with Luther's rite of 1523, where we see a significant difference: "The almighty God and Father of our Lord Jesus Christ who hath regenerated thee through water and the Holy

---

[38] Paul VI, Apostolic Constitution, *Divinae consortium naturae* (15 August 1971). In *The Rites*, Vol. One, 472–78.
[39] Ibid., 477–78.

Ghost and bath, forgiven thee all thy sin, anoint thee with the salutary oil to eternal life." This prayer makes no mention of the Holy Spirit, and the anointing with oil was omitted in the 1526 rite.

Thus the ELCA action and prayer represent what Catholics understand as confirmation, although this was not the intention of the *LBW* drafters.[40] They wanted to provide a fuller ritualization of the gift of the Spirit in order to affirm that baptism is the fullness of initiation[41] and that the Holy Spirit is the gift of baptism rather than the effect of some subsequent event.[42] Whatever the intention, this rite restores the proper order of the postbaptismal anointing associated with the gift of the Spirit by placing it right after baptism and before the reception of the Eucharist, whenever that occurs.

In ritualizing the gift of the Spirit with specifically pneumatological allusions, in having the postbaptismal anointing occur immediately after baptism, and in returning to a sacramental practice faithful to a period of the tradition prior to the disintegration of the rites of initiation, rites such as the current Lutheran rite are compatible with Roman Catholic theology, even though Lutherans do not consider this postbaptismal anointing to be confirmation. Here, though, it must be noted that what

[40] Jeffrey A. Truscott, in *The Reform of Baptism and Confirmation in American Lutheranism* (Lanham, MD, and Oxford: Scarecrow Press, 2003), 68–69, believes that the Roman Catholic confirmation formula of 1971/1973 was not the textual source for the *LBW* baptismal rite. He argues for the influence of the rite of the Consultation on Church Union, *An Order for the Celebration of Holy Baptism with Commentary*. My argument is not about the source of the liturgical texts but about their similarity and the consequences for a convergence of sacramental belief that result from praying such similar texts.

[41] This is also the position of Anglicans: "Walk in Newness of Life: The Findings of the International Anglican Liturgical Consultation, Toronto 1991," in *Christian Initiation in the Anglican Communion*, ed. David R. Holeton, Grove Worship Series No. 118 (Nottingham: Grove Books, 1991); also in David R. Holeton, ed., *Growing in Newness of Life: Christian Initiation in Anglicanism Today: Papers from the Fourth International Anglican Liturgical Consultation, Toronto 1991* (Toronto: Anglican Book Centre, 1993), 227–56.

[42] Truscott, *Reform of Baptism*, 109. Earlier Truscott cites Hans Boehringer, the drafter: "We had 'confirmation' immediately after the baptism because we wanted to show that baptism and confirmation were the same thing, or that confirmation is merely a continuation of baptism. The problem was that you could say that, but no one in the Lutheran tradition knew that. . . . The purpose of this formula, 'You have been sealed by the Holy Spirit,' etc., was to combine anointing and sealing with the marking of the cross." In other words, the intent was to provide a fuller baptismal rite that could be acceptable to Lutherans and yet ritualize more fully the gift of the Holy Spirit, much in the manner of Roman Catholic confirmation (p. 70).

constitutes "confirmation" is very ambiguous when one is comparing different traditions. Confirmation involves imposition of hands, anointing, and prayer for the Spirit, although it has carried multiple meanings across various traditions and even within one tradition. The Lutheran practice is much closer to the Rite of Christian Initiation of Adults, since in the RCIA the anointing after baptism is omitted and the rite proceeds immediately to the celebration of confirmation after the explanatory rites of baptism, the clothing with a baptismal garment, and the presentation of a lighted candle. The RCIA in effect identifies Roman Catholic confirmation with postbaptismal chrismation.[43] If one considers the law of praying as indicative of the law of believing (*lex orandi, lex credendi*), one can affirm a strong convergence between the Lutheran and Catholic traditions in these present rites. Nevertheless, obstacles preventing the full effect of this convergence include the Lutheran conviction that baptism in the trinitarian name constitutes full initiation in water and the Holy Spirit regardless of any additional rites and gestures, the current Lutheran rite of Affirmation of Baptism, and the Roman Catholic practice of separating confirmation from baptism.

Confusion generally reigns in the relation between baptism and initiation more broadly considered, including therefore confirmation, a confusion traceable to the disintegration of the ancient unified rite of initiation inclusive of baptism, postbaptismal chrismation, and Eucharist. In the ancient church one would not have argued that this unified rite did not constitute full initiation and it would not have made sense to attempt to ask the question of the individual parts. Catholics certainly agree with Lutherans that baptism in the trinitarian name confers the Spirit, and Lutherans, without rendering prayer inefficacious, must affirm that the Spirit is given when invoked in the act of chrismation. Arguably there is a need for a rite that explicitly identifies this gift of the Spirit, whether that be some version of Luther's postbaptismal prayer in his 1526 service or the current prayer asking for the sevenfold gift of the Spirit. The issue is not whether the Spirit is given in baptism or whether a person is fully a Christian in baptism, but whether the sacramental ritualization of initiation must necessarily be both christological and pneumatological and culminate in the communal breaking of bread that identifies the Christian baptismal life. Ritual minimalism would argue to the sufficiency of water baptism in the trinitarian name. Never-

---

[43] See Maxwell E. Johnson's critique of this in *Rites of Christian Initiation* (2007), 444ff.

theless, a broader pattern is evident in the experience of Pentecost, which includes baptism, reception of the gift of the Spirit, attention to apostolic teaching, fellowship, the breaking of bread, and the prayers (Acts 2:38-42). The issue is not that a minimal ritual is inefficacious or deprives the baptized of the Spirit or membership in the church, but that a more expansive ritual is more revelatory of the richness and complexity of what is accomplished in Christian initiation. This more expansive ritual has biblical warrant beyond the bare bones of the dominical command of Matthew 28:19. This more expansive ritual is not empty ritualism, but is truly efficacious—and therefore sacramental in the Roman Catholic understanding of sacrament—because we do not lay on hands and pray for the Spirit without the Spirit being present or break bread in obedience to Jesus' request to do so without Jesus being present.

Ambiguity exists in how one should interpret the Lutheran postbaptismal anointing with respect to the rite of Affirmation of Baptism, since it includes the exact same prayer for the gifts of the Spirit as one of two options for the blessing during the imposition of hands. The Affirmation of Baptism significantly is not named "confirmation," although in the introduction to the rite it is obvious that it replaces what was formerly known as confirmation in the recommendation that it be used as "part of a process of formation in faith in youth or adulthood (confirmation)." The rite is designed to serve three occasions: confirmation understood as the completion of a period of catechetical instruction, reception of other Christians into membership in the Lutheran Church through reception into a local congregation, and restoration of the lapsed to active participation in the church.[44] It may be repeated at various times in the life of a baptized Christian and may be used by congregations for such festivals as the Baptism of the Lord and Pentecost.

The Rite of Affirmation is not understood as a completion of baptism, but as an affirmation of the Spirit's continued presence and gifts. In fact, it is important that this rite of affirmation *not* be understood as equivalent to the Roman Catholic sacrament of confirmation since it is patently a *human* act of affirming one's faith and baptism, not a *divine* initiative, a distinction that has been at the root of much misunderstanding of the theology of confirmation in all traditions.[45] Furthermore, it is not an

[44] Philip H. Pfatteicher, *Commentary on the Lutheran Book of Worship: Lutheran Liturgy in its Ecumenical Context* (Minneapolis: Augsburg Fortress, 1990), 68.

[45] In 1968 a joint study group representing the American Lutheran Church, the Lutheran Church in America, and the Lutheran Church-Missouri Synod defined

initiatory step to full incorporation in the church, it does not add anything to baptism, and it is not a necessary rite.

It is unfortunate that this same prayer for the gifts of the Spirit occurs in both the postbaptismal anointing and in the Affirmation of Baptism, for while the Rite of Affirmation tries to distance itself from being interpreted as the equivalent of Roman Catholic confirmation, these elements create a ritual similarity even while the meaning and use of the ritual diverges. In fact, Maxwell Johnson, a Lutheran liturgist, has commented that Lutherans now have two rites of confirmation, one according to a liturgical-sacramental model and one according to a catechetical-educational model.[46] On the other hand, the anointing, imposition of hands, and prayer to the Spirit after baptism enact the meaning of confirmation as a seal of baptism and restore the proper relationship between baptism and postbaptismal chrismation in an integrated rite of initiation, even though for Lutherans they are not a sacrament of confirmation.

Before leaving the topic of confirmation, a corrective word is needed regarding Roman Catholic confirmation viewed from the perspective of proponents of disciple's or believer's baptism. Representatives of these traditions often refer to the Roman Catholic sacrament of confirmation as a moment of personal affirmation of faith that they would require at the moment of baptism. Paul Fiddes, for example, comments: "In the Reformed tradition, completion of initiation in confirmation was seen to be necessary to leave place for the confession of personal faith."[47] Insistence on personal faith for baptism and the search for this in a rite of confirmation may be contributing to a distortion of the interpretation of postbaptismal chrismation or confirmation in ecumenical discussions. Here confirmation is clearly seen as an affirmation of personal faith rather than as a sacramental seal of baptism initiated by God. It reverses what Roman Catholics consider essential in sacramental theology by making confirmation a human initiative of profession of faith rather than a divine initiative of offer of grace.

---

confirmation as "a pastoral and educational ministry of the church that is designed to help baptized children identify with the life and mission of the adult Christian community and that is celebrated in a public rite." Cited in Pfatteicher, *Commentary*, 71.

[46] Maxwell E. Johnson, "The Shape of Christian Initiation in the Lutheran Churches: Liturgical Texts and Future Directions," *Studia Liturgica* 27 (1997): 33–60, at 43.

[47] Paul S. Fiddes, "Baptism and the Process of Christian Initiation," *The Ecumenical Review* 54, nos. 1/2 (2002): 48–65, at 53.

Traditions Practicing Believer's/Disciple's Baptism

Although a number of evangelical and Pentecostal churches, many of them independent, practice believer's or disciple's baptism, the discussion here will limit itself to Baptists. Anthony R. Cross writes: "there is no single Baptist theology or practice of baptism, only theologies and practices, and this diversity accords with Baptist ecclesiology which continues to tend toward independency, each local church and individual minister exercising their liberty in the administration and interpretation of Christ's laws."[48] Consequently, when attempting to identify a Baptist practice and theology of baptism, one can only say "some Baptists" believe this, or "some Baptists" practice that.

Nevertheless, even though there is no *one* Baptist theology and practice of baptism, the common elements are that baptism is for someone who has personally professed belief in the Lord Jesus Christ and confessed repentance. It is administered by immersion in water in the name of the Father, the Son, and the Holy Spirit. Thus the process of initiation consists of proclamation of the Gospel and evangelization, confession of faith, and immersion into the Trinity. In some churches this may be followed by a laying on of hands, reception to membership, and admission to communion. However, one can be a member of some Baptist churches without being baptized, one can be baptized without being a member of the local congregation in some churches, and one can be admitted to communion in some churches without prior baptism. The practice of bringing baptism, reception, and communion together in one event of initiation in some congregations shows the influence of both the ecumenical and the liturgical movements in Baptist life and worship.

The fluidity of the relationship between baptism, church membership, and admission to communion raises the question of the meaning of baptism for Baptists from the perspective of a process of initiation. Is it a witness to or symbol of the conversion and faith already professed, as is the case for Pentecostals and many evangelicals, or does it effect something? Is it an act of obedience or an act empowering obedience? Is it a divine act of grace conveying the benefits of the Gospel?[49] Interestingly,

---

[48] Anthony R. Cross, *Baptism and the Baptists: Theology and Practice in Twentieth-Century Britain* (Waynesboro, GA; Carlisle, Cumbria: Paternoster Press, 2000), 455.

[49] These are questions posed by R. E. O. White, as reported in Stanley K. Fowler, "Is 'Baptist Sacramentalism' an Oxymoron? Reactions in Britain to *Christian Baptism* (1959)," in *Baptist Sacramentalism*, ed. Anthony R. Cross and Philip E. Thompson, 129–50 (Waynesboro, GA; Carlisle, Cumbria: Paternoster Press, 2003), 131.

it does not effect church membership, which requires a distinct action. When individual Baptists such as George Neal have pointed out that in the New Testament baptism was closely associated with forgiveness, regeneration, the gift of the Holy Spirit, union with Christ in his death and resurrection, and salvation, they have received quick criticism.[50] Baptist criticisms of the sacramental view are generally that this denies the "faith alone" character of salvation, that baptismal regeneration is equivalent to traditional Catholic doctrine of *ex opere operato* interpreted as a kind of magical ceremony, that a sacramental view misinterprets key Scripture texts such as Acts 2:38, John 3:5, 1 Corinthians 6:11, Ephesians 5:26, and Titus 3:5, which are capable of nonsacramental readings, that a sacramental view of baptism excludes the unbaptized from salvation and the church, and that a sacramental view is contrary to historic Baptist theology.[51] Nevertheless, some currents of Baptist thought are open to the possibility of a baptismal sacramentalism.[52] The discussion continues, not only between Baptists and their ecumenical partners, but among Baptists themselves.

Conclusion

The restoration of the Rite of Christian Initiation of Adults in Catholicism, wherein adult baptism is normative for determining the theology of initiation at whatever age it is administered, offers an opening for fruitful dialogue with the advocates of believer's baptism as it does for other Christian traditions. Within this rite conversion of life, renunciation of evil, and profession of faith are inseparable from baptism in the name of the Father, Son, and Spirit. Nevertheless, it may challenge the inherent individualism of traditions for which the emphasis is on personal conversion and confession of faith, for all these elements are inconceivable

---

[50] Ibid., 342.

[51] These are the criticisms of *Christian Baptism: A Fresh Attempt to Understand the Rite in Terms of Scripture, History, and Theology*, ed. Ernest A. Payne (London: Lutterworth Press, 1959), the result of a working group in London as reported by Stanley K. Fowler, who describes the study as "a watershed in the twentieth-century reformulation of baptismal doctrine among British Baptists in "Is 'Baptist Sacramentalism' an Oxymoron?" 141–45.

[52] See Stanley K. Fowler, "Is 'Baptist Sacramentalism' an Oxymoron?" and idem, *More Than a Symbol: The British Baptist Recovery of Baptismal Sacramentalism.* Studies in Baptist History and Thought, vol. 2 (Waynesboro, GA; Carlisle, Cumbria: Paternoster Press, 2002).

apart from insertion into a vibrant faith community. The communal nature of the RCIA is evident through the companionship of sponsors who accompany the catechumen through the process, the cohort of catechumens who experience the process together, and, most importantly, the faith community that receives them, supports them in prayer, and shows the way in Christian living through the example of their lives.

The meaning of Christian initiation is most evident in the Easter Vigil. In this holy night the faith community gathers to listen to God's word recount the story of salvation history and to participate in the liturgical celebration of Christ's passage from death to resurrection, the most important feast of the church year. The assembled faithful witness the reception of the sacraments of initiation in a unified rite and renew their own baptismal promises and profession of faith. The entire process of the RCIA represents Christian initiation in its fullness and is the lens through which initiation at any age is to be understood. In Christian initiation a person renounces sin, professes faith in Father, Son, and Spirit, receives the life of God's grace, is incorporated into the ecclesial body of Christ, undertakes a cruciform manner of life patterned on Christ's death and resurrection, and is anointed by the Spirit to participate in Christ's mission of proclaiming the kingdom of God. The event of initiation is preceded by a long period of learning the Christian way of life, engaging in conversion, and growing in faith. The period following the event of initiation, the period of postbaptismal catechesis known as mystagogia, is a time of further growth in faith and understanding of the sacramental experience.

These past two chapters have examined the pattern of initiation in a number of Christian traditions, since ecumenical dialogue suggests that these traditions may find more common ground in this larger pattern than they have been able to find in the event of baptism itself. However, the divergence within the traditions is not simply a different sequence of initiation, that is, whether personal faith is professed before or after baptism, whether or not a laying on of hands and prayer for the seal of the Spirit occurs before or after Eucharist. A deeper question would be: into what is the person being initiated? Here potentially lies greater confusion. Is one initiated into the church, into Christ's life, into discipleship as a pattern of life, or into some combination of these?[53] All the traditions would agree on the latter. Where a ritual for admission to

---

[53] So would say Fiddes, "Baptism and the Process of Christian Initiation," 59. However, he also describes baptism as participation in the fellowship of the Triune God.

membership in a church exists, it would appear that baptism does not constitute membership in the church. Here, however, various traditions might distinguish between the church of Christ or membership in a particular congregation. If baptism is truly regenerative, it would seem to initiate a person into a life of grace in Christ. What this reveals is that the problem of mutual recognition of baptism cannot be solved simply by identifying common patterns, regardless of the order of events, apart from the meaning or theology of baptism. In other words, mutual recognition requires not only agreement on the pattern of initiation, even while admitting certain variations, but also the meaning of initiation. For example, only the meaning of initiation can explain why baptism is oriented to the Eucharist as the completion of a process of initiation. The ecumenical movement seems to have laid aside the problems of the meaning of baptism as intractable in order to examine the patterns of initiation, only to find that the problem of meaning is not only still there, but is present in a more complex form, since multiple relationships pertain among the various elements of initiation.

Nevertheless, the churches cannot fall prey to a sort of baptismal Gnosticism whereby we achieve mutual recognition if only we get our theology right intellectually. At a very fundamental level, when churches baptize they intend to do what Jesus commanded, and they do it in imitation of his own baptism in the Jordan. Such obedience and engagement in Christian discipleship represents a profound commonality among those who engage in this practice. If it is indeed true that the ecumenical movement has discerned a common pattern in baptismal practice, then our work has only begun. The task that must engage Christian churches as a consequence of this common practice is to allow our self-understanding to be shaped by this practice so that there is no longer any discrepancy between the act of baptism and our explanation of it, between the practice of baptism and our understanding of the church as a baptismal community, between our immersion in the death and resurrection of Jesus and our anthropology.

These two chapters have shown that the practice of baptism and the patterns of initiation of many Christian churches share remarkable similarities. They have also pointed out some of the tensions between these practices and such self-defining ecclesial doctrines as justification by faith alone or God's sovereign election or covenant theology. The theological task is complex, for it is not simply a matter of testing our theology of baptism against theologies of justification, faith, or church. We must also allow our theologies of justification, faith, and church to be shaped by our practice of baptism. Some of the unresolved problems to be examined in the following chapters are the relation between faith and baptism and the relationship between baptism and justification, the relationship between baptism and Eucharist, and the relationship between baptism and an underlying theology of the church.

Chapter Six

Baptism, Faith, and Justification

One of the curiosities of history is that Catholics were out of communion with Lutherans and many other ecclesial communities issuing from the Reformation for five hundred years with respect to the doctrine of justification, while at the same time differences in the doctrine and practice of baptism were not considered to be church dividing.[1] Baptism has been called a sacrament of justification, yet theological treatments of justification remain all too often uninformed by a theology of baptism. Moreover, there seems to be an inconsistency between the requirements of justification by faith and the doctrine and practice of baptism, particularly the baptism of infants.

This chapter inquires into the relationship between a doctrine of justification by faith and the doctrine of baptism as a sacrament of justification. It focuses on the relationship between Lutherans and Catholics. Although Reformed theology of faith would differ little from Luther's,

---

[1] Lutheran–Roman Catholic unity on baptism was confirmed in the U.S. Joint Statement, "One Baptism for the Remission of Sins" (1966): "We were reasonably certain that the teachings of our respective traditions regarding baptism are in substantial agreement, and this opinion has been confirmed at this meeting." In *Building Unity: Ecumenical Dialogues with Roman Catholic Participation in the United States*. Ecumenical Documents IV, ed. Joseph A. Burgess and Jeffrey Gros (New York: Paulist Press, 1989), 90.

its theology of justification is more consistently forensic, as is evident in Calvin's refutation of Osiander (1498–1552), a Lutheran who taught that justification was not simply an act by which God declares the person just, but an act by which one is actually made just.[2] Furthermore, the efficacy of baptism in effecting justification is also conditioned by Calvin's doctrine of divine sovereignty and election, the tension between the Reformed emphasis on sanctification and the Lutheran doctrine of *simul justus et peccator*, and tensions between the Lutheran anthropocentric emphasis on *sola fide* and the Reformed theocentric emphasis on God's sovereignty and honor and glory.[3] Thus a comprehensive treatment of baptism, faith, and justification in the Reformed tradition would need its own chapter. Aside from this, the consensus agreement between Lutherans and Catholics in the *Joint Declaration on the Doctrine of Justification*, signed October 31, 1999, invites a testing of the relationship between faith and justification in these two traditions by means of this consensus document.[4]

This chapter first clarifies what is meant by faith, demonstrating a contemporary convergence toward a personalistic concept of faith that was not present at the time of the Reformation.[5] It then examines the extent to which justification and baptism are linked in Lutheran and Catholic confessional documents as well as in the *Joint Declaration on the Doctrine of Justification*. It concludes the section on faith by suggesting that a weakness of this document, as with many discussions of faith, baptism, and justification, is the failure to take into account the relationship between a faith community and an individual's confession of faith.

The chapter then takes up the topic of justification, first presenting the baptismal and transformational theology of justification in the canons and decrees of the Council of Trent. It then examines Lutheran documents, which show a tension between Luther's teaching on justification by faith

---

[2] John Calvin, *Institutes*, vol. 1, ed. John T. McNeill (Louisville: Westminster Press, 1960), Book 3.

[3] See Gabriel Fackre, "The *Joint Declaration* and the Reformed Tradition," in *Justification and the Future of the Ecumenical Movement*, ed. William G. Rusch (Collegeville, MN: Liturgical Press, 2003), 61–85. Fackre cautions against the firm linkage of baptism and justification in the *JDDJ*, pointing to the danger posed by a domestication of grace that precludes both the freedom of God and the response of faith (p. 75).

[4] The Lutheran World Federation and the Roman Catholic Church, *JDDJ* (Grand Rapids and Cambridge: Eerdmans, 2000).

[5] Some of this material was developed and published earlier in "Lutherans and Roman Catholics: Two Perspectives on Faith," *One in Christ* 37, no. 2 (2002): 46–60.

alone, often with a forensic emphasis, and regeneration through baptism. The *Joint Declaration on the Doctrine of Justification* is used as a test case to determine a relationship between baptism and justification that both Lutherans and Catholics can agree upon today. The chapter concludes that the distinction between justification through baptism and justification by faith alone is a false dichotomy since they do not represent two separate avenues to justification. Baptism is itself an act of faith, so that in being baptized a person is justified by both faith and baptism.

A Lutheran Understanding of Faith

Faith saves because of its object, the promised mercy of God. According to the *Apology of the Augsburg Confession* (1530), "faith does not justify or save because it is a good work in itself, but only because it accepts the promised mercy" (Article IV, 55). For Lutherans, faith occurs in the dynamic dialogical relationship of Christ's promise of forgiveness of sin received in faith by the believer on the strength of the faithfulness of the testator, Christ. From a Lutheran perspective the doctrine of justification can only be understood within this relationship of direct address. It is as if the eyes of the one who receives the promise are riveted on Christ. This promise, coextensive with the Gospel, is the living word of Christ addressed *pro me*.

The dialogical character of faith is underscored by its auditory character. As Carl Braaten has noted, for Luther the Gospel is not just a written text but an auditory event.[6] Faith comes by hearing.[7] The believer hears this word in existential inwardness addressed to him or her in personal specificity. It is not addressed to humankind in general, but to me, lost and condemned unless I hear that word of promise addressed to me personally. Furthermore, this promise is not a bargain along the line of "if you do your part I'll do mine." Nor is it only directed toward future hope; it is a proclamation of present grace.[8] Faith is pure receptivity and appropriation of the Gospel promise. It is a direct personal encounter with Christ the Word in the word of the Gospel. In the context of the

---

[6] Carl E. Braaten, *Justification: The Article by Which the Church Stands or Falls* (Minneapolis: Fortress Press, 1990), 94.

[7] "Romans, Chapter Ten," *Luther, Lectures on Romans*, trans. and ed. Wilhelm Pauck (Philadelphia: Westminster, 1961), 301.

[8] Ibid., 95.

direct address it means keeping our eyes on Christ. True faith is existential faith, the faith of personal experience. Luther writes:

> At this point, experience must enter in and enable a Christian to say, "Hitherto I have heard that Christ is my Savior, who conquered sin and death, and I believed it. Now my experience bears this out. For I was often in the agony of death and in the bonds of the devil, but he rescued me and manifested himself. Now I see and know that he loves me and that what I believe is true."[9]

This kind of faith is fiducial faith, that is, the faith of trust or confidence described by Luther thus:

> The other way is to believe in God, as I do when I not only believe that what is said about Him is true, but put my trust in Him, surrender myself to Him, and make bold to deal with Him, believing without doubt that he will be to me and do to me just what is said of Him. . . . That faith, which in life or death dares to believe that God is what He is said to be, is the only faith that makes a man a Christian and obtains from God whatever it will.[10]

This existential, fiducial faith is very different from intellectual faith, which Luther says even the devil has. Even the devil admits that Jesus Christ lived, died, and rose. What the devil fails to believe, however, is that Christ died *for him*.

This interpretation of the nature of faith is susceptible to two misinterpretations. The first is to turn faith into another kind of work wherein the person is the primary actor who earns justification by the work of faith. This is *my* faith. By professing my personal belief I claim the assurance of my salvation. However, faith is never my work, because it is the work of the Holy Spirit within me.[11] The *Apology*, written by Philipp

---

[9] Martin Luther, "Sermons on the Gospel of St. John (1537)," in *Luther's Works* (Saint Louis: Concordia, 1961), 151.

[10] Luther, "A Brief Explanation of the Ten Commandments, the Creed, and the Lord's Prayer" (1520), in *Werke*, vol. 7, at 25; *Works of Martin Luther*, vol. 2 (Philadelphia: Muhlenburg Press, 1943), 368. Cited by Avery Dulles, *The Assurance of Things Hoped For: A Theology of Christian Faith* (New York: Oxford University Press, 1994), 45.

[11] This is a danger in many confirmation programs for teenagers. They are so caught up in their personal ratification of their baptism that this faith starts to look like their work. According to this way of thinking, confirmation becomes a personal work of faith rather than the gratuitous gift of the Spirit.

Melanchthon (1497–1560), states, "Faith does not justify or save because it is a good work in itself."[12] Faith is not our work, a response of our free will, but the awareness we have in the power of the Spirit that salvation is *for* us. In other words, faith alone is grace alone, for faith itself is not our effort but the reception of the promise wrought in us by Christ in the Spirit. When Luther asserts that we are justified by faith alone he means that, placing no hope in ourselves, we accept Christ as our righteousness. In this environment, justification by faith underscores the absolute gratuitousness of God's offer of salvation. We are justified by grace alone through faith alone on account of Christ alone.

A second misinterpretation makes faith autonomous and individualistic. An awareness of two characteristics of faith helps us to avoid this pitfall. First, Hans Schwartz has rightly noted that Luther's faith is not autonomous, but rather theonomous. The source of faith is not in the believer but in the word of God. Faith comes through the word of the Gospel, which promises the free gift of salvation to those who believe. Faith comes from the Holy Spirit, and the person of faith is subject to God's authority, living for God and from God.[13]

Second, although faith is intensely personal, it does not exist in isolation. Faith requires the support of a community of faith. The faith and prayers of others serve to strengthen our faith and we are called upon to mutually strengthen and encourage one another in faith. However, as I will develop later, in the Roman Catholic tradition the community does more than support an individual's personal faith. Nor can we identify a faith community as the collectivity of individuals who first have faith and then join a community of faith. At some level a person is initiated into the faith of the community. There is a communal dimension to faith not accounted for in Luther's doctrine.

Baptism and Faith

In the *Large Catechism* Luther responds to the objection that we are saved by faith alone without works and external things added to faith. He answers that faith must have something to believe, something to

[12] Philipp Melanchthon, *Apology of the Augsburg Confession*, 4:56, in *The Book of Concord: The Confessions of the Evangelical Lutheran Church*, ed. Robert Kolb and Timothy J. Wengert (Minneapolis: Fortress Press, 2000), 129.

[13] Hans Schwarz, *True Faith in the True God: An Introduction to Luther's Life and Thought* (Minneapolis: Augsburg, 1996), 58.

which it may cling and upon which it may stand. Faith clings to the water, the external sign, believing it to be baptism. In the water, through its incorporation with God's word and ordinance and the joining of God's name to it, there is salvation and life. Faith cannot be separated from the object to which it is attached and secured on the grounds that the object is something external. Baptism does not rest on faith, but on the Word of God, who instituted it.[14] However, baptism without faith contributes nothing toward salvation and receives nothing. Here Luther attempts to stake out a middle ground. First, baptism is not a human work but God's work. Second, this work of God requires a human response of faith. In other words, baptism is God's work grasped in faith. Because the lack of faith does not render baptism invalid, baptism is never repeated, even if first received in the absence of faith. Where faith is lacking, however, baptism remains an unfruitful sign. According to Luther, in baptism we have the promise that we shall be saved and have eternal life both in soul and in body. The water and the word constitute one baptism. The soul is saved through the word in which it believes and the body is saved because it is united with the soul and apprehends baptism in a bodily way.[15]

Luther and Infant Baptism

The connection between faith and baptism raises the question of infant baptism.[16] Luther observes that many people who have been baptized as infants show evidence that they have received the Holy Spirit and have been sanctified. Second, he notes that the validity of baptism does not depend on faith, but on God's word and commandment. He says: "Faith does not make baptism; rather, it receives baptism."[17] Furthermore, he holds that no one has proved that infants do not believe.[18] He cites a number of Scripture texts that attest to the innocence of children. The logic is that since they are innocent they must be graced. If they are

[14] "On Baptism," (1528), in *Luther's Works: Sermons I*, vol. 51 (Philadelphia: Muhlenberg Press, 1959), 186.

[15] *The Large Catechism*, IV:46–49.

[16] *The Large Catechism*, IV:46, in Kolb and Wengert, eds., *The Book of Concord: The Confessions of the Evangelical Lutheran Church*, 462. See Eero Huovinen, *Fides Infantium: Martin Luthers Lehre vom Kinderglauben* (Mainz: Philipp von Zabern, 1997).

[17] *Large Catechism*, IV:53.

[18] "Concerning Rebaptism" (1528), in *Luther's Works, Church and Ministry II*, vol. 40 (Philadelphia: Muhlenberg Press, 1958), 241, 254, *passim*.

graced, they must have faith. In support of this he cites the innocent bloodshed in the offering of children to idols by the Jews, the slaughter of the Holy Innocents, and the leaping in the womb of the unborn John the Baptist.[19] He also recalls that Christ said that the kingdom of heaven belongs to children (Matt 19:14) and commanded that the children be brought to him (Matt 19:14). Just as children were accepted through the covenant of circumcision, Luther thought that God would also accept children through the covenant of baptism.[20] Luther also says in "The Babylonian Captivity of the Church": "Infants are aided by the faith of others, namely those who bring them for baptism, although this is not an argument in the catechisms."[21] Even though the belief of infants is only hinted at in the *Large Catechism*, Luther held, if somewhat tentatively, that infants do believe because faith itself is a work of God. He understands this as not an active "grasping" or "clinging," words normally applied to the faith of adults, on the part of the child, but rather as a passive reception of faith as a pure gift of God.[22] This is not far from the teaching of Thomas Aquinas that baptism infuses the virtues. Thomas cites Augustine as saying: "a little child becomes a believer by the sacrament of faith itself, which causes the habit of faith, even though not yet by that faith which is rooted in the will of the believer."[23] The logic in the context of infant baptism would be that the faith infused by baptism enables the recipient to respond to the gift of baptism in faith. Both the gift and the ability to receive the gift are gratuitous gifts of God and not human works. Finally, Luther thought that we baptize on the command of God with the intent and hope and prayer that the infant may believe.[24]

Catholic Understandings of Faith

The divisive issue between Lutherans and Catholics has never been whether or not we are justified by faith. The Council of Trent explicitly affirmed faith in Christ as the sole source of justification: "we are said

---

[19] Ibid., 242.

[20] Ibid., 244.

[21] "The Babylonian Captivity of the Church," 197.

[22] See Edmund Schlink, *The Doctrine of Baptism*, trans. Herbert J. A. Bouman (St. Louis: Concordia Publishing House, 1972), 144. See also the discussion in Jonathan D. Trigg, *Baptism in the Theology of Martin Luther* (New York: Brill, 1994), 102–9.

[23] ST III, q. 69, a. 6.

[24] "On Baptism," 187.

to be justified by faith because faith is the first stage of human salvation, the foundation and root of all justification, without which *it is impossible to please God* and come to the fellowship of his children."[25]

When the Council of Trent responded to the questions about faith raised by the Reformation in connection with the Decree on Justification, drawn up in the second half of 1546, the Catholics were themselves divided among three positions: the Augustinian, the Scotist, and the Thomist. The Augustinians affirmed on the basis of texts from Paul and Augustine that faith has the power to effect justification. The Thomists described justification as effected by the gift of habitual grace, which was inseparable from the theological virtues of faith, hope, and charity. The Scotists, emphasizing the act of faith more than the infused virtues, considered faith as one of a series of acts necessarily preceding the justification of an adult.[26]

The council wished to avoid condemning any of these three positions and incorporated elements of each in its text. Chapter 5 of the Decree on Justification reaffirms the Augustinian position on the necessity of the illumination of the Holy Spirit for even the beginning of faith (canon 3) and stresses the active cooperation of the human subject in the process of justification (canons 4–6). Chapter 6 supports the teaching of Scotus in naming faith as the first of six preparatory acts. Here faith is described as primarily an assent to the truth of what has been divinely revealed and promised: "People are disposed for that justice when, roused and helped by divine grace and attaining the faith that comes from hearing, they are moved freely towards God and believe to be true what has been divinely revealed and promised, and in particular that the wicked are justified by God *by his grace through the redemption which is in Christ Jesus.*"[27]

Chapter 7 discusses the disposition and preparation of justification itself. Following Thomas, the council cites baptism, the sacrament of faith, as the instrumental cause of justification. The formal cause of justification is the justness of God: "not that by which he himself is just, but that by which he makes us just and endowed with which we are renewed

---

[25] Council of Trent, Decree on Justification, Session VI, 13 January 1547, chap. 8. The translation of the texts of the Council of Trent is from Norman P. Tanner, ed., *Decrees of the Ecumenical Councils*, vol. 2, *Trent to Vatican II* (Washington, DC: Georgetown University Press, 1990), 674. Italics in original.

[26] Ibid., 48.

[27] Council of Trent, Decree on Justification, chap. 6, in Tanner, *Decrees*, 672. Italics in original.

in the spirit of our mind, and are not merely considered to be just but which are truly named and are just, each one of us receiving individually his own justness according to the measure which the holy Spirit apportions to each one as he wills, and in view of each one's dispositions and co-operation."[28] In the process of justification we receive forgiveness of sins and the infused virtues of faith, hope, and charity. Faith without hope or charity does not unite us perfectly with Christ or make us living members of his body. Faith without works is dead. Faith working through love avails for justification.

Chapter 8 accepts in a qualified way the Augustinian idea that we are "justified by faith and freely" (DS 1532).[29] The council states that "we are justified by faith because faith is the first stage of human salvation, the foundation and root of all justification, without which *it is impossible to please God* and come to the fellowship of his children." Furthermore, we receive justification freely because "nothing that precedes justification, neither faith nor works, would merit the grace of justification; for *if it is by grace, it is no longer on the basis of works; otherwise . . . grace would no longer be grace.*" Here the council refutes semi-Pelagianism. Faith is not a point of departure for justification, but rather accompanies and sustains the whole process of justification.[30]

Chapter 9 states that a person's sins cannot be said to be forgiven simply because he is certain that they have been forgiven, and relies solely on that conviction. Furthermore, it states: "neither should it be declared . . . that no one is absolved from sin and justified except one who believes with certainty that he has been absolved and justified, and that absolution and justification are effected by this faith alone—as if one who does not believe this is casting doubts on God's promises and on the efficacy of the death and resurrection of Christ."[31] The act of faith does not effect absolution and justification. These are the work of the promise and the gratuitous mercy of God. The Reformers would not object, since for them faith is but the act of grabbing hold of God's promise of forgiveness.

Chapter 12 warns against rash presumption about predestination. We are not to hold for certain that we are unquestionably included among

[28] Council of Trent, Decree on Justification, chap. 7, in Tanner, *Decrees*, 673.
[29] Cited by Dulles, *The Assurance of Things Hoped For*, 49.
[30] Council of Trent, Decree on Justification, chap. 8, in Tanner, *Decrees*, 674. Italics in original.
[31] Council of Trent, Decree on Justification, chap. 9, in Tanner, *Decrees*, 674.

the predestined, as if one justified is either no longer capable of sin, or, if that one sins, may feel sure of repentance. We cannot be certain of our salvation because of the sin incompatible with justification of which we are capable.

While the Lutheran looks primarily at the promise of Christ, the Roman Catholic emphasizes what may transpire through human freedom. The Lutheran position is christocentric; the Catholic analysis is anthropocentric. For the Reformers justifying grace is completely identical with God's forgiving love and thus is a reality on God's side alone. Luther says: "Here, as ought to be done, I take grace in the proper sense of the favor of God—not a quality of soul, as is taught by our more recent writers."[32] For Roman Catholics justifying grace is a reality in the soul of the human being. The primary difference is whether we view justification from the side of God or the side of what is effected in the human being.

The same difference in perspective affects our perception of faith. For the Reformers faith is theocentric. For Catholics it was a theological habit of soul informed by grace. The fiducial faith of the Reformers is insufficient for justification, as canon 23 states: "If anyone says that faith which justifies is nothing else but trust in the divine mercy, which pardons sins because of Christ; or that it is that trust alone by which we are justified: let him be anathema." Ironically, Trent considered fiducial faith to be a human work since it considered faith primarily as an action of the person who believes, that is, the subject of the act of faith. The Reformers, on the other hand, considered fiducial faith to be theocentric and christocentric because it primarily considered the object of faith rather than the subject of faith.

The fathers of the Council of Trent followed the medieval tradition by considering faith first as the assent of the understanding to the revealed Word of God, and as the "objective" belief expressed in the church's creed and its proclaimed doctrine.[33] This is an understanding of faith as notional belief rather than the faith of the heart. It is also well to remember that the council fathers' context affected their teaching on faith. They were considering a "catalogue of errors" in Protestant statements. Thus the very context was a series of propositions to be assented to in faith or refuted. This context underscored the notional aspect of faith.

---

[32] *Antilatomus, Werke*, 8, 106, 10; *Luther's Works*, 32, 227. Cited in Karl Lehmann and Wolfhart Pannenberg, eds., *The Condemnations of the Reformation Era: Do They Still Divide?* (Minneapolis: Fortress Press, 1990), 33.

[33] Ibid., 49.

This intellectualist approach to faith was further emphasized after the council. For example, Domingo de Soto, Ruard Tapper, and Thomas Stapleton emphasized the strictly intellectual character of faith as an assent to revealed truth more than the Council of Trent itself and denied that faith necessarily involves trustful confidence of being justified.[34] Robert Bellarmine (1542–1621), another major figure of the Catholic Reformation, considered faith to be an obedient submission of the intellect prompted by the inclination of the will, drawn by grace.[35] He held fiducial faith to be faulty because (1) faith could not be certain and infallible if it rested on anything but God's word, (2) nowhere in the word of God am I told that I myself am saved or my sins forgiven, and (3) faith is only one of several disposing causes of justification, others being fear of punishment, repentance, and love. He held the true cause of justification to be not faith, but God's righteousness inhering in us.[36] This places the source of justification squarely in God's activity rather than in human response. Bellarmine's intellectualist view of faith reached a sort of culmination in Vatican I, which described faith as full submission of intellect and will "by means of which with the grace of God inspiring and assisting us, we believe to be true what he has revealed, not because we perceive its intrinsic truth by the natural light of reason, but because of the authority of God himself, who makes the revelation and can neither deceive nor be deceived."[37] This follows the propositional notion of revelation in chapter 1 of the Dogmatic Constitution on the Catholic Faith from Vatican I, which speaks of the revelation of the "eternal laws of his [God's] will." Faith, from Trent to Vatican II, was primarily considered to be intellectual assent to these decrees.

Contemporary Developments in the Catholic Understanding of Faith

Vatican II's Dogmatic Constitution on Divine Revelation (*Dei Verbum*) begins its account of divine revelation by identifying the fullness of revelation with Jesus Christ.[38] This will correspond to a personalistic

[34] Dulles, *The Assurance of Things Hoped For*, 51.
[35] Ibid.
[36] Ibid., 51–52.
[37] Vatican I, Session III, Dogmatic Constitution on the Catholic Faith, chap. 3.
[38] DV 2.

notion of faith as a "total and free self commitment to God," although this constitution surprisingly treats the nature of reception of revelation by faith in only one paragraph and largely repeats what had been said about faith at Vatican I:

> In response to God's revelation our duty is "the obedience of faith" (see Rom 16:26; compare Rom 1:5; 2 Cor 10:5-6). By this a human being makes a total and free self-commitment to God, offering "the full submission of intellect and will to God as he reveals," and willingly assenting to the revelation he gives.[39]

The text then notes the necessity of God's grace, which both anticipates and accompanies our act of faith, of the assistance of the Holy Spirit, and of the growth in understanding of revelation that is possible to us. Clearly the act of faith is not a human work, although it engages our whole selves with special mention of our intellect and will. Assent of intellect and will corresponds to the more propositional concept of revelation that prevailed at Vatican I. Even though the text places Vatican I's emphasis on the assent of faith by intellect and will in the broader context of total self-commitment, it does not develop this personal aspect of faith in any detail, nor does it develop the dialogical character of faith.

A fair summary may be that although Vatican II's document repeats Vatican I's propositional description of revelation as the "eternal decrees of his [God's] will concerning the salvation of humankind" at the end of chapter 1, it subordinates this propositional concept of revelation to a personalistic concept of Jesus Christ as the fullness of revelation. This personalistic presentation, however, failed to carry through to a correspondingly robust personalistic account of faith.

A more adequate treatment of faith in the Roman Catholic tradition is given in the *Catechism of the Catholic Church*. Here faith is situated within the personalistic context of invitation and response:

> *By his Revelation*, "the invisible God, from the fullness of his love, addresses men as his friends, and moves among them, in order to invite and receive them into his own company." The adequate response to this invitation is faith.[40]

---

[39] DV 5, in Tanner, *Decrees*, 973.
[40] *Catechism* 142.

> *By faith*, man completely submits his intellect and his will to God. With his whole being man gives his assent to God the revealer. Sacred Scripture calls this human response to God, the author of revelation, "the obedience of faith."[41]

The text then draws on a personal typology of faith, presenting Abraham and Mary as models of faith. It encompasses the complexity of faith as both personal adherence to God and assent to the truth of revelation in the statement, "Faith is first of all a personal adherence of man to God. At the same time, and inseparably, it is a *free assent to the whole truth that God has revealed.*"[42]

Faith Born of Word and Sacrament

A consideration of faith from a Catholic perspective must also examine its role within the sacraments and the interrelationship among word, sacrament, and faith. The mission to baptize is implied in the mission to evangelize, the preaching of the word to elicit faith. The dominical command is: "Go therefore and make disciples of all nations, baptizing them in the name of the Father and of the Son and of the Holy Spirit, and teaching them to obey everything that I have commanded you" (Matt 28:19-20). In this text the act of baptizing is the middle term within the *inclusio* of making disciples and teaching. The implied preaching of the word of God and the faith that is assent to this word is preparation for baptism. The Decree on the Ministry and Life of Priests from Vatican II similarly connects preaching the word and sacramental ministry: "The People of God is formed into one in the first place by the Word of the living God. . . . The preaching of the Word is required for the sacramental ministry itself, since the sacraments are sacraments of faith, drawing their origin and nourishment from the Word."[43]

The sacraments in the Roman Catholic Church presuppose faith and also nourish, strengthen, and express it.[44] The church does not require a perfect and mature faith for baptism, but "a beginning that is called to

[41] *Catechism* 143.
[42] *Catechism* 150.
[43] *Presbyterorum ordinis*, 4, par. 1, 2. Cited in *Catechism* 1122.
[44] *Catechism* 1123.

develop."[45] The Rite of Acceptance into the Order of Catechumens asks of a candidate: "What do you ask of God's Church?" The response is "faith!"[46] The presupposition is that the church's faith precedes that of the catechumen who is invited to adhere to it.[47]

The baptismal rite includes a threefold confession of faith from the catechumen or the parents and godparents:

Celebrant: Do you believe in God the Father almighty,
creator of heaven and earth?

Response: I do.

Celebrant: Do you believe in Jesus Christ, his only Son, our Lord,
Who was born of the Virgin Mary,
Was crucified, died, and was buried,
Rose from the dead,
And is now seated at the right hand of the Father?

Response: I do.

Celebrant: Do you believe in the Holy Spirit,
The holy catholic Church, the communion of saints,
The forgiveness of sins, the resurrection of the body,
And life everlasting?

Response: I do.

The celebrant and the congregation then give their assent to the profession of faith in these words or in some other way in which the community can express its faith:

This is our faith. This is the faith of the Church. We are proud to profess it, in Christ Jesus our Lord.

All: Amen.

The baptismal profession of faith is an interrogative form of the Apostles' Creed divided into its three articles, one for each person of the Trinity, to which the catechumen gives assent. The acclamation given by the celebrant and the congregation attests that the faith of the person being baptized and the faith of the church are one and the same faith. Thus the catechumen, through an individual profession of faith, joins a

[45] *Catechism* 1253.
[46] Rite of Christian Initiation of Adults, 50.
[47] *Catechism* 1124.

community of faith and commits himself or herself to growing in that faith throughout the catechumenate.

The Rite of Christian Initiation of Adults shifted the emphasis in Christian formation from an intellectual model of instruction in the faith to a model of personal conversion. More than an intellectual conversion, the conversion required by the RCIA encompasses affective, moral, and communal dimensions of a person's life. Just as conversion is a process of development during the catechumenate, so is growth in faith, especially when it is seen to be growth in a personal relationship with God. Thus the kind of faith required by the RCIA is consistent with the notion of revelation promoted by the Dogmatic Constitution on Revelation.

Two Views of Faith: A Summary

This presentation of the nature of faith within the Lutheran and Catholic traditions has shown faith to be a complex reality. "Faith" encompasses both the objective content of faith expressed in the teaching of the church and a more subjective response of the believer to the Gospel in which the human person entrusts himself or herself to God. Faith is both adherence of the intellect to revelation and submission in obedience to God. When Catholics hear the Lutheran doctrine expressed as justification by "faith alone," they tend to understand faith differently than Lutherans do. In spite of Vatican II's personalistic emphasis in *Dei Verbum*, the Dogmatic Constitution on Divine Revelation, which identifies Jesus Christ as the sum of revelation and invites us to enter into a personal relationship with him, Catholics still carry around vestiges of a more propositional notion of revelation and tend at times to identify faith with an intellectual assent to truth. Thus there is a tendency for Roman Catholics to think that the Lutheran doctrine allows Lutherans to intellectually believe, then do what they will and still be saved. However, Lutherans understand faith as placing one's trust wholly in the Creator and Redeemer and thus living in communion with him.[48]

This understanding of fiducial faith, theocentric and christocentric in nature, does not reduce a trusting faith to a human work. This faith affects all dimensions of the person and leads to a life of hope and love. Faith is a way of living, not merely intellectual assent to religious truths. The Reformers understood faith as the forgiveness and fellowship with

[48] *JDDJ*, 26.

Christ effected by the word of promise. Faith is unconditional trust in the merciful God now and at the final judgment. It is a personalistic or holistic notion of faith involving the disposition of the whole person, not just intellect and will.

The character of faith differs according to one's dominant theology of revelation. A personalistic concept of revelation results in a dialogical address/response dynamic of faith. Roman Catholics have appropriated a more personalistic notion of faith through the identification of Jesus Christ as the fullness of revelation by the Second Vatican Council, the development of a personalistic description of faith in the *Catechism*, and an emphasis on conversion and growth in faith in the Rite of Christian Initiation of Adults.

This convergence on the nature of faith provides a foundation for an examination of the relationship between a doctrine of justification by faith and the doctrine of baptism as a sacrament of justification. The *Joint Declaration on the Doctrine of Justification*, a consensus statement of the Lutheran World Federation and the Roman Catholic Church, provides a basis for this inquiry since it represents a common understanding of justification between the two traditions.

Faith in the *Joint Declaration on the Doctrine of Justification*

Lutherans and Roman Catholics signed the *Joint Declaration on the Doctrine of Justification* on October 31, 1999. By signing the Official Common Statement the two partners in dialogue confirm two points. First, Lutherans and Roman Catholics affirm that they have reached a high level of consensus on basic truths regarding the doctrine of justification. Second, they declare that the mutual condemnations from the time of the Reformation concerning the doctrine of justification do not apply to the teaching on justification as set forth by Lutherans and Roman Catholics in the *Joint Declaration*. This is not simply one dialogue document among many; for the first time the Roman Catholic Church and the Lutheran churches of the world intend to declare in a binding manner that an understanding has been reached on a question of faith and doctrine that has been divisive for centuries.

The key statement of the *Joint Declaration on the Doctrine of Justification* occurs in section 15: "Together we confess: By grace alone, in faith in Christ's saving work and not because of any merit on our part, we are accepted by God and receive the Holy Spirit, who renews our hearts while equipping and calling us to good works." The emphasis is on justification by grace through faith, a phrase taken from Romans 3:23-25: "For there is no distinction, since all have sinned and fall short of the glory of God; they are now justified by his grace as a gift, through the redemption that is in Christ Jesus, whom God put forward as a sacrifice of atonement by his blood, effective through faith." This statement speaks of being accepted by grace alone through faith rather than being justified by faith alone through grace. This same relationship between faith and grace occurs in another text cited in the *Joint Declaration*, Ephesians 2:8-9: "For by grace you have been saved through faith. And this is not your own doing; it is the gift of God—not the result of works."

It is interesting to compare *JDDJ* 3.15: "by grace alone," 4.3.26: "by faith alone," and 4.6.32: "the mercy of God in Christ . . . alone." Catholics and Lutherans are able to confess "by grace alone," but the phrase "by faith alone" is reserved to Lutherans in this text. The *JDDJ* text only puts "by faith alone" on the lips of Lutherans. The USA bilateral statement "Justification by Faith" (1983) had already observed that (1) an affirmation of our entire hope of justification and salvation resting on Christ Jesus and on the Gospel and (2) an affirmation that our ultimate trust is not in anything other than God's promise and saving work in Christ are not fully equivalent to the Reformation teaching on justification according to which God accepts sinners as righteous for Christ's sake on the basis of faith alone.[49] However, it noted that these affirmations express the central concern of that doctrine, namely, that reliance for salvation should be placed entirely on God. Ultimately, the Reformation doctrine of justification by faith alone serves as a criterion for church practices, structures, and traditions because its counterpart is "Christ alone."[50] In other words, our understanding of faith and "faith alone" is conditioned by our claims of salvation through Christ alone. Herein lies the weight of the consensus achieved in the *JDDJ*. Our two communions confess together that we are saved by Christ. Grace describes the effect of Christ's righteousness in us. Faith describes how we enter into communion with Christ, the communion in grace that results in our justification.

The *JDDJ* affirms justification by faith, but it does not develop any particular understanding of faith, although the context is clearly person-

---

[49] H. George Anderson, T. Austin Murphy, and Joseph A. Burgess, *Justification by Faith*. Lutherans and Catholics in Dialogue VII (Minneapolis: Augsburg, 1985), 157.

[50] Ibid., 160.

alistic. It adopts the perspective of direct address of promise and reception of that promise by stating that sinners "place their trust in God's gracious promise by justifying faith."[51] The document does not describe faith as assent of intellect and will. It says that "such a faith is active in love" so that a Christian cannot and should not remain without works.[52] Here faith is primarily viewed from the perspective of how it relates to the other virtues of hope and love. This section also associates faith with the action of the Holy Spirit in baptism through which sinners are granted salvation.

One's perception of the nature of faith shifts depending on whether one speaks of it in a baptismal context, in the situation of a response to hearing the Gospel preached, or in a declaration of penitential forgiveness. Perhaps one of the greatest weaknesses of the *Joint Declaration* is the absence of any ecclesial references. The terms of the Reformation discussion framed the issues individualistically. Certainly each person is addressed personally by God and responds with a personal act of faith. However, frequently this address is mediated through the community: through the preaching of the word of God, the teaching of the church, the example of holy lives of those who share faith, and communal prayer. A response of faith is given not only within one's heart, but also in the public liturgical prayer of the community that professes the Creed and prays the great doxologies of the church. Within the relationship between our personal faith and membership in a faith community, charity is no longer in danger of becoming a "work" that "merits" justification, but becomes a distinctive characteristic of the community of faith.

Catholic Teaching on Justification

The Catholic Church teaches that that the effects of justification and baptism are one and the same since we are justified through baptism. Of the sixteen chapters in the Decree Concerning Justification, baptism is mentioned in five.[53] Baptism and justification effect interior transformation in Christ. Christians are made righteous and interiorly healed of the wounds of sin. In the Roman Catholic tradition justification "is the

[51] *JDDJ*, 26.
[52] Ibid.
[53] In addition to those chapters just cited, it occurs in chapter 11, which compares the restoration of justification through penance to the original justification in baptism.

acceptance of God's righteousness through faith in Jesus Christ."[54] It is merited for us by the passion of Christ "whose blood has become the instrument of atonement" for our sins.[55] We are justified by Christ through the power of the Holy Spirit. We are justified by faith in Jesus Christ, for by faith we accept God's righteousness.[56] The effect of justification is the forgiveness of sin and interior healing.[57] We are not only declared righteous, but made righteous. Faith, hope, and charity are poured into our hearts.[58] For Catholics, justification entails sanctification. The *Catechism* cites the Council of Trent and Romans 6:19, 22 in this respect, stating: "Justification is not only the remission of sins, but also the sanctification and renewal of the interior man."[59] The text from Romans urges: ". . . just as you once presented your members as slaves to impurity and to greater and greater iniquity, so now present your members as slaves to righteousness for sanctification. . . . But now that you have been freed from sin and enslaved to God, the advantage you get is sanctification. The end is eternal life." Justification is forgiveness of sin, and forgiveness of sin effects the sanctification of the individual. Trent associates the gifts of grace and charity with the remission of sin and justification: "If anyone shall say that men are justified either by the sole imputation of the justice of Christ, or by the sole remission of sins, to the exclusion of grace and charity, which is poured forth in their hearts by the Holy Spirit and remains in them, or even that the grace by which we are justified is only the favor of God: let him be anathema."[60]

The presupposition is that a person is not only declared righteous, but is also made righteous. A change occurs in the person whose sin is forgiven. As sin affects the state of a person before God, so also does grace. In scholastic terms this meant a "translation from that state in which man is born a child of the first Adam, to the state of grace and of the adoption of the sons of God through the second Adam, Jesus Christ, our Savior."[61] This is described as "a new birth." In fact, the Council of Trent used the language of "being born again" saying: ". . . if they were not born again in Christ, they would never be justified, since in that new

---

[54] *Catechism* 1991.
[55] Ibid., 1992.
[56] Ibid., 1991.
[57] Ibid., 1990.
[58] Ibid., 1991.
[59] Council of Trent (1547); DS 1528, cited in *Catechism* 1989.
[60] Council of Trent, Decree Concerning Justification, canon 11.
[61] Council of Trent, Session VI, chap. 4.

birth there is bestowed upon them, through the merit of His passion, the grace by which they are made just."[62] Thus Trent's interpretation of justification is very baptismal in its transformational language. Trent's description of justification speaks of "the grace by which they are *made* just, and the translation from that *state* in which man is born a child of the first Adam, to the *state* of grace."[63]

Justification has been merited for us by the passion of Christ.[64] No one can merit the initial grace of forgiveness and justification.[65] However, Catholics hold that after this initial grace, again through the grace of the Holy Spirit, "we can then merit for ourselves and for others the graces needed for our sanctification, for the increase of grace and charity, and for the attainment of eternal life."[66] Human merit is itself a grace and is due to God,[67] and with regard to God, there is no strict right to any merit on the part of human beings.

Chapter 16, the final chapter in Trent's Decree on Justification, offers a final summary statement of the Roman Catholic position on justification:

> Our own personal justice is not established as something coming from us, nor is the justice of God disregarded or rejected; what is called our justice, because we are justified by its abiding in us, is that same justice of God, in that it is imparted to us by God through the merit of Christ. However, it must not be overlooked that, though so much is attributed in scripture to good works (Christ indeed promises that anyone who gives a cup of cold water to one of the least of his little ones will not lack his reward; and the Apostle bears witness: *This slight momentary affliction is preparing for us an eternal weight of glory beyond comparison*) yet no Christian should ever either rely on or glory in himself and not in the Lord, whose goodness towards all is so great that he desires his own gifts to be their merits.[68]

This is a fine statement that our justification is not our own and comes from Christ alone through grace alone while at the same time appealing

---

[62] Council of Trent, Session VI, chap. 3.

[63] Council of Trent, Decree Concerning Justification, Session VI, chaps. 3 and 4 (emphasis added).

[64] *Catechism* 1992.

[65] Ibid., 2010.

[66] Ibid.

[67] Council of Trent, Decree on Justification (cf. DS 1545).

[68] Council of Trent, Decree on Justification, chap. 16, in Tanner, *Decrees*, 678. Italics (citing 2 Cor 3:5) in original.

to scriptural foundations for a doctrine of merit. Adolf von Harnack, Protestant historian of dogma, has said: "The Decree on Justification, although a product of art, is in many respects remarkably well constructed; indeed, it may be doubted whether the Reformation would have developed itself if this Decree had been issued at the Lateran Council at the beginning of the century, and had really passed into the flesh and blood of the Church."[69]

Baptism and Justification in Catholic Teaching

Sometimes the question is posed to Catholics: Does the water of baptism save or does Christ's atoning blood save? The teaching on justification makes it clear that justification is through Christ alone in the power of the Spirit. The Tridentine teaching on baptism must be understood in terms of the scholastic categories of the day, which included a distinction between formal, final, efficient, and instrumental causality. The formal cause of justification, that is, the form or shape that justification takes, is the justice of God by which we are healed. The final cause, that is, the end or purpose of justification, is the glory of God and of Christ and life everlasting. The efficient cause, that is, that by which justification is made possible, "is the merciful God who washes and sanctifies, gratuitously signing and anointing with the holy Spirit of promise, who is the pledge of our inheritance." The meritorious cause, that is, that which merits justification, is Jesus Christ who "merited for us justification by His most holy passion on the wood of the cross and made satisfaction for us to God the Father." These causes are all God. Only then is baptism, which is the sacrament of faith, the instrumental cause of justification, the tool used by God for the work of justification. The instrumental cause is that by which the other causes take effect, but this would not be possible without the presence of the other causes. When viewed in relation to the other causes, it is the least of them, since it cannot stand alone.

Thus it would be false to say that "salvation is in the water" or baptism justifies apart from Christ or that justification comes from a human act if that act were not also the act of Christ. Roman Catholic teaching since the time of Augustine and the Donatist controversy has taught that Christ is the principal actor in the sacraments. Christ baptizes through the ministrations of the church.

[69] Adolf von Harnack, *History of Dogma*, vol. 7 (New York: Dover Publications, 1968), 57. Cited in Dulles, *The Assurance of Things Hoped For*, 50.

In the Catholic *Catechism* the connection between baptism and justification is made very directly, both from the side of a theology of baptism and within a theology of justification. The Council of Trent speaks of being justified by being born again in Christ.[70] The translation from that state of the first Adam to the adoption in grace through the second Adam, Jesus Christ, is effected through the laver of regeneration or its desire. The council at this point picks up the Johannine terminology of John 3:5 on the necessity of baptism.[71] The Council of Trent names baptism as the instrumental cause of justification and names it as the sacrament of faith without which no one can ever be justified.[72]

Baptism and Justification in Lutheran Teaching

Baptism and justification are rarely associated with each other in Lutheran confessional documents. The word "justification" does not occur in the sections dealing with baptism in either Luther's *Small Catechism* or his *Large Catechism*. Nor does the third part of the *Smalcald Articles* on "How One is Justified before God and of Good Works" contain a reference to baptism. A reference to baptism does not occur in the *Augsburg Confession* in Article 4 on justification.

Conversely, the word "righteous" does not occur in connection with baptism in the *Large Catechism*, although it occurs once in the *Small Catechism*. In the *Augsburg Confession* justification is not mentioned in Article IX, which states the necessity of baptism for salvation. The strongest connection occurs in the *Apology of the Augsburg Confession*, which states: "But those who are righteous have it as a gift, because after the washing [of baptism] they were justified.[73]

Although we are here speaking of nonconfessional writing, it is perhaps significant to note a shift in two sermons by Martin Luther on righteousness. In a 1518 sermon, "On Threefold Righteousness," he describes a civic righteousness, an intrinsic righteousness, and an imputed righteousness. Within his discussion of intrinsic righteousness he identifies baptism as conferring righteousness: "This [righteousness] is conferred

---

[70] Council of Trent, Session VI, chap. 3.

[71] Ibid., chap. 4.

[72] Ibid., chap. 7.

[73] Philip Melanchthon, *Apology of the Augsburg Confession*, article 4, 103, in *The Book of Concord: The Confessions of the Evangelical Lutheran Church*, ed. Robert Kolb and Timothy J. Wengert (Minneapolis: Fortress Press, 2000).

through baptism; this is properly what the Gospel announces, and is not the righteousness of the law, but the righteousness of grace."[74] However, this may have been corrected in his 1519 sermon, "On Twofold Righteousness," based on Philippians 2:5-11, which expresses a more Reformed theology of justification.[75] Here righteousness is the alien righteousness of Christ that is infused from outside us and the second is the fruit of this, namely, our own righteousness. The teaching on a twofold righteousness was incorporated into the third article of the *Formula of Concord*.

One reason for the apparent disjunction between a theology of baptism and a theology of justification may be the polemical context of both discussions. The sixteenth-century documents on baptism are more directly concerned with refuting the Anabaptists; hence the emphasis on the connection between the word and the water in the Lutheran documents and the support for infant baptism on the part of both Lutherans and Catholics. Lutheran texts on justification are preoccupied with a faith/works polemic, emphasizing salvation through grace by faith. Justifying grace is identical with God's forgiving love and is a reality on God's side alone.[76]

Convergences between Catholics and Lutherans

Both Lutheran and Roman Catholic texts on baptism incorporate language such as "rebirth," "new creature," "rising," or "resurrection." The language of regeneration and new birth has been retained in the Lutheran baptismal liturgy since its initial form in 1523, in the more radical revision of it in 1526, and in the 2006 rite of *Evangelical Lutheran Worship*.[77]

[74] Martin Luther, "Sermon on Threefold Righteousness," from Philippians 2. From the texts in *Martin Luthers Werke: Kritische Gesamtausgabe*, vol. 2 (Weimar: Böhlau, 1884), 41–47, in *Dr. Martin Luther's Catechetische Schriften*; and in J. G. Walch and G. Stoeckhardt, eds., trans. Glen Zweck, vol. 10 of *Dr. Martin Luther's Saemmtliche Schriften* (St. Louis: Concordia Publishing House, 1885), cols. 1254–63. Available at http://www.iclnet.org/pub/resources/text/wittenberg/luther/web/3formsrt.html (accessed May 20, 2008).

[75] Martin Luther, "Two Kinds of Righteousness," trans. Lowell J. Satre, in *Luther's Works, American Edition*, vol. 31 (Philadelphia: Muhlenberg Press, 1957), 297–306.

[76] Karl Lehmann and Wolfhart Pannenberg, eds., *The Condemnations of the Reformation Era: Do They Still Divide?* (Minneapolis: Fortress Press, 1990), 33.

[77] Trigg, *Baptism in the Theology of Martin Luther*, 77; Max Thurian and Geoffrey Wainwright, *Baptism and Eucharist: Ecumenical Convergence in Celebration*, Faith and Order Paper No. 117 (Grand Rapids: Eerdmans; Geneva: World Council of Churches, 1983), 47–50.

In short, both Lutherans and Roman Catholics use transformationist language in describing the effects of baptism as contrasted with language of imputation, associated with Lutheran understandings of the effect of grace in justification. Although this is very close to the Lutheran description of the "drowning" of the old Adam, it does not figure prominently in Lutheran descriptions of justification.

On the basis of descriptions of baptism one can say that the theologies of the effects of baptism are similar and certainly not church dividing. Baptism effects righteousness, is necessary for salvation, forgives sin, including original sin, even though concupiscence, described as "the material element" or tendency to sin, remains. Baptism is commended for infants. It gives access to a qualitatively new life in Christ.

In part the tensions involved in theologies of faith, baptism, and justification arise from the specific background and practical references to Christian life in the church for the doctrine of justification in the sixteenth century. For Protestants, their articulation of the doctrine of justification addressed the contemporary theological understanding of penitence and the confessions of sin in the sacrament of penance and the promise of forgiveness in Christ's name.[78] The Council of Trent's Decree on Justification, on the other hand, considers justification in the light of baptism and a baptismal life lived out until the final judgment.[79] This difference determines how individualistically or communally the doctrine is framed, the nature of faith within justification, and how one envisions the effects of justification. Nevertheless, penance and baptism are not two dichotomous events setting up dichotomous theologies of justification. Penance is an extension or application of baptism inasmuch as it is the "second plank" after the shipwreck of sin, the first being baptism.[80] Baptism is the primary sacrament of reconciliation. The justification represented in both sacraments results from the same boundless and gratuitous love of God that is ours through Jesus Christ.

Authors have documented the inconsistency in Luther's own writing on baptism and his explication of justification.[81] James Atkinson has

---

[78] Lehmann and Pannenberg, *Condemnations of the Reformation Era*, 39. The type of Occamism taught at Erfurt, where Luther studied theology, was Occam as modified and interpreted by Gabriel Biel, whose doctrine of justification is found in the context of his analyses of the sacrament of penance. See Heiko A. Oberman, *The Harvest of Medieval Theology: Gabriel Biel and Late Medieval Nominalism* (Durham, NC: Labyrinth Press, 1983), 134.

[79] Ibid.

[80] Jerome, *Ep.* CXXX.

[81] Cited in Trigg, *Baptism in the Theology of Martin Luther.*

commented: "There is no satisfactory way of reconciling Luther's clear teaching on justification by faith alone with his views on baptismal regeneration. His contemporaries saw this chink in his armour, and so have many radicals who succeeded them."[82] Luther's work was far ranging, engaged multiple opponents, and was more often polemical rather than systematic in method. The heritage of this inconsistency remains in ecumenical discussions on justification today.

The *Joint Declaration on the Doctrine of Justification* and Baptism

The *Joint Declaration on the Doctrine of Justification* is a test case for the reconciliation of the two points of departure for a theology of baptism as it relates to justification. The *Joint Declaration on the Doctrine of Justification* mentions baptism in six paragraphs. Three of these are in statements representing joint agreement,[83] two in statements referring to Catholic understanding,[84] and one within a Lutheran understanding of the justified as sinner.[85] Roman Catholic and Lutheran confessional teaching on baptism as a sacrament of justification is consonant with the consensus statements in the *Joint Declaration on the Doctrine of Justification*.

Concerning the biblical message of justification:

> 11. [Justification] occurs in the reception of the Holy Spirit in baptism and incorporation into the one body (Rom 8:1f, 9f; 1 Cor 12:12f).

Concerning justification by faith and through the Holy Spirit in baptism:

> 25. By the action of the Holy Spirit in baptism, they are granted the gift of salvation, which lays the basis for the whole Christian life.

Concerning the justified as sinner:

> 28. We confess together that in baptism the Holy Spirit unites one with Christ, justifies and truly renews the person.[86]

---

[82] James Atkinson, *Martin Luther and the Birth of Protestantism* (London and Baltimore: Penguin, 1968), 192. Cited in Trigg, 4.

[83] *JDDJ*, 11, 25, 28.

[84] Ibid., 27, 30.

[85] Ibid., 29.

[86] Ibid., 11.

The statement explicitly says that justification occurs in the reception of the Holy Spirit in baptism and that baptism justifies and truly renews the person. It reinforces the theology that baptism and justification are God's action rather than being a human work of the church or the recipient of the sacrament.[87] As we have seen, these statements are faithful to the tradition of both Lutherans and Catholics, but it perhaps raises the Lutheran teaching on the effects of baptism to a new visibility or emphasis by connecting it more explicitly with a theology of justification.

The *JDDJ* brings together the idea of justification as transformation and the teaching on being justified and yet a sinner, the traditional Catholic claim of being "made" righteous and the traditional Lutheran claim of being "declared" righteous. It says: "We confess together that God forgives sin by grace and at the same time frees human beings from sin's enslaving power and imparts the gift of new life in Christ."[88] The *JDDJ* avoids the traditional roadblocks to agreement on the doctrine of justification by situating justification within the context of interpersonal relationship with Christ through the power of the Spirit, a relationship established in baptism. The interior change in the justified person occurs as a result of his new identity as Christian, defined as one who lives by being united to Christ and called to a life of Christian discipleship.[89] The change in state of being is ultimately relational. The baptized is inserted into a communion of relationships with God as Father, Son, and Spirit.

Baptism and Faith

The issue between Lutherans and Catholics has never been whether or not we are justified by faith. The Council of Trent explicitly affirmed faith in Christ as the sole source of justification: "we are said to be justified by faith because faith is the first stage of human salvation, the foundation and root of all justification, without which it is impossible to please God and come to the fellowship of his children."[90]

---

[87] *Large Catechism*, 6, 10, 35.

[88] *JDDJ*, 22.

[89] John J. McDonnell, "The Agreed Statement on Justification: A Roman Catholic Perspective," *Ecumenical Trends* 28, no. 4 (May, 1999): 7–12, at 11 (71–76 of the whole volume, at 75).

[90] Decree on Justification, chap. 8. Much of the material in this section is taken from Susan K. Wood, "Lutherans and Roman Catholics: Two Perspectives on Faith," *One in Christ* 37, no. 2 (2002): 46–60.

Baptism is a sacrament of faith. Faith is necessary for the sacraments, and one of the purposes of the sacraments is to beget and confirm faith.[91] From the Lutheran perspective the sacraments are a means to obtain justifying faith.[92] Edmund Schlink expresses the relationship between faith and Baptism within the Lutheran confession thus:

> If the Gospel is received by faith, it cannot be done without a desire for Baptism. For the Gospel concerning Jesus Christ is also the call to Baptism in the name of Christ. In the approach to Baptism the obedience of faith toward the Gospel is realized. At the same time faith in Christ and the approach to Baptism are not side by side without relation to each other. Just as faith in the Gospel that is heard is faith in the Christ who confronts him in the Gospel, so also Baptism is to be desired by faith in the saving activity of Christ through Baptism. . . . This does not mean that Baptism is to be made a second means of appropriating salvation alongside faith, but faith and Baptism belong together.[93]

In other words, faith leads to baptism since faith in Jesus Christ leads one to fulfill his ordinances and to join oneself to Christ sacramentally in his redemptive death and resurrection. Conversely, baptism is meaningless apart from faith. Faith and baptism are not two separate avenues of attaining salvation but two mutually conditioned responses to the Gospel.

Baptism and the Faith of the Church

An area for exploration in an ecumenical context with Lutherans is not the necessity of faith for the reception of baptism, but the relative emphasis on individual faith versus the faith of the church in our respective traditions. Catholicism emphasizes the need for a community of believers, for "it is only within the faith of the Church that each of the faithful can believe."[94] Roman Catholics consider all the sacraments as forms of liturgical prayer. Liturgical prayer is the public, official prayer of the church, not the prayer of a private individual. In the profession

---

[91] *Apology of the Augsburg Confession*, VII, 3, 10, 30–31; also *Smalcald Articles*, 2, IV, 9.
[92] Ibid., VIII, 4–5.
[93] Schlink, *Doctrine of Baptism*, 123.
[94] *Catechism* 1253.

of faith within liturgical prayer, the "I" of "I believe" is not only the individual, but the whole church professing its belief.[95] Our response of faith is given, not only in our hearts, but also in the public liturgical prayer of the community when we profess the Creed and pray the great doxologies of the church. Thus there is a complex dynamic between the faith brought to the sacrament by an individual and the faith of the community that invites, supports, and sustains that faith.

Documents from the Second Vatican Council attesting to the communal character of faith include the Preface to *Dei Verbum*, linking adherence to the Gospel with fellowship in the believing community,[96] and *Lumen Gentium*'s reference to the people of God's "supernatural sense of the faith." With the help of the Holy Spirit the faithful are able to cling without fail to the word of God, penetrate its meaning more deeply, and apply it more fully in their lives.[97]

In an alternative way of viewing this, an individual first comes to personal faith, confessing Jesus Christ as Lord and Savior, and then unites with other Christians for support in that personal affirmation of faith. The first reality—communal faith—is the paradigm for infant baptism. The second—individual adult faith—is the paradigm for adult believer baptism. Luther conceded a measure of causal efficacy to the sacraments but considered them to have salutary value insofar as they aroused or strengthened faith.[98] He also supported infant baptism as illustrative of the gratuity of grace. However, there also exists in Reformation thought a suspicion, if not a rejection, of mediating authority in favor of the direct, existential, intensely personal experience of faith. In a Lutheran context this may represent a certain tension in the Lutheran worldview between the ecclesial practice of baptism inherited from its Catholic origins and Luther's view of faith acquired in his adult experience of reading Romans 4:4-6. This tension may reflect the fact that the Catholic theology of justification originates in the experience of baptism while the Lutheran forensic model finds its origin in the sacrament of penance, hence the forensic and declaratory nature of justification. This difference represents one of the major asymmetries in the two approaches to justification.

---

[95] This point is made by Henri de Lubac in *La foi chrétienne: essai sur la structure du Symbole des Apôtres* (Paris: Aubier-Montaigne, 1970), 217–34.

[96] DV 1.

[97] LG 12.

[98] Dulles, *The Assurance of Things Hoped For*, 44.

Since the restoration of the catechumenate after Vatican II and with the promulgation of the Rite of Christian Initiation of Adults, adult baptism is normative for Roman Catholic understanding of the sacrament even though statistically more infants may be baptized than adults. Adult baptism is normative because of the faith engaged and also because the rite involves a conversion of life not experienced by an infant. In the case of infant baptism there is faith by proxy, the faith of parents, godparents, and the Christian community. Children "are baptized in the faith of the Church, a faith proclaimed for them by their parents and godparents, who represent both the local Church and the whole society of saints and believers."[99] From earliest times the Roman Catholic Church has baptized infants as well as adults. The introduction to the rite notes that the church has always understood the words "unless a man is reborn in water and the Holy Spirit, he cannot enter the kingdom of God" to mean that children should not be deprived of baptism. There is nothing automatic or magical in the reception of the sacrament, for if it is not responded to in faith, it remains incomplete and not active in the life of the individual. Thus there must be assurance that a baptized child is to be raised in an environment of faith for the sacrament to have the power to make one's life truly baptismal in its orientation to Christ. Neither familial pressure nor the desire to fulfill an established social convention is a sufficient reason for infant baptism. Infant baptism requires, however, a postbaptismal catechesis in the faith, and the church does not baptize infants unless there is reasonable assurance of this postbaptismal catechesis.[100] If there is no evidence that the faith professed by proxy for the child will develop into a living personal faith, the baptism should be delayed.[101]

The primary difference between those communions that baptize infants and those that practice believer's baptism is not primarily whether faith is present or not—since faith is required for the reception of all the sacraments—but rather where faith is located. Baptists and other groups issuing from the Anabaptist arm of the Reformation require a personal profession of faith on the part of the person who is baptized. In the Catholic tradition, faith is expressed by proxy by the godparents and the

[99] Ibid.

[100] Code of Canon Law (Washington, DC: Canon Law Society of America, 1983), 868.1.2. Sacred Congregation for the Doctrine of Faith, "Instruction on Infant Baptism," Vatican City, 1980, 30.

[101] See Congregation for the Doctrine of the Faith, Instruction *Pastoralis actio*, no. 28 (October 20, 1980); *Acta Apostolicae Sedis* 72 (1980) 1137–56.

parents. In other words, the faith is located first in the Christian community that initiates the child into the community of faith. A child is welcomed into the faith of the community. The community of faith is where the Gospel is proclaimed and where a person is drawn to belief through hearing. In this way of thinking the community of faith precedes the individual believer.

Baptism as an Act of Faith

The question whether one is justified by faith or by baptism should not be posed in an either/or fashion. Baptism is an act of faith. The very gesture of presenting oneself or a child for baptism manifests the desire to be associated with Christ and his church and is thus an act of faith. The rite of baptism includes a profession of faith in the Triune God. Baptism only justifies when it is received in faith. However, as we have seen, this faith is not only the personal faith of an individual, but also the faith of the ecclesial community that welcomes an individual into its faith. When the church baptizes, it professes its faith.

Baptism is an act of faith because it is actually a prayer form, and prayer implies faith. Too often we think of sacraments as objects received for personal benefit, even received in faith, rather than looking on them as the liturgical prayer of the church by which it joins itself to Christ in his redemptive paschal mystery or as a response to God's promise. Prayer is always directed to the Father, through Christ, in the power of the Spirit. Thus even though Catholic theology has insisted on the anthropological transformation effected in baptism, attention must not terminate in the individual but must look ahead to the theonomous and eschatological terminus of the sacrament. The transformation of the individual has a purpose, namely, the reconciliation of all with the Father through union with Christ in his death and resurrection through the power of the Spirit.

Baptismal faith is not individualistic, a purely private concern between a person and God. It is fundamentally ecclesial. The act of being baptized in the public liturgical prayer of the church manifests the willingness to live out faith in the context of the faith community that receives the baptized.[102] It is baptism in this local community that gives the baptized

---

[102] See Cosmas Alule, *Baptism and Faith: Their Relationship in our Salvific Encounter with God Today in the Light of the New Testament Baptismal Theology and Vatican II Sacramental Theology* (Frankfurt am Main: Peter Lang, 2000), 242–48.

their ecclesial identity as Catholic, Lutheran, Presbyterian, or Anglican. No rite says "I baptize you a Catholic, a Lutheran, or a Baptist." The faith of the community that baptizes and receives and nurtures the newly baptized in faith determines the ecclesial identity of the person baptized.

The ecclesial character of baptismal faith is intimately connected to the communal dimension of salvation. As we have noted earlier, *Lumen Gentium* states, "He [God] has, however, willed to make women and men holy and to save them, not as individuals without any bond between them, but rather to make them into a people who might acknowledge him and serve him in holiness."[103] The subject of redemption is in the first place always the people. An individual participates in redemption as a member of the people.[104] An individual is born again as a member of this people "through the word of the living God (see 1 Pet 1:23), not from flesh, but from water and the holy Spirit (see Jn 23:5-6)."[105] In this text of *Lumen Gentium* word and sacrament are united as are faith and sacrament. Faith, baptism, and salvation have a socio-ecclesial dimension.[106]

At the end of the day one is justified by Christ alone through grace alone. This puts the questions of justification by faith or justification by baptism into perspective. From a human perspective we access the grace of justification through faith expressed in baptism, whether that be baptism in water in the Triune name or through inchoate or explicit desire for baptism. Even though baptism must be received in faith, even if it is the faith of the church interceding for an infant, baptismal reality does not owe its existence to the faith of the baptized person.[107] The sacrament is effected through the Holy Spirit acting through the church.

Faith is absolutely essential for a baptismal life. One cannot lay down one's life in imitation of Christ's death apart from faith. One cannot exercise a common priesthood through participation in the liturgical life of the church apart from faith. One cannot consciously work for the transformation of the world into the kingdom of Christ apart from faith. One cannot engage in a life of discipleship apart from baptism. Baptism not only initiates a person into a baptismal way of life, it shows the way back to the Father within the trinitarian pattern of relationships.

[103] LG 9.

[104] Karl Rahner, *The Church and the Sacraments* (New York: Herder & Herder, 1963), 88.

[105] LG 9.

[106] Alule, *Baptism and Faith*, 244.

[107] Comité Mixte Baptiste-Catholique en France, *Du Baptême à l'Église: Accords et divergences actuels* (Paris: Cerf, 2007), 10.

Chapter Seven

Baptism and the Church

In the scriptural account of the early church, baptism, the Eucharist, and participation in the *koinonia* of Christian life follow as a response to the proclamation of the Gospel. In Acts 2:16-42, in response to Peter's proclamation that God had made the Jesus who had been crucified both Lord and Messiah, the people ask: "Brothers, what should we do?" (v. 37). Peter replies: "Repent and be baptized every one of you in the name of Jesus Christ so that your sins may be forgiven; and you will receive the gift of the Holy Spirit" (v. 38). Those who welcome his message are baptized (v. 41), and "devoted themselves to the apostles' teaching and fellowship [*koinonia*], to the breaking of bread and the prayers" (v. 42). In drawing nearer to Christ they drew nearer to each other. The sequence of initiatory events: proclamation, profession of faith, baptism, life in community, and participation in the Eucharist reflect the fact that initiation finds its fulfillment in ecclesial life and worship. There is a direct trajectory both between baptism and life in the church and between baptism and participation in the Eucharist.

A tradition's understanding of baptism is profoundly linked to its view of the church. The answer to the question, "What does baptism do?" is dependent on a tradition's ecclesiology. Different traditions come to different conclusions about baptism because of their different understanding of the nature and boundaries of the Christian community and how that community is constituted. This certainly raises the question whether the mutual recognition of baptism needs to begin with a dialogue about the nature of the church rather than with baptism: that is, whether mutual recognition of the sacraments, particularly baptism and Eucharist, leads to the mutual recognition of churches, or whether the mutual recognition of churches, the ability to recognize in one another the church of Christ in faithfulness to the apostolic tradition, leads to the mutual recognition of the foundational sacraments of the church. Undoubtedly both are necessary, although each seems to have the other as its prerequisite.

This chapter examines the relationship between baptism and the church. This necessarily includes the nature of Christian initiation as an ecclesial event, the relationship between baptism and church membership, and, most importantly, the correspondence between the understanding of the church and the doctrine of baptism in various traditions. The chapter will examine how these various ecclesiologies are related to the corresponding theologies of baptism and argues that there is a direct correlation between what a tradition considers baptism to be and its theology of the church.

The Rite of Christian Initiation: A Profoundly Ecclesial Process

The Rite of Christian Initiation in the Roman Catholic tradition makes it clear that baptism is an ecclesial event and that there are a number of ecclesial effects of the rite.[1] First, initiation into the church is a public rather than a private process. There are a number of steps that take place before the assembled community. At the beginning of the rite of acceptance into the Order of Catechumens the candidates are asked: "What do you ask of God's Church?"[2] In the second step, the rite of election or enrollment of names, the church judges the readiness of the catechumens to advance toward the sacraments of initiation on the basis of the testimony of godparents and catechists. The church then elects them, an eloquent indication that baptism is not something we undertake entirely of our own initiative or alone.[3] The rite instructs that before the rite of election

---

[1] Margaret Mary Kelleher enumerates these in "Ecclesial Nature of Baptism," in *Dictionary of Sacramental Worship*, ed. Peter E. Fink (Collegeville, MN: Liturgical Press, 1990), 87.
[2] Rite of Christian Initiation of Adults, 51.
[3] Ibid., 119.

the bishop, priests, deacons, catechists, godparents, and the entire community, in accord with their respective responsibilities and in their own way, should, after considering the matter carefully, arrive at a judgment about the catechumens' state of formation and progress. After the election, they should surround the elect with prayer, so that the entire Church will accompany and lead them to encounter Christ.[4]

Within the rite of election itself the bishop celebrant or his delegate declares in the presence of the community the church's approval of the candidates.[5] Also within this rite the catechumens affirm their desire "to enter fully into the life of the Church through the sacraments of baptism, confirmation, and the Eucharist,"[6] indicating that these sacraments of initiation are gates into the life of the church.

The formal rituals before the assembly are supported by the relationships forged outside of times of formal worship. Justin Martyr, in his mid-second-century text known as the *First Apology*, not only asks those preparing for baptism to pray and fast and ask forgiveness of sin but also instructs the community to pray and fast with them.[7] Thus there was community solidarity with the catechumens in their process of initiation.

Second, the growth in faith required of the catechumen is not merely intellectual assent to the doctrines of the church. The faith required is a commitment to paschal living that entails a radical transformation of life and values to be lived publicly. Thus the RCIA entails a shift from an educational, "inquiry" model of initiation to one that emphasizes conversion. This conversion takes place within and is molded by the liturgy, the public prayer of the church, specifically by a lectionary catechesis. It also occurs in communion with a particular faith community that ideally models lives of conversion. Catechumens learn what it means to be a Christian by observing this in the concrete lives of others.

Third, the rite requires a vibrant church community into which the catechumen can be initiated. There is a reciprocal cycle: the catechumen is initiated into a vibrant community that is in turn made more vibrant because of the addition of a committed, converted member. The various

---

[4] Ibid., 121.
[5] Ibid., 122.
[6] Ibid., 132.
[7] Justin Martyr, *First Apology*, 61.

aspects of our community life that contribute to this vitality include the liturgy, social activities, social justice outreach, and education, to name but a few. Faith comes to expression in all these activities. The RCIA initiates a cycle whereby faith is brought to articulation, and this articulation in turn increases faith, which then seeks expression in various ecclesial activities. This is as true for the neophyte as for the congregation. In short, the process of initiation presupposes an ecclesiology of the church as a committed, converted people of God and in turn contributes to such an ecclesiology.

The case of infant baptism further underscores the communal and ecclesial nature of baptism. Eugene Brand suggests that "rather than speaking of infant baptism, we should speak of the baptism of infants born into the Christian congregation."[8] The goal is not a mechanistic and indiscriminate baptism, but one that has the potential of leading to a mature faith. Generally speaking, infants should not be baptized unless there is some assurance that the parents will raise the child in the faith. Canon 868 prescribes:

> For the licit baptism of an infant it is necessary that there be a founded hope that the infant will be brought up in the Catholic religion; if such a hope is altogether lacking, the baptism is to be put off according to the prescriptions of particular law and the parents are to be informed of the reason.[9]

The ecclesial community also has a responsibility with respect to the child. The introduction to the Rite of Baptism for Children states:

> Before and after the celebration of the sacrament, the child has a right to the love and help of the community. During the rite, in addition to the ways of congregational participation mentioned in the General Introduction to Christian Initiation no. 7, the community exercises its duty when it expresses its assent together with the celebrant after the professions of faith by the parents and godparents. In this way it is clear that the faith in which the children are baptized is not the private possession of the individual family, but the common treasure of the whole Church of Christ.[10]

---

[8] Eugene L. Brand, *Baptism: A Pastoral Perspective* (Minneapolis: Augsburg, 1975), 40.

[9] Code of Canon Law (1983), 868, §1.2.

[10] Rite of Baptism for Children, 4.

Not only the family, but the whole congregation has a responsibility for the baptized baby. In fact, the whole program of religious education and parish formation grows out of the parish's baptismal responsibility. Baptism gives a parish—identified as a community of Christian formation gathered around font, pulpit, and table—its identity as a parish.[11] Baptism—and the evangelization and Christian formation that accompany it—distinguishes parishes from other kinds of eucharistic communities. Reciprocally, the faith community that is that parish gives the baptized their particular ecclesial identity, for no baptismal rite says that a person is baptized a Lutheran, Anglican, or Roman Catholic. The community that received the baptized person and hands on its faith to the new Christian determines the faith identity of the newly baptized.

The ecclesial dimension of baptism is associated with the conviction that all who are baptized into Christ have become one in Christ Jesus (Gal 3:27-28). This unity in Christ is expressed by Paul in the image of the body: "For just as the body is one and has many members, and all the members of the body, though many, are one body, so it is with Christ. For in the one Spirit we were all baptized into one body—Jews or Greeks, slaves or free—and we were all made to drink of one Spirit" (1 Cor 12:12-13). By being baptized into the death and resurrection of Christ we become his body, not individually, although there is a transformation in grace whereby we are transformed into the likeness of Christ, but corporately.

Here the trajectory between baptism and Eucharist, the sacrament of Christ's body and blood, is evident. They are both sacraments of the same body and we participate in the body through different sacramental modalities. The communion into which we are baptized is both Christic and ecclesial. In terms of sacramental symbolism, the water bath symbolizes our immersion in the death and resurrection of Christ and the Eucharist represents our communion in Christ with the sacrament that memorializes his paschal mystery. The Eucharist is the repeatable communal form of the incorporation into Christ achieved under different sacramental signs in baptism. Both sacramentalize an individual's participation in the paschal mystery. Both sacramentalize an individual's communion in the church.

---

[11] See Susan K. Wood, "Presbyteral Identity within Parish Identity," in *Ordering the Baptismal Priesthood: Theologies of Lay and Ordained Ministry* (Collegeville, MN: Liturgical Press, 2003), 175–94.

Definitions of Church Membership
and Church Boundaries

An ecumenical consultation sponsored by the Faith and Order Consultation of the World Council of Churches on the sacramentality of baptism in Prague, 2000, while observing the great diversity in Christian practices, made this comment on the relationship between baptism and church membership:

> Among the churches "membership" now seems to occur at varying points along a continuum of practises. Some churches have developed rites for the dedication of children. In some communions, catechumens are considered church members, as reflected in their right to a Christian burial. Some traditions consider faith to be sufficient for church membership, even prior to baptism. For yet others, full membership seems to come only with confirmation, even if this is separated from baptism by several years. Theologically and liturgically, membership appears to be "incomplete" prior to admission to the eucharist; yet some baptized are barred from the eucharist because they have not reached a certain age, or because they are not yet confirmed. This wide diversity of practice among—and sometimes within—the churches indicates discrepancies between theology, symbol, and practice.[12]

The document then observes that church membership is really a narrower question within a larger and richer theme, that of Christian initiation, since the notion of membership "is too often based on an understanding of the church as an organization, rather than as the *ekklesia* of believers in communion with Christ, with the Spirit, and with one another."[13] A quick survey of various traditions reveals the differences among them and the issues involved.

The Anglican-Reformed International Commission observes: "There is a difference between our two communions in the way they define membership. Reformed churches have tended to define it primarily as membership in a local congregation, while Anglicans, by the practice of episcopal confirmation, have emphasized membership in the wider

---

[12] Faith and Order Consultation, "The Sacramental Dimension of Baptism," Prague, 29 May–4 June 2000, provisional document dated September 20, 2000, §69.
[13] Ibid., §70.

church."[14] In addition to this difference of scale, one also finds a distinction between a description of the church as the assembly of the saints, known only to God, and thus with boundaries invisible from an earthly perspective, on the one hand, and the visible church community or congregation identified as the locale where the sacraments are rightly administered and the Gospel is purely preached on the other hand.

In the Lutheran tradition, the *Augsburg Confession* identifies the church as "properly speaking, the assembly of saints and those who truly believe."[15] The *Apology of the Augsburg Confession* responds to the Roman Confutation that stated: "The seventh article of the confession, in which it is affirmed that the church is the assembly of saints, cannot be admitted without prejudice to faith if by this definition the wicked and sinners are separated from the church."[16] The *Apology* makes the clarification that "we grant that in this life hypocrites and evil people are mingled with the church and are members of the church according to the external association of the church's signs—that is, the Word, confession of faith, and sacraments—especially if they have not been excommunicated."[17] It further notes that the sacraments do not lose their efficacy when they are administered by the wicked and that the church can legitimately make use of sacraments administered by evil people. Nevertheless, it asserts that even though wicked people are associated with the true church according to the external rites, nevertheless, the church defined as the living body of Christ is the assembly of the saints since those in whom Christ is not active are not members of Christ.[18] It rejects an understanding of the church as an external government consisting of both the good and the wicked. The true church "is a spiritual people . . . a true people of God, reborn through the Holy Spirit."[19] The people of God according to the Gospel are only those who receive the promise of the

[14] Anglican-Reformed International Commission (1981–84), "God's Reign and Our Unity," §57.

[15] *Augsburg Confession*, VII.

[16] Roman Confutation, part 1, art. VII, cited in n. 237 of *The Book of Concord: The Confessions of the Evangelical Lutheran Church*, ed. Robert Kolb and Timothy J. Wengert (Minneapolis: Fortress Press, 2000), 174.

[17] *Apology of the Augsburg Confession*, Articles VII and VIII: The Church, §3.

[18] The first thesis of the Berne Reformation Mandate (1528) cited in Christian Link, "The *Notae Ecclesiae*: A Reformed Perspective," in *Toward the Future of Reformed Theology: Tasks, Topics, Traditions*, ed. David Willis and Michael Welker (Grand Rapids and Cambridge: Eerdmans, 1999), 241.

[19] *Apology of the Augsburg Confession*, VII, §14.

Spirit. The ungodly are not in the church even though they intermingle with the church and hold offices in the church.

Thus for the Lutheran Confessions the true church is an invisible church in the sense that no one but God knows its members. As Luther said, "The church is a so deeply hidden thing that no one can see it or know it but can only grasp and believe it in baptism, the Lord's Supper, and the word."[20] There are not two churches, the visible congregation and the church of the saints. The church of the saints exists within the visible congregation. The invisible church of the justified exists within the mixed church comprised of both wheat and tares. Yet, paradoxically, the mixed church is indeed "church" because the marks of the church are to be found there, especially the word, confession of faith, and the sacraments. The connection between these two uses of "church" is that these marks or signs of the church elicit and support faith. Nevertheless, a tension exists in these two descriptors of the church as a community of saints and as an assembly.

The hiddenness of the church in Protestant traditions raises questions about the relationship between baptism and the boundaries of the church. As Jonathan Trigg notes, "But what is baptism, if it is not in some sense a boundary of the Church. . . . *Prima facie* it must surely be allowed that a sacrament of initiation defines, or at the very least plays some part in defining, not only the beginning of a new life but also the extent and membership of the community to which it is the entrance."[21] Does one truly become a member of the church through baptism? Is the church the community of the baptized? The Lutheran response would affirm this, but qualifies it according to a doctrine of faith. Baptism is efficacious through faith as justification is efficacious through faith. Thus the *Apology* states that "the church consists of those persons in whom there is a true knowledge and confession of faith and truth."[22] This rules out an *ex opere operato* notion of baptismal efficacy if this is defined apart from the faith of the person being baptized.[23] Membership in the church is contingent on faith as is baptism, and justification depends on faith. The *Small Catechism* instructs that baptism "brings about forgiveness of sins, redeems

---

[20] *Werke,* 51m 507, 13ff. = *LW* 41, 211; *Against Hanswurst,* 1541. Cited by Jonathan D. Trigg, *Baptism in the Theology of Martin Luther* (New York: Brill, 1994), 179.

[21] Ibid., 174–75.

[22] *Apology of the Augsburg Confession,* §22.

[23] The *Apology* states: "Again, what need will there be for faith if the sacraments justify *ex opere operato* without a good impulse in those using them?" (§21).

from death and the devil, and gives eternal salvation to all who believe it, as the words and promise of God declare" by the "Word of God, which is with and alongside the water, and faith which trusts this Word of God in the water."[24] The Flood Prayer in the Baptismal Booklet of Martin Luther, included in the second edition of the *Small Catechism* published in 1529 and presently included in the *Book of Concord*, asks that God "would look graciously upon N. and bless him with true faith in the Holy Spirit so that through this same saving flood all that has been born in him from Adam and whatever he has added thereto may be drowned in him and sink, and that he, separated from the number of the unbelieving, may be preserved dry and secure in the holy ark of the Christian church. . . ."[25] This prayer reflects an ecclesiology of the church comprised of believers. Entrance to this church is granted by way of baptism, the sacrament of faith. Christians are initially received into the Christian community through baptism.[26] Subsequent unbelief or sin inconsistent with faith removes a person from the ark of the Christian church.

Recent ecumenical discussions have softened the polemical disagreements about an "invisible" or "visible" church. The Lutheran–Roman Catholic Joint Commission's document, *Church and Justification*, acknowledges the tension in the Lutheran description of the church as both an outward association recognizable by the marks of the church and an invisible association of the saints.[27] This document does not discuss the visibility or invisibility of the church in terms of boundaries, but from the perspective of faith. Only the eyes of faith recognize an assembly as the people of God.[28] For Lutherans there is an analogy between the hidden church and the hidden God on the cross. Both are unrecognizable by earthly standards; both must be discerned in what seems opposed to them in sinful structures and in suffering and death.

Catholics, too, share the difficulty of church membership "according to the heart" and membership "according to the body."[29] *Lumen Gentium* says:

---

[24] *Small Catechism*, "The Sacrament of Holy Baptism," 5–6, 9.

[25] *The Book of Concord*, 374.

[26] *The Large Catechism*, in *The Book of Concord*, 426.

[27] Lutheran–Roman Catholic Joint Commission, *Church and Justification* (Geneva: Lutheran World Federation, 1994), §139. It also notes that Melanchthon, in the *Apology of the Augsburg Confession*, rejected a view of the church as a kind of "Platonic republic." Ibid., §136, citing *Apol* 7, 20; *Book of Concord*, 171.

[28] *Church and Justification*, §141.

[29] Ibid., §142.

> Fully incorporated into the society of the church are those who, possessing the Spirit of Christ, accept its entire structure and all the means of salvation established within it and who in its visible structure are united with Christ, who rules it through the Supreme Pontiff and the bishops, by the bonds of profession of faith, the sacraments, ecclesiastical government, and communion. A person who does not persevere in charity, however, is not saved, even though incorporated into the church. Such people remain indeed in the bosom of the church, but only "bodily" not "in their hearts."[30]

On the one hand, this passage picks up Bellarmine's definition, cited earlier, of a church as a society with all its emphasis on the visibility of the church. On the other hand, full incorporation into the church requires charity. Simply being a member of the visible church does not guarantee salvation.

Although Vatican II did not solve the problem of membership in the church presented by the incidence of membership "in the body" but not "in the heart," it did provide a synthesis between the spiritual or transcendent reality of the church and its visible social reality.[31] It did this not only through the category of sacramentality, but also by comparing it to the mystery of the Incarnate Word:

> The one mediator, Christ, established and constantly sustains here on earth his holy church, the community of faith, hope and charity as a visible structure through which he communicates truth and grace to everyone. But the society equipped with hierarchical structures and the mystical body of Christ, the visible society and the spiritual community, the earthly church and the church endowed with heavenly riches, are not to be thought of as two realities. On the contrary, they form one complex reality comprising a human and a divine element. For this reason the church is compared, in no mean analogy, to the mystery of the incarnate Word.[32]

The council's teaching that the church "is at once holy and always in need of purification" shows that it does not simply identify the salvation community that has already been graced with beatitude with visible church structure and its sinful members, nor does it separate them, even though it distinguishes between them.

[30] LG 14.
[31] *Church and Justification*, §144.
[32] LG 8.

The consensus statement between Lutherans and Catholics in *Church and Justification* reads:

> Catholics and Lutherans are in agreement that the saving activity of the triune God calls and sanctifies believers through audible and visible means of grace which are mediated in an audible and visible ecclesial community. They also agree that in this world the salvation-community of Christ is hidden, because as a spiritual work of God's it is unrecognizable by earthly standards, and because sin, which is also present in the church, makes ascertaining its membership uncertain.[33]

This consensus statement is possible because it speaks of the hiddenness of the "salvation-community" rather than "church." The "salvation-community" is hidden because only God knows who is saved. The church is not simply identified with the communion of saints but is a mixed community of saints and sinners this side of the eschaton and is a complex society with a visible structure. Conversations among ecumenical partners on this point must identify when the spiritual and therefore "invisible" dimension of the church and the "visible" dimension of its embodiment as an assembly gathered around word and sacrament are treated in a dialectical way and when these two aspects are treated synthetically. The dialectic potentially drives a wedge between the two expressions of the church, while a synthetic approach develops two complementary aspects of the church.

How one speaks of belonging to the church is theologically significant. Vatican II did not use the category "membership," preferring to speak of "incorporation" or "communion." "Membership" is an either/or category; one is either a member or not. Both "incorporation" and "communion," on the other hand, admit of degrees. These degrees can potentially encompass distinctions between bodily inclusion in the social dimension of the church and inclusion in the spiritual community incorporated in grace without dichotomizing a "visible" church and an "invisible" one.

This suggests that the problem of membership in the church through baptism may be better posed in terms of incorporation and communion rather than membership. In baptism, through the gift of grace received in faith, we enter the one church in its complex reality as assembly gathered by word and sacrament and as spiritual communion. Even though

---

[33] *Church and Justification*, §147.

a person remains bodily in the church, that person may lose grace and therefore may no longer be in communion with the spiritual dimension of this complex reality. At all costs both Lutherans and Catholics, to be faithful to their traditions, must avoid speaking of two churches, an earthly one and a heavenly one. There is but one church, a complex entity, even though both traditions are challenged to describe it adequately.

Painting with a very large brush, one can identify three ecclesial groupings, each with a distinctive relationship between baptism and ecclesial identity: Catholics, Orthodox, and Anglicans, for whom baptism and the Eucharist incorporate a person into Christ and the church and for whom these sacraments are constitutive of the church; traditions issuing from the Reformation for whom the church is constituted by the word of God as a *creatura verbi*, a creature of the word; and those traditions practicing believer's baptism for whom the church is a committed assembly.

Catholics, Orthodox, Anglicans: Sacraments as Constitutive of the Church

For both Catholics and Orthodox the sacraments of baptism and Eucharist are constitutive of the church. Both incorporate an individual simultaneously into the body of Christ and into the church, the ecclesial body of Christ. One is a member of the church by virtue of being a member of Christ.

Baptism effects incorporation into the church. This is much more than external church membership or membership in an ecclesial organization, for membership in the church is inseparable from union with Christ. The ecclesial and christological nature of baptism is evident in such New Testament texts as Galatians 3:27-28, which notes that all who are baptized into Christ have become one in Christ Jesus, and 1 Corinthians 12:13, where Paul reminds the Corinthians that all who were baptized were made one body, in one Spirit. In Acts 2:41 the baptized are added to the community that day. The baptized experience a communion (*koinonia*) with one another expressed in a common life (Acts 2:42), which is the outgrowth of their participation in the life of Jesus Christ (1 Cor 1:9), their participation in the body and blood of the Lord (1 Cor 10:16-17), and their share in the one Spirit (Phil 2:1; Acts 2:42, 44-45). The oneness of the church of Jesus Christ does not exist because of something we do or achieve as churches, but because of the one Christ into whom we are baptized. The unity of the church is the unity of Christ. This mystery of

Christ dead and risen is present in both the sacraments of baptism and the Eucharist.

Baptism and the Eucharist are not only different sacramental modalities of incorporation in Christ; they are intrinsically related to each other and to the church. Both sacraments realize what they signify, namely, the body of Christ in the plenitude of the members of Christ's body joined to Christ their head. The church is not only built up numerically through the addition of new members through baptism in an extrinsic way; it is constituted as the body of Christ by baptism as it is by the Eucharist through communion in the body of Christ, effected through these two sacraments. Communion in Christ is inseparable from communion with the church. The relationship is one of simultaneity and mutual interdependence. Jean-Marie Tillard expresses it thus: ". . . strictly speaking, a person is not made a member of the church because he is made a member of Christ. He is, in the same and unique moment, inserted into communion with the Head which does not exist without the Body and with the Body which does not exist without the Head."[34]

An agreed statement between the Orthodox and Roman Catholics expresses this understanding of the relationship between baptism, the Eucharist, and the church:

> Believers are baptized in the Spirit in the name of the Holy Trinity to form one body (cf. 1 Cor. 12:13). When the Church celebrates the eucharist, it realizes "what it is," the body of Christ (1 Cor 10:17). By baptism and chrismation (confirmation) the members of Christ are "anointed" by the Spirit, grafted into Christ. But by the eucharist, the paschal event opens itself out into Church. The Church becomes that which it is called to be by baptism and chrismation. By the communion in the body and blood of Christ, the faithful grow in that mystical divinization which makes them dwell in the Son and the Father, through the Spirit.[35]

---

[34] J.-M. R. Tillard, "Perspectives nouvelles sur le baptême," *Irénikon* 51 (1978): 171–85, at 172.

[35] Joint International Commission, "The Mystery of the Church and of the Eucharist in the Light of the Mystery of the Holy Trinity" (1982), in *The Quest for Unity: Orthodox and Catholics in Dialogue. Documents of the Joint International Commission and Official Dialogues in the Unites States 1965–1995*, ed. John Borelli and John H. Erickson (Washington, DC, and Crestwood, NY: United States Catholic Conference and St. Vladimir's Seminary Press, 1996), 54–55.

In other words, what the scholastics called the *res* or the fruit of the sacrament of the Eucharist is the unity of the church, which is to say the ecclesial body of Christ in union with its Head. Through baptism we are grafted into Christ. By communing with the sacramental body of Christ we become one body (1 Cor 10:16-17), which is the constitution of the ecclesial body. Thus there is an intrinsic relationship between sacramental realism (belief in the real sacramental presence of Christ in the Eucharist) and ecclesial sacramental realism, wherein the church is also sacramentally present in the Eucharist.

From this relationship follows an intrinsic link between baptism and Eucharist. The incorporation in Christ effected in baptism finds a visible completion in eucharistic communion. The Eucharist is the visible, sacramental sign of all the baptized in communion in the body of Christ within a concrete community that experiences its identity as the body of Christ. Tillard expresses this intrinsic relationship in the strongest terms:

> Where baptism does not lead to a genuine eucharist, even if the content of the faith essentially conforms to revelation, the incorporation to Christ lacks sacramental contact with the Body of the Lord and the experience of *koinonia* with all in communion with this unique and indivisible Body of Christ. This sacramental visibility of the reality of incorporation is neither purely symbolic nor purely "expressive" of the profound mystery of the Church: it actualizes what it signifies.[36]

Tillard contrasts the visibility of this sacramental communion and constitution of the church with the interior experience of the Spirit and hidden communion with Christ within Protestant traditions. According to these traditions only God knows the degree to which someone is within the fullness of the church since interior sanctity escapes our judgment. Catholic traditions, on the other hand, while acknowledging the importance of this interior dimension, refuse to limit the church in this way, but see ecclesial fullness in the union of the invisible interior dimension of communion and its visible expression.

This relationship between the invisible interior dimension of the church and its visible expression gives the church a quasi-sacramental structure since the outward, visible manifestation of the church reflects an inner

---

[36] Tillard, "Perspectives nouvelles," 181.

spiritual component.[37] This complex relationship between outward sign and inward spiritual dimension, the one inseparable from the other, is one reason for the insistence on the visibility of the church, although it must be noted that at the time of the Reformation the dominant view of the church was that of a society rather than a sacrament. The great theologian of the Catholic Reformation, Robert Bellarmine, defined the church institutionally: "The one true Church is the society of men bound together by profession of the same Christian faith, and by communion of the same sacraments, under the rule of legitimate pastors and in particular under the one vicar of Christ on earth, the Roman Pontiff. . . . And it is as visible as the kingdom of France or the Republic of Venice."[38] The emphasis in this definition of the church is on observable characteristics and actions: profession of faith, communion of the sacraments, and the rule of pastors. This post-Reformation Catholic polemical reaction against Reformation ecclesiology focused on the church almost exclusively as a visible entity identified by creed, sacramental structure, and hierarchy. More spiritual conceptualizations of the church came later with the retrieval of the notion of the church as the body of Christ in Pius XII's encyclical *Mystici Corporis* (1943) and the application of the category of sacrament to the church by the Second Vatican Council. This history of Roman Catholic ecclesiology is significant for ecumenism, for it represents a nuancing that softens the polemics of the sixteenth century.

Although all churches agree that the church is a sign and an instrument, the language of sacramentality as applied to the church is an ecumenical stumbling block. The World Council of Churches document, *The Nature and Mission of the Church: A Stage on the Way to a Common Statement*, notes that the churches that identify the church as a sacrament do so because they understand the church to be an effective sign of communion of all human beings with each other and the Triune God. Those churches that reject the concept do so because they consider that this does not sufficiently distinguish between the church and sacraments. They consider the sacraments to be "means of salvation by which Christ sustains the Church, and not actions by which the Church realizes or actualizes

---

[37] LG 1 says: "*Cum autem ecclesia sit in Christo* veluti *sacramentum seu signum et instrumentum intimae cum Deo unionis totiusque generis humani unitatis . . .*" (emphasis added). The force of *veluti* is that the church is "sort of" a sacrament.

[38] Robert Bellarmine, *De Controversiis: Christianae Fidei Adversus Haereticos* (Rome: Giunchi et Menicanti, 1836), II: book 3, chap. 2, 90.

itself."[39] This position clearly opposes the kind of theology articulated by Tillard, which represents the liturgical ecclesiology of the Catholic and Orthodox churches. Some churches also reject a concept of the church as sacrament because they consider the church to be a communion that, while being holy, is still subject to sin. The WCC document also observes that "behind this lack of agreement lie varying views about the instrumentality of the church with regard to salvation" even though "those who have become accustomed to call the church 'sacrament' would still distinguish between the ways in which baptism and the Lord's supper on the one hand, and the church on the other, are signs and instruments of God's plan."[40] In fact, as the German Catholic-Lutheran dialogue has noted, the use of this term "serves to illustrate that the church, although it is the body of Christ, may not simply be identified with Christ, the 'primal sacrament.'"[41] Thus the concept of sacramentality as applied to the church is meant to distinguish between Christ and the church, avoiding too close an identification between them, at the same time as it shows the church's dependence on Christ and its task to represent him visibly in the world.

The Christian's relationship to Christ is inseparable from that person's relationship to the corporate body, the church. In the theology of Thomas Aquinas baptism is a relational act that places a person in community with Christ, the head of the ecclesial body, and with the gathered assembly.[42] Furthermore, baptism constitutes the baptized as a "liturgical person" oriented to worship in the official prayer of the church that is both public and paschal. The Second Vatican Council's Dogmatic Constitution on the Church taught that "the faithful are appointed by their baptismal character to Christian religious worship."[43] That same council's Constitution on the Sacred Liturgy states: "It is very much the wish of the church that all the faithful should be led to take that full, conscious and active

---

[39] World Council of Churches, *The Nature and Mission of the Church: A Stage on the Way to a Common Statement*, Faith and Order Paper No. 198 (Geneva: World Council of Churches, 2005), 29. See also the discussion in the document by the Bilateral Working Group of the German National Bishops' Conference and the Church Leadership of the United Evangelical Lutheran Church of Germany, *Communio Sanctorum: The Church as the Communion of Saints*, trans. Mark W. Jeske, Michael Root, and Daniel R. Smith (Collegeville, MN: Liturgical Press, 2004), §§86–88.

[40] *The Nature and Mission of the Church*, 30.

[41] *Communio Sanctorum*, §87.

[42] See ST IIIa, 63, 1; IIIa, 70, 1; and IIIa, 63, 1.

[43] LG 11.

part in liturgical celebrations which is demanded by the very nature of the liturgy, and to which the Christian people, 'a chosen race, a royal priesthood, a holy nation, a redeemed people' (1 Pet 2:9, 4-5) have a right and to which they are bound by reason of their Baptism."[44] A person is incorporated into a priestly community by baptism, but without the Eucharist the priestly exercise of that community is missing, at least with respect to its highest expression.

The Rite of Christian Initiation of Adults, in the instruction for the celebration of the sacraments of initiation, describes the activities of the priesthood of the baptized. These include the right to join the community in common prayer, have a part in the general intercessions, bring gifts to the altar, exchange the sign of peace, share in the offering of the sacrifice, express the spirit of adoption as God's children, which they have received in baptism, through the recitation of the Lord's Prayer, and commune in the Eucharist.[45] These activities are symbols of full membership in the church and exercises of the priestly identity of the church.

The liturgy defines the nature of the church as a priestly community. Individual Christians, lay or ordained, do not have a priestly role apart from the priestly community that is the church. The church is priestly because it is the mystical body of Christ who was priest. The priestly character of the church community is most evident in its worship of the Father in the celebration of the Eucharist, the source and summit of the church's activity and the culmination of Christian initiation. In baptism, through our union with Christ the high priest, we participate in the same service that Christ rendered to the Father in his suffering, death, and resurrection. In the words of Edward Schillebeeckx, "a baptized member of the Church receives the commission and therefore the competence, duty and right to take an active part in the ecclesial mystery of Easter. This activity is primarily the sacramental activity of the Church, above all in the Eucharist, in which the mystery of Easter is realized in the fullest sense."[46]

Some members of the Anglican communion share the Orthodox and Catholic view of baptism and Eucharist constituting the church. The Report of the Anglican-Reformed International Commission (1981–84),

---

[44] SC 14.
[45] §217.
[46] Edward Schillebeeckx, *Christ the Sacrament of the Encounter with God* (Kansas City: Sheed & Ward, 1963), 163.

"God's Reign and Our Unity," affirms baptism as being constitutive of the church:

> Baptism, by which Christ incorporates us into his life, death and resurrection, is thus, in the strictest sense, constitutive of the Church. It is not simply one of the Church's practices. It is an event in which God, by engaging us to himself, opens to us the life of faith and builds the Church. As Jesus was baptized, anointed by the Spirit from the Father, and declared to be the Son, so we are incorporated into the Church in the triune name, and are commanded: "Go therefore and make disciples of all nations, baptizing them in the name of the Father and of the Son and of the Holy Spirit, teaching them to observe all that I have commanded you" (Matt 28.19f.).

The commission, however, connects this more Catholic interpretation with a more Protestant theology of the church as constituted by the word of God. It observes that baptism is never an uninterpreted action. As the voice from heaven proclaimed its meaning, so preaching proclaims in the power of the Spirit that "this Jesus is the Christ," and every baptism proclaims his name. Word and action are inseparable.[47]

The same document makes a similar claim regarding the Eucharist: "Along with baptism, the Eucharist is fundamental to and constitutive of the life of the Church. It is the sacrament given to the Church by her Lord for the continual renewal of her life in him."[48] This statement appears open to an interpretation close to an Orthodox or Catholic liturgically based identification of the church.

The Reformation: The Church as *Creatura Verbi*

Generally speaking, churches issuing from the Reformation view the church as born from the word of God. The church is a *creatura verbi*, a creature of the word. Paul Avis identifies the question raised by the link between the two aspects of the church as the Reformers conceived it—the invisible, spiritual reality and its physical manifestation—as being whether the marks of the church, among which word and sacrament hold a privileged position, are *constitutive* of the church or merely *descriptive*

---

[47] Anglican-Reformed International Commission (1981–84), "God's Reign and Our Unity," §54 (d).
[48] Ibid., §71 (g).

of where the church is to be found in its visible manifestation.[49] Even though Avis concludes that the marks of the church are indicative and not constitutive of the church in the thought of the Reformers, the word of God is arguably unique as being both constitutive and indicative of the church. Luther defines the church in terms of the preached word, for where that word is, there is faith, and where there is faith, there is the church.[50] The word of God builds the church.[51] More precisely, the church is constituted and defined not just by any word, but by reference to the Gospel.[52]

The same would not be as true of the sacraments, for all the other notes of the church are subordinated to and serve the preaching of the word, and thus are signs of where the true church is located. Nevertheless the sacraments, as visible words, also serve a function of proclamation and from that proclamation a function of gathering the church. However, since the word of God is none other than Jesus Christ, this principle underscores the christological center of the church. In the post-Reformation period a polemical wedge was often driven between word and sacrament, the Protestant churches emphasizing word and the Catholics emphasizing sacraments. However, this is a false dichotomy if understood absolutely, for the Reformers unambiguously identified the church by word and sacrament even while linking the latter to the former, and the Catholic reform attempted to improve clergy education and provide for more adequate preaching.[53] Both emphases—word and sacrament—have

---

[49] Paul D. L. Avis, *The Church in the Theology of the Reformers* (Atlanta: John Knox Press, 1981), 7. Martin Luther enumerated seven marks of the church in his treatise *On the Councils and the Church* (1539): the word of God; the sacraments of baptism and the altar, rightly administered according to Christ's institution; the offices of the keys and the ministry; public prayer including the Lord's Prayer; the Apostles' Creed; the Decalogue; and the bearing of the cross.

[50] *Werke*, 2.208.

[51] Ibid., 43.596.

[52] Avis, referring to the work of Edmund Schlink, *The Doctrine of Baptism*, trans. Herbert J. A. Bouman (St. Louis: Concordia Publishing House, 1972), 25.

[53] Council of Trent, Session V, 17 June 1546, Second decree: On Instruction and Preaching; Session XXIV, 11 November 1563, Decree on Reform, canon 4. Nevertheless, as the actual practice of the churches developed after the Reformation it would be fair to say that the Protestant traditions clearly emphasized preaching and the Catholics, the sacraments. The Second Vatican Council (1962–65) addressed this imbalance by urging that the administration of every sacrament include Scripture readings and a word of explanation with pastoral application by the sacramental minister (SC 24, 35). This Liturgy of the Word *precisely as liturgy* forms part of the ritual action of the sacrament. Furthermore, the council's teaching that preaching is

a christological center, for the subject of the preaching is the Gospel, which is to say, Jesus Christ. The same is true of the sacraments of baptism and Eucharist. To say that the sacraments constitute the church is to say that Jesus Christ constitutes the church.

Karl Rahner was a Catholic theologian who contributed to a renewed Catholic appreciation of the role of the word in sacramental theology. He proposed that a theology of the word in the church as the eschatological presence of God could be a fresh common point of departure for both the Catholic and Protestant traditions.[54] Although at the time of his writing there had been very little developed theology of the word in Catholic theology, he believed that this could be "the basis for a theology of the sacraments in which the sacrament figures as the supreme human and ecclesiastical stage of the word in all its dimensions."[55] In the polemical climate of the Reformation, too often word and sacrament were seen as different entities. Rahner suggested that this dichotomy could be overcome by understanding the sacrament as a "word-event within a theology of the word."[56] The sacraments are embodied proclamations. Baptism and the Eucharist proclaim the death and resurrection of the Lord. In this proclamation the saving event is itself made present in sacramental sign, and the grace of that event is extended in a personal way to the recipient of the sacraments.

Finally, a theology of word and sacrament come together in their common role of eliciting faith. The traditions of the Reformation emphasize the role of the word in eliciting faith, which serves as an identifier of the church. We are called to faith through the word and the homily. The Second Vatican Council emphasized the dynamic role of the sacraments in the process of maturing in faith: "[Sacraments] not only presuppose faith, but by words and objects they also nourish, strengthen, and express it. That is why they are called sacraments of faith. They do, indeed, confer grace, but in addition, the very act of celebrating them is most effective in making people ready to receive this grace to their profit, to worship God duly, and to practice charity."[57] A coming-to-faith is an essential

---

the first responsibility of priests and bishops supports this emphasis on the word. The homily within the sacramental rituals forms an intrinsic part of the Liturgy of the Word.

[54] Karl Rahner, "What is a Sacrament?" *Theological Investigations*, vol. 14, trans. David Bourke (London: Darton, Longman & Todd, 1976), 136.

[55] Ibid.

[56] Ibid., 138.

[57] SC 59.

moment within all sacramental acts and one that is inseparable from reception of the word.

The Reformed Tradition:
Baptism within a Church of the Elect

The Reformed tradition shares with other Protestant traditions a view of the invisible church of the elect and the mixed visible church where the saints and reprobate mingle. Likewise, it emphasizes the birth of the church from the word of God. In contrast to Luther, Calvin's ecclesiology is characterized by a concern for church order and discipline. However, with respect to what concerns us here the most distinctive aspect of his theology as it impacts baptism and the church is his theology of God's election. Although Calvin describes the church in terms of its marks, only the elect are truly members.

The doctrine of election in Reformed theology is subject to multiple and varied interpretations, each potentially having a different impact on the question at hand. For the present it is only possible to sketch these out in the broadest terms. The classic interpretation, indebted to John Calvin, has been to think of the elect and the reprobate as two classes within the empirical church, with the true, invisible church being known only to God. This is also the view that conceives of election in individualistic terms: God preordains some individuals, and therefore presumably not others, to salvation. This view seems to be supported on biblical grounds in such texts as Deuteronomy 7:7-8; Jeremiah 1:5; Romans 11:2; and Ephesians 1:4. Several problems ensue. First, God's choice seems to be gratuitous rather than gracious. Why are some individuals chosen and others not? Neither being chosen nor not being chosen is due to any merit on the part of an individual or to any fault. Nor is an individual's fate affected either by his or her willing or acceptance of God's gift.[58] Second, since this election is prevenient and particular, the danger is that it seems to render both baptism and the church superfluous as means of grace. God's choice operates outside of and prior to any experience of the means of grace. Election is by grace alone, and it is an unmediated grace. Baptism is only efficacious for the elect. Nor can we say that baptism is efficacious on account of faith, for faith is the work of election,

---

[58] Calvin, *Institutes*, III, 24, 3.

but election does not depend on faith.[59] The elect will profess faith, be baptized, and be members of the visible church, but none of these is a guarantor of election. Falling from faith is a sign of the absence of election from the beginning. Calvin reconciles God's universal offer of mercy and the doctrine of election thus:

> For however universal the promises of salvation may be, they are still in no respect inconsistent with the predestination of the reprobate, provided we pay attention to their effect. When we receive the promises in faith, we know that then and only then do they become effective in us. On the contrary, when faith is snuffed out, the promise is abolished at the same time. . . . God is said to have ordained from eternity those whom he wills to embrace in love, and those upon whom he wills to vent his wrath. Yet he announces salvation to all men indiscriminately. I maintain that these statements agree perfectly with each other. For by so promising he merely means that his mercy is extended to all, provided they seek after it and implore it. But only those whom he has illumined do this. And he illumines those whom he has predestined to salvation.[60]

This citation notes the necessity of faith, significant both for the doctrine of justification by faith and for the continuity of the Reformed doctrine of baptism with Luther's teaching on baptism as a promise received in faith, at the same time as it reconciles these doctrines with the doctrine of predestination. Only those illumined by God possess the sure and unbroken truth of the promises. Only the predestined persevere in faith. Presuming that the baptized is elect, baptism has a strengthening, assuring, nourishing, and deepening function by bearing witness that the baptized belongs to God's covenant of grace, is implanted into Christ, is accepted into the community, and has the remission of sins. Baptism is not the cause of salvation, but mediates knowledge and certitude of salvation for the elect. It seals the application of the Gospel to the one being baptized who receives it as a sign and pledge that the promise given through the word of proclamation is really true in his or her regard. The point of departure of this analysis is the election, salvation, and faith of individuals.

Karl Barth's teaching attempts to address some of these concerns raised by a doctrine of election by identifying Jesus Christ as God's elect. The

[59] Ibid.
[60] Ibid., 24, 17.

point of departure of his analysis is not the salvation of an individual believer and the election of individuals, but what God accomplished in Jesus Christ. In his view, potentially everyone is included among the elect by being contained within the corporate Christ.[61]

Barth's mature work on baptism in the fourth volume of his *Church Dogmatics* (1969) reverses his earlier (1943) position on baptism.[62] In the later work Barth distinguishes sharply between baptism with the Holy Spirit and baptism with water. He makes the second dependent upon the first and rejects the sacramental nature of baptism, identifying it as a human act, an obedient response to God requiring freedom and personal faith. He summarizes the meaning of baptism as the human work of basic confession of faith, which consists in a washing of the candidates with water.[63] This confession leads to conversion of life and hence to a Christian ethic of life lived within a community already engaged in this manner of life.[64] The relationship between baptism with the Holy Spirit and baptism with water lies within a dialectic of God's gratuitous election through the Holy Spirit—an event that is in no way dependent upon baptism—and human response to this election in baptism. Thus baptism is a human rather than a divine act; more precisely, it is a human act in response to a divine act. Consequently, he rejects the practice of infant baptism since infants are incapable of free, obedient, and faithful response.

As for the relationship between baptism and the church, Barth makes a very fine distinction when he states that a person "becomes a Christian in his human decision, in the fact that he requests and receives baptism with water. But he does not become a Christian through his human decision or his water baptism."[65] The Holy Spirit brings about the change in a person by which a person, in virtue of God's faithfulness to him or her, becomes faithful to God in return, is baptized, and thus becomes a Christian. However, it is the action of the Holy Spirit in him or her and not the agency of water baptism that makes the person a Christian, even

---

[61] Karl Barth, *Church Dogmatics*, II.2, ed. Geoffrey W. Bromiley and Thomas F. Torrance (Edinburgh: T&T Clark, 1957), esp. §33.

[62] Karl Barth, "Baptism as the Foundation of the Christian Life," in *The Christian Life (Fragment), Church Dogmatics*, IV.4 (Edinburgh: T&T Clark, 1969). See Karl Barth, *The Teaching of the Church Regarding Baptism* (London: SCM Press, 1948). This lecture was originally delivered May 7, 1943.

[63] Barth, "Baptism as the Foundation," 73.

[64] Ibid., 138, 149.

[65] Ibid., 32–33.

though the action of the Holy Spirit leads him or her to the profession of faith and baptism with water that identifies one as a Christian. Baptism with the Holy Spirit does not dispense with baptism with water, but makes it possible and even demands it.[66]

Barth describes the change wrought by baptism with the Holy Spirit:

> . . . if it is to be possible for a man to be faithful to God instead of unfaithful, there must be a change which comes over this man himself. Nor may this change be simply an awakening of his natural powers, nor his endowment with supernatural powers, nor his placing by God under another light and judgment by which he may stand before God. It must be an inner change in virtue of which he himself becomes a different man, so that as this different man he freely, of himself, and by his own resolve, thinks and acts and conducts himself otherwise than he did before.[67]

This passage at once refutes a Catholic theology of supernatural grace and a Lutheran theology of imputed grace as well as any variation of Pelagianism. Baptism with the Holy Spirit "cleanses, renews and changes man truly and totally,"[68] an effect which other traditions such as the Catholics and the Orthodox would attribute to baptism with water. For Barth, however, the human activity of being baptized with water does not mediate grace, although a person enters the historical Christian community, that is, the church as a religious society, by way of baptism with water. However, it is only baptism with the Holy Spirit that is identical with a person's reception "into the church as the assembly of those who . . . continuing in a circle around Jesus are engaged in doing the will of God as His people" (Vulgate, Mark 3:34).[69] As we have already seen, in Reformed thought the historical community is not coterminous with the church of the elect.

With respect to the church as the administrator of baptism with water, Barth states: "The Church is neither author, dispenser, nor mediator of grace and its revelation."[70] One of the greatest differences between Catholic and Orthodox ecclesiology, on the one hand, and the ecclesiology of traditions issuing from the Reformation, on the other hand, is

---

[66] Ibid., 41.
[67] Ibid., 18.
[68] Ibid., 34.
[69] Ibid., 37.
[70] Ibid., 32.

over this issue of mediation, that is, whether an institution comprised of fallible and sinful members can mediate God's grace. For Barth baptism is not efficacious of grace, justification, or salvation. Nevertheless, the community is not dispensable, for its work is to recognize a person's faith and thus his membership in the church and in the body of Jesus Christ and to baptize him.[71] No one can dispense with the baptizing community and baptize himself. Barth also departed from Calvin in thinking that the ability to baptize was not restricted to any particular ecclesiastical office but could be granted to any member of the community, but as a member of the community, not as a private individual.[72] In Barth's theology, even though he finds that, after Pentecost, Christian baptism has a gathering and uniting character, baptism proclaims but does not establish fellowship.[73] Thus, for him, it is in no way constitutive of the church.

A second issue is that whereas Catholic teaching considers the church to be a complex entity, comprised of a human and a divine element, Barth's dialectical theology sharply divides the human institution, the religious society, from the heavenly church or the assembly of the elect. Barth cleanly separates baptism with the Holy Spirit from baptism with water, God's Word and command expressed in his gift and human obedience in faith, the church as a religious society from the church as the assembly of the saints, and divine agency from human agency. His dialectical theology does not admit of human and divine synergism or the possibility of human instrumentality as mediatory of God's grace. His dismissal of the sacramental character of baptism is consistent with this dialectic, as is his assumption that baptism with the Spirit is a separate event from baptism with water.[74] One consequence of this separation is that he considers the baptism of John and that of the community after Pentecost to be one and the same baptism.[75]

Colin Gunton proposes a third interpretation of the doctrine of election, suggesting a community-centered doctrine of election of Israel as

[71] Ibid., 49.
[72] Ibid., 49–50.
[73] Ibid., 82.
[74] Ibid., 77. Some Catholic scholarship attempts to integrate the two. See Kilian McDonnell and George T. Montague, *Christian Initiation and Baptism in the Holy Spirit: Evidence from the First Eight Centuries*, 2nd ed. (Collegeville, MN: Liturgical Press, 1994).
[75] Barth, "Baptism as the Foundation," 86.

the people of God and the church as the body of Christ.[76] His analysis rests on the election and calling of particular communities rather than particular individuals. He places the church in the context of creation as ordered to an eschatological perfection in which all things are reconciled in Christ (Col 1:20). From this perspective "the elect are not primarily those chosen for a unique destiny out of the whole; rather, they are chosen out of the whole as the community with whom the destiny of the whole is in some way bound up."[77] Whereas Barth saw the whole human race *immediately* in Christ, Gunton, borrowing insights from John Owen,[78] suggests that the whole human race is *mediately* in Christ as Israel and the church. Election means being part of the community identified as the body of Christ engrafted in some way to share Israel's election (Rom 11:17-22). One is incorporated into this body and into this community and thus shares in this communitarian election through baptism: ". . . if the church is the body of Christ, those incorporated by baptism are more than merely called. There is an ontological change, because they have entered a new set of relationships—with God, with other people, and with the created order."[79] In this theology of election the means of grace, here the sacraments and the church, are no longer contingent, but truly the means by which one is literally incorporated into the election of the community. Those so incorporated participate in the reconciling mediation of the community serving God's universal purposes on behalf of all creation. The election of these communities does not imply the perdition of everyone else, but simply that they are the servant church, instruments of God's purposes. Undoubtedly much remains unanswered in this evocative essay, not least the relationship of those incorporated into the elected communities to those not so incorporated, how God's final reconciliation is accomplished through this mediation, and what its eschatological form will be. Nevertheless, Gunton offers the beginnings of an alternative view of election that allows for a robust theology of baptism that is truly efficacious and transformative of human nature.

Of these three interpretations of the Reformed tradition, only Calvin represents mainstream Reformed thought regarding the relationship

---

[76] Colin Gunton, "Election and Ecclesiology in the Post-Constantinian Church," in *Reformed Theology: Identity and Ecumenicity*, ed. Wallace M. Alstron Jr. and Michael Welker (Grand Rapids: Eerdmans, 2003), 97–110, at 104.

[77] Ibid.

[78] John Owen, *The Works of John Owen*, 24 vols. (London: T&T Clark, 1862).

[79] Gunton, "Election and Ecclesiology," 107.

between election, baptism, and the church. Reformed churches have not followed Karl Barth's proposal to restrict baptism with water to those who can freely respond to God's action in their lives with obedient faith. Colin Gunton's suggestion is too brief and recent to have had a reception or even a hearing within his tradition, although it is very promising from an ecumenical perspective.

Practitioners of Believer's Baptism: A Committed Community

From a Baptist perspective, Morris West has noted that the approach to a mutual recognition of baptism based on common elements of an initiation process begs certain questions, notably that of the doctrine of the church. He comments:

> It may be argued that those who practice infant baptism and those who practice believers' baptism start from different "models" of the Church. Those practicing infant baptism see the church as an ontologically given community into which a child is incorporated, whereas Baptists and those practicing believers' baptism view the church as a community which is constituted by the activity of God on the individual who responds consciously and believes and so becomes a participating member of the community.[80]

For Baptists, the faith of an individual precedes in some fashion the formation of a faith community. God's action on an individual brings that individual to a profession of faith, and this leads that person to affiliate with others with a similar experience to form a church that is congregationally defined. In 1927 Wheeler Robinson observed that the one-sided emphasis on the human response of faith in baptism made it possible to talk of faith as if it occurred in a vacuum and the products of faith then came together to form a church.[81] In his view members do not join a church, but rather "constitute it as a society of men and women drawn together by common convictions and needs and entering into a

---

[80] Morris S. West, "Towards a Consensus on Baptism: Louisville 1979," *Mid-Stream* 19 (1980): 107–14, at 109.

[81] Cited in Nigel G. Wright, "'Koinonia' and Baptist Ecclesiology: Self-Critical Reflections from Historical and Systematic Perspectives," *Baptist Quarterly* 35 (1994): 363–75, at 367.

social experience of the Christian faith for which their individual experience has prepared them."[82] The church is a gathered community of the faithful and the focus is primarily on individuals accepting Jesus Christ as their Lord and Savior. The experience of faith is primarily personal, individual, and experiential. From this perspective the church is not liturgically constituted. This means that an individual does not necessarily enter the church by way of baptism; potentially this separates church membership and baptism both ritually and in fact.

Baptist ecclesiology is grounded in a regenerate church membership, which is the basis of their insistence on believer's baptism as a perquisite to membership for those churches practicing closed membership. The Baptist conviction is that "Christian faith is a personal voluntary commitment of one's self to Jesus Christ as Lord and Saviour; and that the church is a gathered fellowship of persons who have made such a commitment to Christ."[83] The requirement of a public profession of faith and repentance prior to baptism and reception in the fellowship of a church is the means used to make the visible churches approximate the membership of the invisible communion of saints.[84] The conviction is that the universal church is most visible in a local congregation of professed believers.[85]

Yet it must be noted that a concept of a universal church is not uniform among all Baptists. Both the "Abstract of Principles" drawn up for the Southern Baptist Seminary in 1859 and the Southern Baptist Convention in 1925 omit references to the universal church. The latter defines a "Gospel church" as "a congregation of baptized believers, associated by covenant in the faith and fellowship of the gospel; observing the ordinances of Christ, governed by his law, and exercising the gifts, rights and privileges invested in them by his word, and seeking to extend the gospel to the ends of the earth."[86] In this definition the church is congregationally defined, associated not by sacrament but by covenant in the faith and

---

[82] This is Wright's summary of Robinson's position.

[83] W. Hubert Porter, "The Baptist Doctrine of the Church and Ecumenicity," 92, in *Report: Consultation on World Mission, Hong Kong, 1963–64*. Papers presented at the Consultation on World Mission held at the Christian Study Center in Tao Fong Shan, Hong Kong, December 27, 1963–January 4, 1964. Bound typescript, n.d.

[84] Wayne A. Dalton, "Worship and Baptist Ecclesiology," *Foundations* 12 (1969): 7–18, at 11.

[85] See "A Statement Approved by the Council of the Baptist Union of Great Britain and Ireland, March 1, 1948," §2 in H. Leon McBeth, *A Sourcebook for Baptist Heritage* (Nashville: Broadman Press, 1990), 369.

[86] John H. Leith, ed., *Creeds of the Churches* (Garden City, NY: Doubleday, 1963), 348.

fellowship in the Gospel. The church "observes" the "ordinances" of Christ, but is not constituted by them.

Ecumenical conversations between Baptists and other traditions tend to affirm the necessity of viewing local churches in relationship with wider ecclesial entities. Thus the Baptist-Reformed statement, "Baptists and Reformed in Dialogue," the report of the theological conversations of 1973–77 between the Baptist World Alliance and the World Alliance of Reformed Churches, makes the following three affirmations:

- The one holy universal Christian church becomes concrete in the local congregation.

- At the same time the local congregation is necessarily related to other local congregations.

- The wider church relationships (area, national, regional, worldwide) have ecclesiological significance.[87]

Alan Sell cautions, however, regarding the interpretation to be given to "congregation" in these affirmations:

> In all of this the term "congregation" has a rather Presbyterian ring. If it is understood to mean the "congregation of the saints" there should be no difficulty; if it were (wrongly) taken to mean "all who comprise a worshipping congregation—members and adherents and passing atheists alike" then Baptists (and Congregationalists within the Reformed family) would feel an ecclesiological threat.[88]

In other words, the invisible church of the sanctified finds concrete expression in the local community of committed believers. However, not all members of the local community are necessarily members of the invisible church.

According to Robert G. Torbet, what gave rise to the Baptists as a distinct group of Christians was the issue "whether or not it is possible to have a visible church of visible saints, a truly regenerate church membership."[89] This position identifies Baptists in a general sense with the Free Church movement, but also distinguishes them from such groups as the

---

[87] Cited in Alan Sell, "Ecclesiology in Perspective: Conversations with Anglicans and Baptists," *Reformed World* 38, no. 3 (1984): 168–76, at 174.

[88] Ibid.

[89] Robert G. Torbet, *A History of the Baptists*, rev. ed. (Valley Forge, PA: Judson Press, 1963), 32.

Congregationalists, who admitted the children of regenerate members. Norman Maring and Winthrop Hudson comment that what resulted—or so it was hoped—was "not a sinless community, but a committed community."[90]

The majority of Baptist churches practice closed membership, which means that membership is closed to all except those baptized as believers. Those coming from other churches must be baptized, even though this baptism may serve more as a reaffirmation of faith than a first confession of faith. In contrast, Baptist churches that practice open membership admit all who profess repentance toward God and faith in our Lord Jesus Christ, and whose lives bear evidence of their Christian profession. These members are usually received after baptism by immersion, but the church welcomes all who conscientiously follow Jesus Christ.[91]

Conclusion

Among the many nuances in both theologies of baptism and theologies of the church, we can draw these very general conclusions. First, baptism is an ecclesial event. The community baptizes in imitation of Jesus, who submitted himself to baptism in the Jordan and commanded his followers to do likewise. Baptism is not an individualistic action that is just between the person being baptized and God. Nor can a person self-baptize. Thus baptisms should normally be celebrated within the public worship of the assembled community.

Next, the fact that baptism is received, not taken or self-administered, means that it is a gift given. Thus it cannot be solely an act of obedience, a one-sided human act. While Karl Barth sharply distinguished divine initiative in baptism with the Holy Spirit and human response in baptism with water, the paradigm of baptism, Jesus' baptism in the Jordan, indicates that both divine initiative and human response occur in one and the same baptismal event. Nor can we suppose that baptism would not impart the gift of the Spirit, into whose name we are baptized. When Jesus submitted himself to John's baptism, this personal action was accompanied by the theophany of the appearance of the Spirit and the

---

[90] Norman H. Maring and Winthrop S. Hudson, *A Baptist Manual of Polity and Practice* (Valley Forge, PA: Judson Press, 1963), 37, cited by Dalton, "Worship and Baptist Ecclesiology," 13.

[91] Ibid., 14.

voice of the Father. In this event the gift of the Holy Spirit is associated with baptism with water.

The giftedness of baptism gives the community a mediating function. Depending on the tradition, this would at least be God's promise of grace mediated through the word proclaimed by the community. Proclamation does not occur in a vacuum. Other traditions would say that the community also mediates sanctifying grace, justification, and rebirth. The community itself is not the source of these effects, which can only come from God through the power of the Holy Spirit, but when the word is proclaimed, when the community acts in obedience to the dominical command to baptize into the name of the Trinity, God's renewing grace is present by the very fact of the promise. The sacramental effect is attached to the sacramental event as the embodied word-promise of God, making it tangible within an incarnational principle of an enfleshed word. The sacramental event is impossible apart from the community to whom it is entrusted.

Baptism builds up the church, an obvious effect as the community receives the baptized and thereby increases its numbers. However, there is more than a quantitative increase, for baptism fills out the diversity of the church in the Pauline sense of there being many different members of the one body, each with a different function. The depth dimension of the church is enhanced through an intensification of the presence of the Spirit in the holiness of the members manifested in their baptismal conversion of life. Thus the height, width, and depth of the church, symbolic of its pleroma, or fullness, is filled out not just by the number of church members added, but by the quality of life, the depth of faith, and, ultimately, by the indwelling presence of Father, Son, and Holy Spirit into whom the members are baptized.

Incorporation and communion, rather than membership, are more fruitful concepts with which to think about affiliation with the church through baptism. Communion allows for various degrees and intensities of affiliation. It is less static and more dynamic than membership. Incorporation has the benefit of reflecting the Pauline reference to the body of Christ (1 Cor 12:12-31), with the diversity of gifts. Its christological reference links to the theology of baptism in Romans 6 as participation in the death and resurrection of Christ, for this participation would be as members of his ecclesial body.

These terms may potentially contribute to a partial ecumenical resolution of the membership in the visible/invisible church problem. Although membership in a historical community may be established through baptism, communion with the assembly of the saints both on earth and in heaven is what is actually achieved in Christ. One does not speak of membership in the community of saints, but precisely of the "communion" of saints. The use of perfect and imperfect communion was employed by Vatican II to show the various degrees of ecclesial relationships. In an ecumenical context, ecclesial traditions seek "full communion" through ecumenical dialogue.

This shift in terminology, however, does not address a theology of particular, personal election of some and the nonelection of others, for there is no tradition of degrees of election. It also does not solve the difference between the two theologies, one of a complex church comprised of human and divine elements, and the other of a church defined as the assembly of the sanctified where the issues are the capability of an institution to mediate grace and the relationship of sinful "members" to the church. For this latter, a stronger distinction between the assembly of the saints in the eschaton and the mixed and provisionary character of the pilgrim church may be a solution. The church only reaches its completion in heaven.[92] In the meantime, although holy, it is always in need of purification.[93]

Finally, as argued earlier, the polemical distinction between word and sacrament, the church as constituted by baptism and Eucharist or as constituted as a creature of the word is a false distinction if used to separate churches that are more catholic from those that are more evangelical. The church is constituted by Christ through the proclamation of his word and through incorporation into his body through the sacraments of baptism and the Eucharist. Ultimately there is one church and one baptism because there is one Christ who is the Word of the Father. The unity of word and sacrament lies in the person of Christ.

[92] LG 49.
[93] LG 8.

Index of Subjects

Augustinian position on justification, 153–54

baptism and faith, xiii, 150–51, 171–76
baptism and salvation, xii, 10–13, 22, 23, 26, 41, 45, 56, 62, 75, 83, 94, 110, 142, 151, 163, 166, 167, 169, 170, 172, 176, 184–85, 198, 201
baptism and the Trinitarian formula, 3, 11, 16, 21, 26–27, 49, 54, 74, 78–79, 83, 89, 94, 97–100, 105, 108–9, 111–12, 115, 122, 138, 141, 142–43, 158–59, 171, 175, 176, 189, 194, 207
baptism as a sacrament of justification, xiii, 38, 49, 146, 161, 166–71
baptism as death and resurrection, xii, 1–2, 6–8, 10, 16, 17, 42, 49, 50, 51, 53, 54, 56, 58, 59, 78–80, 87, 89, 94, 107–8, 112–13, 116, 118, 119–20, 135, 142, 143, 144, 168, 172, 175, 181, 193, 194, 196, 207
baptism as eucharistic, 100, 110, 116–18, 190
baptism as full initiation, 123, 130, 137, 138
baptism as transformative, 3, 19, 42, 100, 110, 112, 114, 115–16, 163, 165, 169, 175, 181, 202
baptism by blood, 14, 23, 60
baptism by desire, 14, 16, 23, 176

baptism by immersion, 21, 27, 78–80, 94–95, 100, 105, 108, 120, 141, 206
baptism by infusion, 86, 94–95, 100, 120
baptism by water, 4, 14, 23, 60, 89, 176, 199–201, 203, 206–7
baptism with the Holy Spirit, 60, 199–201, 206
baptismal life as communion, 16–17, 18
baptismal life as cross, 8, 17, 143
baptismal life as mission, 18–19, 102, 143
believer baptism, xiii, 21, 59, 78–82, 90, 93, 140, 141–42, 173–74, 188, 203–6

church as committed assembly, 188, 203–6
church as constituted as a creature of the Word, 188, 194–97, 208
church as constituted by baptism and Eucharist, 9–10, 188–94, 196, 208
church as sacrament, 12, 13, 42, 190–92
confer grace, 23, 33–38, 68, 74, 81, 82–83, 85, 88, 196
confirmation/chrismation, 22, 29, 34, 39–41, 66n91, 83, 91n1, 95, 101, 102, 104, 106, 108–9, 116–17, 121, 123, 134–40, 149n11, 179, 182, 189
contain grace, 33, 47, 84–85, 87–88

Index of Documents

212

Index of Proper Names

John, son of Zebedee, 7
Johnson, Maxwell, 39n40, 121–23, 134n36, 135, 138n44, 140
Joint International Commission for Theological Dialogue between the Roman Catholic, 94

Kavanagh, Aidan, 42, 117, 134–35
Kay, James F., 132

Lathrop, Gordon, 98, 99–100
Leo X, 57
Lombard, Peter, 33, 58, 68, 71n113, 84n171, 87
Lorenzen, Thorald, 79
Lubac, Henri de, 41n46, 173n95
Luther, Martin, xiii, 25, 30, 45–55, 57n49, 58, 59, 61–62, 71, 87, 88, 90, 122–28, 131, 136, 138, 146–52, 155, 167–68, 169–70, 173, 184, 185, 195, 197, 198
Lutheran World Federation, 161
Lutheran-Roman Catholic Joint Commission, 185

Manz, Felix, 58
Maring, Norman H., 206
Martyr, Justin, 97–98, 179
Mary, 158, 159
McBeth, H. Leon, 76n140, 82
Melanchthon, Philipp, 149–50, 185n27

National Conference of Catholic Bishops, 101
Neal, George, 142
Nicodemus, 7
Noah, 68, 115, 126
North American Orthodox-Catholic Theological Consultation, 95n14, 96–97

Office of Evangelism Ministries of the Episcopal Church in the United States of America, 125

Osiander, 147
Owen, John, 202

Paul, 2, 6–8, 41, 42, 48, 50, 51, 87, 89, 153, 181, 188, 207
Paul VI, 57, 136
Peter, 5, 92, 177
Pius X, 40, 57
Pius XII, 57, 191

Rahner, Karl, 14, 25, 28, 196
Riggs, John W., 130–33
Robinson, Wheeler, 203–4

Sacred Congregation for Divine Worship, 100
Schillebeeckx, Edward, 88n182, 193
Schlink, Edmund, 172, 195n52
Schmaus, Michael, 11–12
Schwartz, Hans, 150
Scotus, Duns, 28, 31, 37, 46, 47, 153
Searle, Mark, 39
Sell, Alan, 205
Smyth, John, 79, 81–82
Soto, Domingo de, 156
Stapleton, Thomas, 156

Talley, Thomas J., 3
Tapper, Ruard, 156
Tillard, Jean–Marie, 95–96, 189–90, 192
Torbet, Robert G., 205
Tranvik, Mark, 33
Trigg, Jonathan, 184

West, Morris, 203
William of Occam, 30, 31, 46n13, 169n78
World Alliance of Reformed Churches, 205
World Council of Churches, xiii, 4n5, 20, 100, 182, 191–92

Zwingli, Ulrich, 59, 61–65, 70, 71, 89, 90

Index of Scripture Citations